NEGOTIATING PRIVACY

iPOLITICS: Global Challenges in the Information Age

RENÉE MARLIN-BENNETT, SERIES EDITOR

Governing the Internet:
The Emergence of an International Regime,
Marcus Franda

Intellectual Property Rights: A Critical History,
Christopher May and Susan K. Sell

Knowledge Power: Intellectual Property, Information, and Privacy,
Renée Marlin-Bennett

Launching into Cyberspace:
Internet Development and Politics in Five World Regions,
Marcus Franda

Negotiating Privacy:
The European Union, the United States,
and Personal Data Protection,
Dorothee Heisenberg

NEGOTIATING PRIVACY

The European Union, the United States, and Personal Data Protection

DOROTHEE HEISENBERG

BOULDER
LONDON

Published in the United States of America in 2005 by
Lynne Rienner Publishers, Inc.
1800 30th Street, Boulder, Colorado 80301
www.rienner.com

and in the United Kingdom by
Lynne Rienner Publishers, Inc.
3 Henrietta Street, Covent Garden, London WC2E 8LU

Library of Congress Cataloging-in-Publication Data
Heisenberg, Dorothee, 1963–
Negotiating privacy : the European Union, the United States, and personal data protection / by Dorothee Heisenberg.
(iPolitics/global challenges in the information age)
Includes bibliographical references and index.
ISBN 1-58826-380-0 (hardback : alk. paper)
1. Data protection—Law and legislation—European Union countries. 2. Records—Law and legislation—European Union countries. 3. Privacy, Right of—European Union countries. 4. Data protection—Law and legislation—United States. 5. Records—Law and legislation—United States. 6. Privacy, Right of—United States. I. Title. II. Series. K3264.C65H45 2005
342.2408'58—dc22

2005005663

British Cataloguing in Publication Data
A Cataloguing in Publication record for this book is available from the British Library.

Printed and bound in the United States of America

The paper used in this publication meets the requirements of the American National Standard for Permanence of Paper for Printed Library Materials Z39.48-1992.

5 4 3 2 1

Contents

Acknowledgments

I don't remember exactly what sparked my interest in the EU-US data protection dispute. As with so many interesting topics, I first had the opportunity to learn and think about it in the courses I teach at the Johns Hopkins University School for Advanced International Studies (SAIS). SAIS has provided me the academic freedom to teach about policy-relevant international problems, and I am grateful for the benevolent guidance of my colleague David Calleo over the past five years. SAIS also contributed research funds toward travel for interviews, conferences, and research assistants, and I could not have completed this book without this support.

I had several excellent research assistants who worked on different parts of the project, and my thanks go to Cesar Munoz, Leonora Fitzgibbons, Yunie Kim, Dave Landes, and Marie-Helene Fandel. I also wish to thank Gerry Masson, director of the Johns Hopkins University Information Security Institute, for his generous research support at the beginning of the project.

As this book developed, I became acquainted with a host of scholars and lawyers who shared my interest in the issues involved. It was of great value to me that I could call on them to ask questions about and discuss details of this swiftly evolving field. In this context, I wish to sincerely thank Scott Blackmer, Henry Farrell, Abe Newman, and Greg Shaffer. Scott, in particular, was wonderful in clearing up some of my misconceptions regarding legal questions, but, of course, he is not responsible for any remaining errors or omissions.

I had the good fortune to interview many of the people responsible for the European Data Protection Directive and the Safe Harbor Agreement. On the European side, I would like to thank Susan Binns, Ulf Brühann of the European Commission, and Spiros Simitis, among others. The staff of the Data Protection Office were especially helpful in finding old documents and allowing me access to useful studies. On the US side, I benefited from speaking to David Aaron and the late Barbara Wellbery, who were the principal architects of Safe Harbor. I also wish to thank the contact officers of the Safe Harbor companies who agreed to be interviewed and participate in a survey, most of whom wished to remain anonymous.

Two anonymous reviewers of the manuscript had thoughtful, detailed, and ultimately extremely helpful comments on structuring the book, and I thank them both for their helpful suggestions. Renée Marlin-Bennett, editor of the iPolitics series for Lynne Rienner Publishers, provided exceptionally useful feedback on earlier versions of the manuscript, and her professionalism was a great asset to my rewriting efforts.

Although the subject of this book only peripherally involves computers, it seems fitting to dedicate this book to my computer science husband, Greg.

NEGOTIATING PRIVACY

1

Data Privacy: Setting the International Standard

> "Whether you like it or not, the EU is setting the standards for privacy protection for the rest of the world."
>
> —International Herald Tribune[1]

In 1995, the fifteen states of the European Union (EU) approved the European Data Protection Directive[2] that guaranteed all citizens in the European Union the right to personal data protection.[3] Henceforth, any personal data, from medical records to employment data to credit files, would be protected from unauthorized use anywhere in the world. Starting in 1998, the EU also had the authority to pass judgments on privacy protections around the world along with the ability to stop transfers of Europeans' data to other countries where similarly strict data protection was not guaranteed. Since the US laws for privacy were sectorally based, and did not blanket all personal information, any EU citizen's personal data could not automatically be sent to the US. This element of the Directive was the genesis of the US-EU data protection conflict, a transatlantic problem ultimately resolved by the 2000 Safe Harbor Agreement.

A similar data protection conflict between the US and the EU arose in 2003, when the US passed a law, in order to prevent terrorism, that mandated the release of airline passenger data (the so-called "passenger name record" or PNR) to the Department of Homeland Security for all flights involving the US. Because the airline data were gathered for a commercial purpose and then used for a different one (security), the transfers fell under the European Data Protection Directive and, therefore, had to comply with the EU laws. In June, 2004, the EU Commission signed an agreement allowing European airlines to comply with the US law. However, the European Parliament opposed the June 2004 agreement, and sued the EU Commission in the European Court of Justice, rendering the future of the Passenger Name Record Agreement uncertain.

Transatlantic conflicts are nothing new. Since the establishment of the European Economic Community, there have always been small trade, regulatory, or foreign policy issues that divided the US and Europe. Over time, as the Europeans created more of a state-like entity and enlarged from six to twenty-five member states, it also began to assume a larger global role, especially in commercial matters. The member states eliminated nontariff barriers, ceded greater control to the institutions of the EU, and began trying to forge a European identity with European citizenship and currency.

The United States quietly supported European integration, and also reaped benefits from the increased market size and political stability that the expanding EU created.[4] In general, however, the transatlantic relationship was bifurcated; when there were differences in foreign policy, they were handled bilaterally between the US and the affected member state(s) without using the EU institutions. However, when conflicts involved commercial problems, increasingly, the EU handled these issues. Over time, the EU market became larger than the US market in terms of both gross domestic product (GDP) and population, and the EU became more assertive in commercial matters, setting international product standards,[5] costeering the World Trade Organization (WTO) trade agenda,[6] and scrutinizing foreign companies' mergers for anticompetitive implications.[7]

The data privacy conflict that arose between the EU and the US in 1998 was more important than the other economic conflicts that the close US-EU relationship had spawned. It was bigger because of its potential size—the US estimated that $120 billion worth of trade was at risk, making it thirty times larger than the next largest trade conflict (the Foreign Sales Corporation dispute)—and because it reflected two very different ideas about personal data privacy. The fundamental right to data privacy first became enshrined in the EU Charter of Fundamental Rights signed in 2000, and was later integrated into the June 2004 European Constitution. For the Europeans, data protection had become a fundamental human right, thus, automatically trumping many other rights.

By contrast, although the right to privacy had always been an important and expanding right in the US, it was not at par with explicit, constitutionally guaranteed rights. The US had very strict privacy laws in some sectors, but any data not covered by those sectoral laws were unprotected. In practical terms, this meant that the EU and the US reached very different conclusions about the rights of businesses and individuals relating to personal data, and these differences threatened to derail a large proportion of transatlantic commerce.

It also meant, however, that the conflict had zero-sum characteristics, making it more difficult to resolve than a collective action problem. Either standard was viable internationally, but the two were incompatible with each other, and in order to make commerce possible, one side had to adopt the other's standard. Although it was true that the Europeans were only trying to get data protection for any European data that were transferred to the US, in practice, it would have been impossible to write legislation to monitor, and to enforce, a law requiring compliance with the European data protection laws for European data only.[8] Thus, any legislative solution in the United States would necessarily have been binding on US personal data as well. The conflict was, therefore, whether the Europeans could force the US to do something the Clinton administration was unwilling to do.

Compounding the diplomatic problem was the fact that privacy protection was explicitly exempted from WTO jurisdiction, and thus, the data protection dispute could not be resolved by that supranational body as many of the other EU-US trading conflicts had been. Another traditional method of diffusing "standards" issues, that of mutual recognition,[9] was also impossible because of the Europeans' established definition of privacy as a fundamental human right, meaning a "lowest common denominator" approach would not be acceptable to them.

The clash between the EU and the US, in short, had become a classic international conflict: international institutions and regimes did not cover the issue area, and compromise looked impossible. Negotiations began in early 1999, but a year later they had still not found a solution. In early 2000, partly because of the pressure created by the imminent departure of the chief US negotiator, Ambassador David Aaron, the Safe Harbor Agreement was finalized. That agreement (detailed in Chapter 3) allowed individual US companies to sign up to a list kept by the Department of Commerce, and warrant that they were following the requirements of the European Data Protection Directive in house. The Safe Harbor Agreement resolved the potential problem of blocking data flows and commerce between the EU and the US. The agreement itself, however, was the stuff of significant controversy: on the EU side, the European Parliament, which did not have the institutional ability to veto the agreement, voted to reject the agreement, saying it was unsatisfactory in important ways that had been elaborated by the national data protection authorities. Meanwhile, on the US side, the incoming Bush administration pledged to renegotiate the Safe Harbor Agreement, declaring the EU had no right to dictate to the US.

In a similar vein, the US-EU Passenger Name Record conflict was also abridged by an agreement granting "adequacy" to the US procedures for using the EU citizens' personal data. The data protection authorities in Europe expressed significant reservations about those procedures, and the European Parliament rejected the agreement, but again the European Commission elected to conclude the negotiations.

Making Sense of the Outcome

Given the many contradictions that characterize the Safe Harbor and Passenger Name Record Agreements, how should one understand the outcomes between the US and the EU on personal data protection? Since the issue is still relatively new, one should distinguish the short term and the long term effects. In the short term, the Safe Harbor Agreement did not result in an official bilateral treaty on data privacy, nor did it set in motion negotiations for a multilateral regime for other non-EU states to join. It did, however, prevent egregious abuses of Europeans' personal data, and it did prevent the EU from blocking an estimated $120 billion of transatlantic trade. In the short run, the Safe Harbor Agreement appears to have been a victory for the US commercial interests that were actively involved in preventing European style regulations in the US. Any abstraction from the negotiations on data privacy would likely conclude that the final agreement was closer to the preferences of the US than those of the EU. The EU was able to force the US to deal with privacy issues, but the negotiated outcome was clearly not the preferred solution of the EU.

In the long term, however, the Safe Harbor Agreement looks much less like a victory for the US commercial interests that were its main proponents. Neither did the agreement establish a new norm of industry self-regulation that was copied by other countries, nor did it create a flood of companies seeking to sign up for the Safe Harbor status. It did not prevent the EU from establishing a de facto international privacy regime, in the sense that the EU's standard is used by most other countries around the world, and it did not forestall greater US state-level regulation that resembled much of the philosophy behind the EU directive. In short, the agreement may come to be seen historically as a costly ceasefire during which most other countries (as well as some US states) allied with the Europeans.

The outcome of the Passenger Name Record Agreement, by contrast, was more of a capitulation by the EU. The European airlines had already been complying with the US requirements, and had more to fear from US retaliation, which could take the form of screening passengers in the US and fining the airlines, than it did from the threat of fines for violating the European Data Protection Directive. The agreement itself, challenged before the European Court of Justice by the only directly elected body of the European institutions, is unlikely to be overturned by the European Court of Justice. The Europeans tried first to establish a multilateral regime under the auspices of the United Nations, something in which the US showed only a passing interest, and then, as a fallback, suggested the creation of a new EU-wide forum for the discussion of personal data protection issues arising from international co-operation on security matters. As with the Safe Harbor Agreement, the fact that the EU was able to force the

US to deal with the privacy issues at all, and to make some minor concessions from the original, showed that the EU's privacy standard was significant. Overall, however, the US largely determined the outcome, and US preferences were dominant. The EU was much more deferential to US preferences in security matters than commercial issues.

In order to understand these two outcomes, it is necessary to review some of the factors that other analysts have used to gain leverage on these problems. Here the discussion centers on five differing explanations that should not necessarily be considered mutually exclusive. The first is a "power" approach, represented by Krasner's (1991) "Life on the Pareto Frontier" argument. The second explanation, elaborated by Shaffer (2000), credits the EU's market power, showing how the EU was able to leverage its growing internal market power by threatening to block data flow to the US, shielded by the WTO exemption for privacy. A third explanation, by Mattli and Büthe (2003), hinges on the institutions in Europe, where more formally organized business groups have communication advantages that encourage their involvement in the setting of standards at the international level earlier and more effectively than their US counterparts. Similarly, Newman (2004) argues that transnational data protection authorities in Europe compelled the EU to act in this issue by leveraging their power to block data flows. The fourth, constructivist, explanation was used by Farrell (2003)[10] who argued that the US-EU dialogue shifted the preferences of decisionmakers in both countries, diffusing the power conflict, and making a hybrid solution possible. Finally, the liberal intergovernmentalist approach, elaborated by Moravcsik (1997), explains the emergence of the US and the EU's negotiating preferences by showing how interest groups in each region had differential impacts on the initial negotiating positions taken by each side. Each of these explanations is reviewed in greater detail below.

Krasner (1991) analyzed the emergence of global telecommunications regimes with the observation that co-operation was the result of power symmetry between states, rather than the conquering of market failure. According to him, co-operation among states was more likely when the relative power among states was equal than when powerful states could simply do as they pleased. The reason for states to co-operate was to avoid adverse consequences from the other states that had the power to inflict them. The regimes created, however, were skewed toward the preferences of the powerful states, and thus ensured that the costs of adjustment fell onto the others.

Krasner identified these types of conflicts as co-ordination problems with distributional consequences: "Though the states agreed on mutually undesirable outcomes [in this case, the halting of data flows and commerce], they disagreed on their preferred outcomes."[11] Krasner does not give a particular way to assess power differentials, beyond stating that if an agreement is reached, power is symmetrical. "Agreement . . . has been limited to areas where states have shared interests and relatively equal power."[12]

In essence, in both data privacy cases, the basic conflict between the EU and the US was a classic power conflict—could the EU make the US do something it did not want to do, namely, pass comprehensive federal privacy legislation and apply European standards to Passenger Name Record data? Or could the US make the EU accept something (less data protection abroad) that it did not want to allow? The fact that an agreement was ultimately reached, and that neither side tried to renegotiate the terms after it had been signed (the Bush administration quietly shelved plans to try to renegotiate the agreement a couple of months after it had looked into the matter more carefully), shows that the agreement had durability, and that both parties were unable to move the agreement closer to their preferred position. According to Krasner, this implies that the US and the EU had symmetrical power. The US was unable to prevent the EU from extending its data protection to the US companies at home, but neither could the EU force the US to extend the kind of protection it wanted, and had to conclude a suboptimal data protection agreement in order to keep transatlantic commerce flowing. Thus, the two states reached the pareto frontier, but ultimately selected a point nearer the US position (no comprehensive federal privacy legislation).

The power framework has a great deal of appeal, especially when one sees the interaction between the EU and other countries in this context. Whereas the US was able to resist the demands of the EU to pass comprehensive privacy legislation, and still get an adequacy ruling, other states were not able to move in that direction, and most of the countries that implemented privacy policies to transfer data to and from the EU eventually adopted legislation that comports with the EU's directive.

However, there are two drawbacks to the power analysis of this issue: the first is that it does not present an iterative or strategic process. Gruber (2000) demonstrated that states do join regimes even when a priori the regimes were not consonant with their preferences. Thus, changing the facts on the ground can change a state's preferences. There are many examples of states joining successful regimes that they initially opposed because it was better to be within the structure than outside it (perhaps the classic case was Britain's entry into the EU). In the case of data protection, it is too early to say whether the US will ultimately join the rest of the world in passing comprehensive privacy legislation, since it is large enough to remain isolated and has reached an equilibrium with the EU at present.

The other drawback to the power approach is that it does not give any explanation of how that power is accrued. The observable outcome, that of the parties having reached an agreement, implies that the EU and the US have power symmetry, but exactly how the EU or the US was able to force the other to the negotiating table is left underspecified.

Looking at just that question, Shaffer (2000) examines the role of using the common internal market as leverage. In his view, the EU was able to force the US to negotiate by virtue of holding transatlantic data flows hostage. Further, since privacy related legislation was specifically exempted from WTO jurisdiction, the US had no recourse to multilateral trade institutions and was forced to confront the EU's privacy demands. This argument has appeal, as economic motives have been a staple in state coercion for a long time. But it does raise the following question: if the EU could prevent data flow, and the US was motivated by the threat to transatlantic commerce, why was the EU not able to get an agreement closer to its preferred spot on the pareto frontier? By all accounts, the Europeans were unhappy with many of the features of the Safe Harbor Agreement, yet the EU Commission and the Council of Ministers decided to accept it. If the market access threat was credible, it is difficult to understand why the EU would settle.

A second answer to the question of how the EU was able to bring the US to the negotiating table and create a new international privacy regime is elaborated by Newman (2004). Newman correctly points out that the market access threat should be credible in a number of policy areas, including corporate governance and securities regulation, but the EU has failed to convert the US to its positions. Thus, not just market power, but what he calls effective market power, "a nation's capacity to deploy domestic political institutions into international political influence,"[13] is necessary. For Newman, the domestic institutions that reinforce the domestic policies in an issue area make the market power effective. Thus, the creation of a group of independent data privacy authorities that traded information among themselves, and had the power to force the EU Commission to act, proved to be the lynchpin of the EU's success. Others have also credited the more comprehensive institutional infrastructure, which the EU developed during its evolution, with yielding benefits at the international level. Mattli and Büthe (2003) demonstrate convincingly that the EU is more effective than the US in setting international product standards in the International Standards Organization because the EU and its member states have formalized institutions to bridge the business-government gap, whereas the US does not. Using an institutional approach to understand why the EU was effective in promoting its standard is conducive to understanding the conflict. Again, however, the argument suffers from the same question: why, if the EU had effective market power, did negotiations result in an agreement that reflected a great deal of EU compromise?

Farrell (2003) tackled that question with a constructivist argument, that the EU's compromises were the result of real preference changes among decisionmakers, brought about by the long and intensive discussions with the US negotiators. His argument was that deliberative discourse among the different actors created conditions that made each side receptive to new ideas about solutions. Rather than seeing the Safe Harbor Agreement as showing EU weakness vis-à-vis the US, Farrell used that outcome to demonstrate how dialogue can change attitudes, interests, and negotiating positions of both parties. He writes:

> Thus, the negotiation of Safe Harbor provides important evidence supporting constructivist accounts of how international actors behave. The two key moments of the negotiations demonstrate the importance of argument and persuasion as a vital explanatory factor. . . . [Aaron's] initial proposal for a 'Safe Harbor' disclosed new possibilities of action to the protagonists . . . [and] actors on the U.S. side were successful in persuading EU member-state representatives to accept a new set of ideas concerning self-regulation and privacy.[14]

The harmonious conclusion painted by Farrell, however, is in sharp contrast with the acrimonious debates within the EU institutions themselves. Although the representatives of the member states were ultimately persuaded to accept the self-regulatory mechanism, the Article 29 Working Party (the member states' data protection commissioners, who had the technical expertise with privacy issues) was against the arrangement. Moreover, the European Parliament voted 279 to 259 against considering Safe Harbor adequate. Safe Harbor exists today only because the Article 29 Working Party and the European Parliament had no power to prevent the Commission from recognizing the agreement. In the words of Internal Market Commissioner Bolkestein to the European Parliament: "If Parliament were ultimately to support the Commission's proposal, then it would not end up out in the cold . . . The United States has no desire to revisit the discussions again and the Commission also takes the view that the talks are over." If this is constructivism, then it would be difficult to distinguish it from power bargaining theories in any meaningful way.

There is, however, an inquiry that is analytically prior to the "how the EU was powerful enough to force the US to negotiate" question. That question is, "Why did the US and the EU disagree about privacy protection in the first place?" By most accounts, the US and the EU should have had fairly similar preferences for data protection; they had agreed on the principles of data protection in international regimes, and similar ideas were the basis for national laws. Bennett (1992), who authoritatively analyzed the data privacy debates in Europe and the US through 1990, concluded that there was convergence in the policy inputs, even as divergence in policy outputs existed because of national structures. By virtue of negotiating and ratifying multilateral privacy framework documents, like the 1980 OECD

Guidelines on the Protection of Privacy and Transborder Flows of Personal Data ("OECD Guidelines"), the EU member states and the US had already agreed to honor the same data protection principles.[15] It is, therefore, fair to ask, why was there a US-EU conflict at all? After all, within the EU itself, different legal systems and institutions were able to comply with the Directive. There was nothing structural in the US legal system that would have prevented the US from adapting legislation to guarantee data privacy in line with its OECD commitments.

Westin (1996) argued that different cultural legacies were the source of the conflict. Whereas the EU preferred a regulatory approach consistent with its administrative infrastructure, the US wanted a decentralized, self-regulatory system that comported with its traditional regulatory approach. Naturally, there are historical and cultural differences between all states, and it would be foolish to overlook these factors completely, especially given how history and institutions are related.[16] On the other hand, the EU managed to implement the directive in various different regulatory frameworks in Europe. More importantly, the claim that the US would be culturally uncomfortable with the comprehensive data protection offered by the Europeans is refuted by opinion polls (analyzed in greater detail in Chapter 2) that show a majority of Americans preferred the federal government to legislate privacy protection. Europeans and Americans also reported similar levels of distrust of businesses to protect their data. If there were few cross-national differences between the US and EU publics on data protection, there were even more similarities in the multinational businesses' response: in EU countries and the US, similar reservations about the proposed system were voiced by business lobbies and industry associations. Thus, the claim that culturally the US would have been an inhospitable ground for the European Data Protection Directive's privacy strictures is undermined by data showing similar preferences of interests across borders. What changed across governments, however, was the access that pro-privacy interests or business interests had to the government. That is the analytical lens that best captures the different preferences and outcomes.

To answer the earlier question of why there was a conflict despite similar outlooks by various interest groups on both sides of the Atlantic, this book uses a liberal intergovernmental approach. Liberal intergovernmentalists derive state preferences from interest groups vying for power within the state. By understanding which groups the state represents in international negotiations, a state's preferences become more robust empirically and more comprehensible. Similarly, negotiation outcomes should be understood in the context of these preferences. Moravcsik (1997) argued that, "the state is not an actor but a representative institution constantly subject to capture and recapture, construction and reconstruction by coalitions of social actors. Representative institutions and practices constitute the critical 'transmission belt' by which the preferences and social power of individuals and groups are translated into state policy. . . . Every government represents some individuals and groups more fully than others."[17]

By analyzing where the negotiating positions of the US Government and the EU Commission originated, it is easier to see patterns of responses, and to explain how and why the Safe Harbor Agreement had the characteristics it did. Only a focus on different interest groups in the creation of each country's negotiating stance can really explain why there was a conflict to begin with, and how it was resolved. In fact, the interest group interactions become essential to understanding the European reaction to the Passenger Name Record dispute in 2003. When one recalls that the European Parliament and Article 29 Working Party had been forced to watch their recommendations being ignored in the final Safe Harbor Agreement two years earlier, it is easier to understand their willingness to take the relatively extreme step of suing the Council of Ministers and the EU Commission in the European Court of Justice.

As the following chapter shows, opinion surveys in both the EU and the US showed that citizens were concerned about how their data were being used, trusted similar institutions to do the right thing with their personal data, and were interested in greater government regulation in this area. Moreover, in both the EU and the US, businesses were opposed to the data protection proposals. Shaping the negotiation positions of both "countries"[18] (for want of a better word in the EU context), however, was the relative access of interests to the negotiators. In the EU, when crafting the European Data Protection Directive in 1990, only pro-privacy interests (the data protection authorities of several member states) were consulted, and businesses were unable to make significant changes to the Directive after it had been drafted by the EU Commission.[19] In the US, by contrast, business interests were consulted almost exclusively and the administration's negotiation position was based on a paper written essentially by telecommunications industry lobbyists.[20] Thus, the power conflict described above did not originate from systematically incompatible structural differences between the US and EU, but rather from the relative positions of interests within each society, and from the type of causal mechanism that linked state bargaining behavior with domestic preferences.

As this book will argue, the resolution of the conflict was also not determined by structural differences in power capability between the EU and the US. On both sides of the Atlantic, important groups preferred an imperfect agreement to nonagreement and a potential trade war. The fact that the dispute was considered a trade dispute, and hence negotiated by the Department of Commerce in the US and the Internal Market Directorate General in the European Commission, meant that keeping commerce flowing was the overriding goal of both sides. Those groups or institutions with strong preferences not to compromise (for example, the National Business Coalition on E-Commerce and Privacy in the US, and the Article 29 Working Party in Europe) became increasingly marginalized as negotiations wore on.

To see the Safe Harbor Agreement in these terms implies that societal preferences changed over the course of negotiations. This is true at the aggregate level, not the individual level. Thus, whereas constructivist accounts of the Safe Harbor Agreement give credit to individual leaders who changed their preferences as they became more engaged in the negotiations and more educated about the proposals of the other side, liberal intergovernmentalists see shifts in the domestic coalitions underpinning the positions of the negotiators, thus, ultimately changing the scope of possible bargains.

The Safe Harbor Agreement was essentially an agreement to avoid the most egregious misuse of Europeans' private data, while at the same time creating a semipermanent "cease fire" that would allow transatlantic data (and hence commerce) to flow, despite not meeting the letter or intent of the European Data Protection Directive. It is important to recognize, however, that the agreement was designed by two countries that realized they could not force the other to capitulate, and that interests on both sides did not get exactly what they had initially preferred. Thus, although the US and the EU were able to move to the pareto frontier (agreement which forestalled trade disruptions), the point on the pareto frontier was closer to the US preferences than the EU's. Power was an important determinant of the outcome in the short run. To make the point about power symmetry more obvious, one need only contrast the reaction of the US to the European Data Protection Directive with that of the rest of the world. All non-EU countries were equally at risk of the EU blocking data transfers if they did not guarantee the protection of those data in ways acceptable to the EU Commission. In the six years since the European Data Protection Directive came into force, most of the other countries around the world have drafted, or tried to pass, legislation that would be deemed adequate by the EU Commission. Indeed, in many cases, legislators explicitly acknowledged their intent to meet the EU's standards so that there would be no data transferral problems.

When the Safe Harbor Agreement was reached, the US negotiators had hoped it would establish a new, hybrid regulatory standard to deal with privacy concerns, and one that would be adopted by other states around the world. However, whereas the US was powerful enough to negotiate the Safe Harbor Agreement, which many in Europe felt did not really meet the adequacy standard, other countries did not ultimately try to emulate Safe Harbor because the EU Commission discouraged it in bilateral adequacy meetings. As a result, large areas of the world have adopted legislation consonant with the European Data Protection Directive, leaving the US fairly isolated in its position. Chapter 5 details some of the other countries' responses to the European Data Protection Directive, and shows that the Europeans de facto set an international standard despite opposition from the US and the lack of international negotiations.

The international community, including the US, had negotiated the multilateral privacy guidelines that established the basis for the European Data Protection Directive in the late 1970s.[21] Under the auspices of the OECD and the Council of Europe, the international community created a consensus on the basic ideas about data privacy. The European approach, which the drafters of the Directive believed mainly codified the 1980 OECD Guidelines that the US had also approved, did not represent a fundamental change in the principles of data protection. Consequently, some Europeans expressed surprise at the US unwillingness to formalize the principles it had agreed to in these international negotiations.

For US businesses and the Department of Commerce, the OECD Guidelines had been appropriate for an earlier technological state of data transfer between countries, but new networking technologies in the 1990s and the widespread use of the Internet made these principles unworkable or, at best, impractical. From the perspective of the US telecommunications industry, these international guidelines and principles were outdated. Yet it seems clear in retrospect that the majority of the US business community and government missed the signals that the Europeans were going to agree on a common standard, and that this standard would be substantially different from one the US thought appropriate. Moreover, the US was at an institutional disadvantage in that it had decided not to create a data protection board in the United States, even though that had been explicitly considered in congressional hearings in 1990,[22] leaving policy initiatives and agenda setting prerogatives to the European Data Protection Authorities. As privacy expert, David Flaherty, stated in his 1990 Congressional testimony:

> The EEC, I am informed, is also about to issue guidelines on data protection for the whole EEC in anticipation of 1992, which I am told they are going to turn into directives for the public and private sector on necessary, essential data protection measures that should be in place in all of the EEC countries. That is going to further the pressure on the US Federal Government and on the private sector to have some body that could represent American interests in these areas.

One can easily imagine a counterfactual[23] data protection scenario that included greater US protection in the early 1990s, perhaps with a data protection board, and new federal, comprehensive legislation, without some of the more bureaucratic features of the European Data Protection Directive that were derided by businesses. Had the US brought together the EU member states and other industrialized countries to establish a new international regime appropriate to the networked technologies, it is likely that the result would have been closer to the preferred point of the US because it would have had allies in Europe (for example, the UK, which ultimately abstained from the Directive) as well as others around the world that did not endorse the Franco-German bureaucratic approach, like Australia, Japan, and India. Once the European Data Protection Directive had been passed, however, the EU was in a much better position to negotiate bilaterally with these other countries because of its size and existing legislation. By taking a laissez faire approach to privacy in the early and mid 1990s, the US allowed the EU to set the global standard because the states within the EU that were in the minority in opposing the European Data Protection Directive draft in 1995 were afterwards legally bound to support the EU's position. Similarly, if the US had immediately called for an international privacy regime conference in the early 1990s, there might have been a critical mass of states that would have moved the privacy proposals closer to the US preferred points. Instead, however, countries like Canada, Argentina, Hong Kong, and others wrote privacy legislation in the ensuing years with an eye toward meeting the EU's standards of adequacy. Thus, any future international regime negotiations would have a critical mass of states incorporating EU standards, leaving the US isolated.

It is, of course, an open question of how long the US can maintain its regime without bowing to the international constraints. With other examples, such as the twelve digit bar code (the US resisted going to thirteen digits for twenty-five years),[24] global trade considerations finally made the US adopt the European international standard. Similarly, by 2001, important US business associations, like the largest electronics trade association, were already calling for federal comprehensive privacy regulation because the US was in danger of having fifty different state standards, making compliance difficult for US businesses domestically.[25]

▪ Why Is Data Protection Difficult to Regulate?

Regulating individual data protection is a challenge to states because there are questions about what defines privacy in a particular setting, about which reasonable people can disagree. Indeed, definitional issues have derailed many a privacy proposal in the US,[26] and there is no agreement on a comprehensive definition of privacy among the legal profession, let alone the public. Internationally, there are different legal contexts, arising from different constitutional orders, legal systems, and interpretations. At the level of a culture, societal expectations create a framework where certain information is generally regarded as more private than other information.

Thus, revealing (or not) details about one's self is greatly determined by the societal context under which the information is sought.[27] Finally, at the level of the individual, certain personalities are more prone to protect privacy than others (introverts versus extroverts, or those who have had a negative life experience with privacy issues, for example). Creating international norms to meet the data privacy needs of all people proves difficult. To a large extent, international multilateral agreements about privacy have been respectful of varying preferences, relying instead on broadly written principles that could be adapted to the national context. In the EU, the Commission itself expressly referred to the principle of "subsidiarity" (allowing each member state to create a law to implement the Directive in its own way), choosing closer adaptation to national legal contexts over more absolute harmonization.

From a very general policy perspective, there are two distinct ways to formulate data privacy protection: the first is to restrict the amount of data collected, and to prevent that collected data from being stored and passed on. Thus, there are laws for getting rid of any personal data that aren't needed currently, and requiring organizations to explain to individuals why certain data are collected or transferred to others. The underlying logic of the protection system is that if there is no readily available information, the abuse of that information cannot exist either. This approach prefers to err on the side of caution and to forego any potential benefit the data could have in the future or another context.

Conversely, society can legislate data privacy by allowing the collection and storage of data, but forbidding certain uses or abuses of that data. The law would react to abuses more than proscribe uses preemptively. The benefit of using those data for a purpose not yet evident is thus preserved, and only the uses that society deems inappropriate are forbidden.

These two basic approaches to legislating privacy are detailed here because the US and the EU took these two separate, and in many ways incompatible, paths toward legislating privacy. The EU's method of creating data privacy is to ensure that "excess" data are not collected and that data cannot be used for other purposes than those for which they were collected. In framing the policy response, the EU was guided by the member states' data commissioners, who took a "fundamental human right" view of data protection, based on their own constitutions, where data privacy was enshrined as a fundamental human right (i.e., not one to be traded off for some other benefit). After the European Data Protection Directive had been passed, the 2000 Charter of Fundamental Rights of the European Union actually enshrined data protection at the EU level, thus bringing the approach full circle.[28]

By contrast, the US followed a framework of assuming data collection is acceptable and potentially beneficial, and legislating only where individual problems highlighted a fundamental problem. The provenance of many of the US privacy laws is often an individual's problems with the status quo. Perhaps the most well known example is the 1988 Video Privacy Protection Act, which prohibits video stores from disclosing customer borrowing information. The act was passed after Supreme Court nominee Robert Bork's video rentals became public during his confirmation hearings.

Promulgation of regulations is only the first step in any regulatory mechanism; implementation and enforcement are the key parts of regulation that can dramatically change the regulatory impact. Therefore, another aspect of why legislating privacy is so difficult is that compliance and enforcement are hard to measure. In the European view, compliance means monitoring the organizations that handle data to ensure that they do it correctly. This is an administratively burdensome approach to enforcement.[29] The US approach relies on consumer complaints as a signal that laws may have been broken. However, complaints require that individuals know their rights and understand that they have been violated. As data protection was still in its (relative) infancy, there was a great deal of ignorance about those rights. Even five years after the European Data Protection Directive had come into force, 68 percent of Europeans were unaware of the data protection in place in Europe.[30] Thus, both sides reached opposite conclusions about data protection efficacy: the US celebrated the fact that there were very few complaints about the system, but the European Commission worried that the lack of complaints reflected the Europeans' incomplete understanding of their rights.[31]

■ The Actors in this Study

Only the European Commission had the authority to take the issue of data privacy out of the purview of the member states and move it to the supranational level. As the sole institution allowed to originate EU legislative acts, the EU Commission was the lynchpin for the creation of the European Data Protection Directive. The EU Commission had been asked by the European Parliament twice (in 1979 and 1982) to harmonize data protection in the community, but had not acted. Other studies have characterized the reluctance of the Commission to act as showing that "the primary concern of the Council and the EU Commission seemed rather to be more the promotion of a European data processing industry than the safeguarding of individual rights."[32]

Abe Newman (2004) argued that the EU Commission's hand was forced by the national data protection authorities from some of the member states. Several member states, including Germany and France (the traditional motor of European integration), had legislated their citizens' data protection since the 1970s. As a network of transnational data protection authorities spread among countries, these states' independent data protection authorities became the catalyst for greater supranational European legislation.

The European Parliament, the traditional upholder of individual European rights, noted the unevenness of data protection laws throughout the EU, and again asked the Commission to consider legislating data protection at the EU level in order to facilitate the single market.[33] In 1990, Parliament was successful. The Commission subsumed the data protection division in the Internal Market Directorate General because, before the Maastricht Treaty introduced a political dimension to community action, the only logic of data protection could be internal market harmonization.

The Council of Ministers debated the Commission's drafts, and incorporated input from the private sector, and the last step in the European legislative process was taken by the European Parliament.

European private sector actors lobbied both the member states and the European Parliament through their industry organizations and individually. UNICE (the Union of Industrial and Employers' Confederations of Europe) and European banking sector organizations, like the Banking Federation of the EC and the European Savings Bank Group, were particularly vocal in their opposition to the Directive. The US firms that would later oppose the European Data Protection Directive later were largely uninvolved in lobbying against the Directive between 1991 and 1995, or kept a very low profile.

Once the European Data Protection Directive had been passed, new sets of actors were formed and involved. The Directive created a new independent supervisory agency in each of the member states, headed by a Data Protection Commissioner.[34] The national data protection commissioner had the right to investigate cases of alleged data mishandling, to intervene in the handling of those data (including embargoing data), and to bring legal proceedings in the national judiciary. Thus, the enforcement of the European Data Protection Directive was entirely at the national level. However, there was supranational co-ordination between the data protection commissioners. The Directive created the Article 29 Working Party and the Article 31 Management Committee ("Article 31 Committee"). Of the two, the Article 29 Working Party was the more substantive, fleshing out the implementation of the Directive and negotiating the essence of new issues to be discussed. The Article 29 Working Party comprised a representative from each of the independent supervisory agencies of the member states, as well as a member of the Commission. The Article 29 Working Party was hosted by the Commission's Internal Market Data Protection Unit, and made all of its decisions by simple majority. As detailed in the next chapters, there have been significant differences of opinion between the Article 29 Working Party and the Internal Market Commission representatives, due to their different backgrounds, functions, and remits. The Article 29 Working Party members have the legal and technical background and expertise, and they generally have a privacy hawk outlook. The Commission was more concerned with keeping commerce flowing. One of the significant intra-EU debates involved whether the EU would grant an adequacy standing to the US Safe Harbor Agreement, meaning all member states would have to accept that the US companies that had agreed to the Safe Harbor principles would be deemed to adequately protect Europeans' data. The Article 29 Working Party opined that the Safe Harbor Agreement was insufficient, while the Commission said it was adequate. The European Parliament, in its advisory role to the Commission on this issue, sided with the experts in the Article 29 Working Party, and did not approve Safe Harbor. However, the Commission pulled rank and deemed it adequate, saying the European Parliament did not have the authority to prevent the Commission from making adequacy rulings. During the negotiations of the Passenger Name Record Agreement, the European Parliament and the EU Commission replayed the Safe Harbor argument almost verbatim, with the same result. There is, thus, a clear institutional divide between the opinions of the Article 29 Working Party and the Commission on a number of issues. This contentious history between the Article 29 Working Party and the EU Commission highlights another factor that deserves explication at this point. Although the Article 29 Working Party is an institutionalized committee established in the European Data Protection Directive, in this book it is often characterized as an "interest," leading some to wonder why it would be classified with other groups that have to fight for government recognition. One significant difference between institutions and interests is that institutions have some legal rights leading them to structure and participate in decisionmaking more officially, and (usually) more effectively than interests. Since, as was pointed out above, this is not true of the Article 29 Working Party, it functionally resembles an interest more than an institution, and is, thus, generally classified as such in this book, despite its official recognition in the European Data Protection Directive.

The Article 31 Committee is less public than the Article 29 Working Party, and represents comitology in the EU institutions. Comprising member state representatives, it delivers judgments on Commission proposals for measures to be taken in data protection matters. It votes by qualified majority whether or not the Commission's proposals should be accepted. Its representatives are not data protection experts, and its members tend to prefer that commerce not be disrupted, although for a long time several Article 31 Committee members held up the Safe Harbor Agreement on privacy protection grounds.[35] It is important to understand the institutional dynamics among the Commission, the Council of Ministers, and the European Parliament, and so a brief digression on comitology is in order.

Described in textbooks as "almost preposterously arcane,"[36] the function of comitology in the EU is to assert the Council of Ministers' prerogatives within the regulatory agencies of the Commission in the implementation phase. Comitology committees are chaired by the EU Commission and comprise representatives of the member states from the appropriate ministries with a mandate to oversee the authority delegated to the Commission, especially in the implementation of legislation and directives. Following a 1999 revision of comitology, there are three different types of comitology committees: advisory, management, and regulatory, reflecting (respectively) the decreasing autonomy of the EU Commission vis-à-vis input by the Council. The Article 31 Committee of the European Data Protection Directive is a management committee, which means that after the Commission submits a proposal, the committee must deliver its opinion within a certain time. If the committee does not approve a Commission proposal by qualified majority voting, the "Commission may immediately implement its version and the Council has three months to act, thus strengthening the Commission's prerogatives vis-à-vis the Council."[37] One of the final amendments of the European Data Protection Directive negotiations demanded by the European Parliament was changing the Article 31 Committee from a regulatory to a management committee, indicating that the European Parliament wanted less Council influence in decisions about the implementation of the Directive. Although the European Parliament is uninvolved in the comitology, most of the institutionalist literature[38] assumes similar interests between the European Parliament and the European Commission. During the drafting of the Directive, the European Parliament believed its interests lay closer to the Commission than to the Council. In the case of determining the adequacy of Safe Harbor and the Passenger Name Record Agreements, however, the European Parliament found itself isolated against the EU Commission and Council. Once the Article 31 Committee accepts a proposal, the European Parliament cannot amend or override its opinion. The legality of the European Commission concluding a transatlantic agreement in the face of opposition by the European Parliament was under review by the European Court of Justice at the time of this writing, but it is believed that the European Court of Justice is unlikely to side with the European Parliament on this issue not least because of the wider implications for comitology.

On the US side, the Department of Commerce was the most important agency negotiating the European Data Protection Directive compliance issues with the European Commission. The Department of Commerce venue was important since it put the policy problem squarely in the privacy "doves" purview. Hypothetically, the administration's newly created privacy czar, Peter Swire (appointed in March, 1999), could have handled the European Data Protection Directive compliance problem, which might have led the issue to be constructed with more of a pro-privacy orientation. Swire was also very well informed about the European Data Protection Directive, having written a book about the subject in 1998.[39] Alternatively, Congress or the Federal Trade Commission might have been more interested in consumer groups' views. However, the natural constituency of the Department of Commerce was business, and this was the primary focus of its policies. Only the Department of Commerce was involved in the formal US-EU negotiations, not Congress or other agencies. By his own account, the Department of Commerce's David Aaron had a relatively free hand to decide how to deal with the threat of data flows to the US being interrupted by the Europeans.

In addition to the Department of Commerce, the Clinton administration's e-commerce advisor, Ira Magaziner, figured prominently, if informally, in configuring the ground rules and pushing the self-regulatory message to the US industries in order to get them to present a coherent front to the Europeans. The history of the European Data Protection Directive and the Safe Harbor Agreement negotiations are often said to show how different countries with the same goals prefer different policy decisions because of their history and culture. The argument goes that the EU, because of its emphasis on government-led solutions, preferred EU level regulation, while the US, with its antibig government cultural attitudes, preferred to solve privacy issues with industry-led solutions. Although these stereotypes contain a grain of truth, a closer look at the history of the privacy negotiations does not confirm that underlying cultural attitudes played a major role. Instead, the willingness of government actors to include business in the formulation of the policy to solve the privacy problem was the most significant difference between the US and the EU. What one sees in both areas is a mass public with considerably similar attitudes toward what rights individuals should have regarding the manipulation of their personal data. Public opinion polls confirm the basic similarities in the concerns and wishes between the European and US publics. Even on those questions where one might expect to see large differences—the "who should regulate" questions, for example—a majority of the US public was consistently willing to have the government regulate business because they did not trust business to regulate itself effectively. A March, 2000 *Business Week*/Harris Poll showed that 57 percent of the US citizens polled thought that "the government should pass laws now for how personal information can be collected and used on the Internet," up from 53 percent two years earlier, and significantly more than those who believed that "the government should recommend privacy standards for the Internet, but not pass laws at this time" (21 percent), and "the government should let groups develop voluntary privacy standards, but not take any action now unless real problems arise" (15 percent).[40] Thus, at the level at which the cultural explanation should have had the most explanatory power (i.e., before the intervening institutions filtered these mass preferences into policy), it does not seem to be valid.

■ Overview of the Book

This book is primarily about the politics of the Data Protection Directive and the Safe Harbor Agreement, rather than the issue of privacy per se. There are numerous studies of privacy laws and conceptions of privacy[41] that are invaluable for a greater understanding of the legal concepts generally. These studies, however, often do not address the questions of negotiating among different standards to come up with a common standard.[42] For example, why would a country with very strong national data protection laws (like Germany) agree to a European initiative that is weaker in certain areas? Why would Britain abstain from a vote to create the European Directive rather than vote against it? Why would the US conclude an agreement with the Europeans that many in the US Congress believed was the illegal extraterritorial application of European law on US companies in the US? Thus, there are two stories to tell about the data protection law—one about privacy, and the other about politics. This book is more about the latter than the former, although in order to understand the substance of certain countries' positions, an understanding of their privacy laws must also be included. For those knowledgeable about the European Data Protection Directive and the Safe Harbor Agreement, the sections of the book explaining these agreements can be skipped entirely.

In the realm of politics, there are also questions of who negotiates and what actors are relevant and important. In particular, the role of transnational business has been highlighted[43] to demonstrate that the role of governments in regulating privacy has been circumscribed to a considerable extent. It is also apparent, however, that the role of transnational business varies according to the state context in which it is embedded. This book will examine the differences between the government-business relationships in the EU and the US. When the European financial services and direct marketing sectors mobilized in 1993 and 1994 to prevent the EU from moving forward with the Directive, their views were largely ignored by the Council of Ministers and the European Parliament, and the Directive was passed with only minor revisions. By contrast, US firms were on much stronger footing in persuading the Clinton administration not to pass comprehensive privacy legislation that would unequivocally satisfy the Europeans.

The emphasis of this book is on understanding how the Europeans were able to create a European standard that harmonized different data protection systems within Europe, and how the short term focus of the US administration toward the data protection issue created an opening for other states to follow the lead of the EU. Only a focus on the historical antecedents of the European Data Protection Directive and the Safe Harbor Agreement can adequately explain the choices of actors.

The subsequent chapters of this book examine the international negotiations of data privacy in greater detail. Chapter 2 examines the provisions of the European Data Protection Directive in detail, and describes the existing privacy laws in the US. The chapter also highlights the bearing of some of the public opinion surveys on data protection policy in both the US and the EU. Chapter 3 details the negotiations of the European Data Protection Directive in the EU, and examines the role of businesses and privacy authorities in the drafting of the proposals and subsequent negotiations. Chapter 4 analyzes the US position and negotiations in response to the implications of Article 25 of the European Data Protection Directive. The role of large multinational technology companies is highlighted and contrasted with the role of pro-privacy consumer groups in setting the US position and negotiation agenda. Chapter 5 reviews some of the responses by other countries to the European Data Protection Directive, and the theoretical and empirical studies of the cost of implementing data protection. Chapter 6 examines the events after the creation of Safe Harbor in May 2000, including the European Parliament's refusal to agree with the Commission's adequacy finding of Safe Harbor, and the Bush administration's attempts to renegotiate Safe Harbor. The final chapter discusses the four main conclusions that emerge from this study.

■ Notes

1. Cherise M. Valles. "Setting the Course On Data Privacy; As U.S. Firms Hesitate, EU Gets Set to Enforce Its Rules." International Herald Tribune (May 28 2001).

2. A directive in the EU requires all of the member states to transpose a set of guidelines written by the EU into national law. In contrast, EU regulations are immediately binding. Directives can occasionally result in laws that are not sufficiently similar across European jurisdictions, but the EU Commission is responsible for monitoring the implementation of directives to ensure compatibility.

3. The term "data protection" (from the German, Datenschutz) is a standard (if inelegant) formulation of the right of individuals to protect information about themselves from being widely disseminated or stored indefinitely. There are other terms that will be used interchangeably in this book to mean the same thing, for example, data privacy, personal information privacy, or personal information protection.

4. Hamilton and Quinlan, 2004.
5. Mattli and Büthe, 2003.
6. Bhagwati, 2004.
7. Morgan and McGuire, 2004.
8. Before the Safe Harbor Agreement, the EU envisaged creating standard contractual clauses for individual companies that were in states without adequate data protection laws.
9. Mutual recognition means that a product which meets the regulatory requirements in one jurisdiction be allowed into another market on the same terms, even if the regulatory requirements in that market are different or higher. This method creates minimal regulation and was used by the EU to eliminate many non-tariff barriers in the single European market in 1986.
10. Farrell, 2003.
11. Krasner, 1991, p. 337.
12. Ibid., p. 348.
13. Newman, 2004, p. 6.
14. Farrell, 2003, p. 295.
15. See Appendix A for a comparison of the European Data Protection Directive and the OECD Guidelines.
16. Pierson, 2000, and 2004.
17. Moravcsik, 1997, p. 518.
18. The EU is not a country, but, for lack of a better word, throughout this book, the EU is sometimes called a country in juxtaposition to the US because it is too cumbersome to use "collection of states," and because the EU has shared competence in the data protection issue area.
19. Moravcsik (1997) terms this "ideational liberalism" – "the impact on state behavior of conflict and compatibility among collective social values or identities concerning the scope and nature of public goods provision." (p. 515)
20. This is termed "republican liberalism" by Moravcsik (1997): "The impact on state behavior of varying forms of domestic representation and the resulting incentives for social groups to engage in rent seeking." (p. 515)
21. Bennett, 1992.
22. Gurak, 1997, p. 24.
23. On the methodological merits of counterfactuals, see Tetlock and Belkin, 1996.
24. *New York Times*. July 12, 2004. The bar code governance headquarters is now based in Brussels.
25. In January, 2001, the spokesperson for the American Electronics Association said, "This is a new position because there's a new environment. The states have been taking the lead [on privacy legislation]. If [we] have to deal with 50 sets of privacy rules, both consumers and businesses will suffer and obviously so will e-commerce." quoted in http://www.computerworld.com/governmenttopics/government/policy/story/0,10801,56513,00.html.
26. Regan, 1995.
27. Hine and Eve, 1998.
28. One should note that since data protection is now a European fundamental right, any potential multilateral agreement must take this fact into account.
29. Indeed, in the Commission's first report on the implementation of the European Data Protection Directive, it noted the complaints by the national supervisory authorities about the lack of adequate resources to actively monitor compliance. Commission, 2003, p. 13.

30. Eurobarometer 196. available at http://europa.eu.int/comm/public_opinion/archives/ebs/ebs_196_data_protection.pdf.

31. Commission of the European Communities, 2003, p. 12.

32. Nugter, 1990, p. 29.

33. Ibid.

34. Some European countries already had this independent agency.

35. I thank Henry Farrell for making this point clearer.

36. Peterson and Bomberg, 1999, pp. 42–43.

37. Ballmann et al., 2002, p. 559.

38. For an opposing argument, see Ballmann et al., 2002.

39. Swire and Litan, 1998. Swire's official title was Chief Counselor for Privacy in the Executive Office of the President at the Office of Management and Budget.

40. *Business Week*/Harris Poll. March, 2000 available at http://businessweek.com/2000/00_12/b3673006.htm.

41. Schwartz and Reidenberg, 1996; Gormley, 1992; Schoeman, 1984; and Westin, 1967.

42. There has been greater emphasis on regulatory competition recently. See Mattli and Buthe, 2003; Egan, 2001; Evenett et al., 2000.

43. Cowles, 2001; Haufler, 2001, 1999; and Spar, 1999.

2

Why the Conflict? Exploring Public Opinion and Business Concerns

In his book *1984*, George Orwell painted a scenario of a surveillance society that horrified readers. Published just four years after the end of World War II, the book reflected an almost universal consensus that governments should never be allowed to monitor their citizens and intrude on an individual's liberty. The protection of an individual's private facts from prying government became enshrined in legislation and constitutions throughout the world after World War II.[1] Most of the data were easily contained within a nation's borders, and different privacy guarantees in different jurisdictions were not a problem of any significant magnitude.

The advent of widespread computer use in the 1960s forced governments to ensure that safeguards were in place. Although governments could more easily store and transfer personal data with computers, the creation and deployment of computers did not fundamentally alter the government's role. As computer technology evolved, however, the adoption of massive mainframe computers in the 1970s and early 1980s by businesses created the need for an overhaul of national legislation to ensure that business was covered by the same strictures as government. Again, however, the technology could be contained within the nation states without creating significant negative externalities for either the individual or the state.[2] The cross border data protection problems that were envisaged were addressed by two multilateral regimes on data protection: the 1981 Council of Europe Convention for the Protection of Individuals with Regard to Automatic Processing of Personal Data, and the 1980 OECD Guidelines on the Protection of Privacy and Transborder Flows of Personal Data. Bennett's (1992) analysis of both international regimes and domestic privacy laws showed convergence and significant agreement across advanced industrialized economies about data protection principles.

The technological innovation of linking personal and business computers in a network in the 1980s and 1990s provided a new and significant source of cross jurisdictional conflict. With the adoption of personal computers and the networking of those computers, individuals, businesses, and governments could transfer private data out of a nation's jurisdiction more easily, and could theoretically pick the least regulated jurisdiction to collect and manipulate personal data, creating data havens. Policymakers began to believe that the new networking technology mandated new multilateral solutions.

Although the technology presented a similar set of challenges to different countries, the state-specific responses to the threats to privacy were moderated through different institutional constraints and historical legacies. Bennett's analysis detailed significant policy convergence in the 1970s and 1980s in the issue of data privacy in the sense that various countries identified a common threat to individuals' privacy and formulated policies to cope with that threat.[3] The multilateral regimes created in the early 1980s were consonant with most countries' domestic laws, including the US, which had created fair information practices and passed laws that bound the government's hands with respect to individual privacy. The implementation of these principles varied across countries, making the final data protection laws diverge, but the consensus on the basic principles enabled data to be shipped across borders, thereby creating a stable equilibrium.

What makes the second act (1990–2004) of the privacy policy drama remarkable is that, despite a reasonably stable status quo before 1990, most countries were compelled to change their approach to privacy again in the 1990s to accommodate pressure from the European Commission, thus leading to genuine policy convergence. There was consensus on not only the necessity of data protection, but also on how to implement it. The method of transmission in this case was EU supranational regulation, not international organizations. Thus, whereas the convergence described by Bennett in the earlier period reflected policy preferences, or policy input convergence, the current convergence brought about by the European Union reflects greater concern regarding policy outcomes, that is, with the actual implementation and enforcement of the principles.

The first part of this chapter examines the European Data Protection Directive in greater detail, and then the federal laws protecting privacy in the US. The second part analyzes public opinion attitudes in the US and Europe about data privacy. It demonstrates, first, that on both sides of the Atlantic, a majority of the public was interested in data protection, especially as people began to believe that the Internet was eroding that privacy significantly. Second, on both sides of the Atlantic, a majority of the public did not trust businesses to handle their data in an appropriate way. Finally, again on both sides of the Atlantic, a majority of the public preferred the government to regulate data protection, even when survey questions explicitly presented the option of businesses self-regulating. There is a common explanation that the regulatory impulse in Europe, and the nonregulatory "let the market rule" philosophy of the US are due to different cultural histories, and thus, the European Data Protection Directive and Safe Harbor Agreement simply reflected these differences. Often, in congressional hearings, businesses would cite these differing cultural histories as a reason why the US should not pass federal omnibus privacy legislation. Certainly, privacy expert Alan Westin, who consulted for businesses in the privacy issue area, often voiced this theme in his many appearances before Congress. As this chapter details, however, the differences between the European and the US public on the issue of personal data privacy, especially privacy on the Internet, were small. Thus, hypothetically, in the US there would certainly have been grassroots support for a federal legislative solution to the transatlantic privacy dispute. Indeed, over time, more and more US states have jumped into the breach to create data privacy protection for their citizens as pro-privacy grassroots movements have been successful.

▪ A Review of the European Data Protection Directive

The European Data Protection Directive[4] sets out the principles of data protection that must be incorporated in each member state's data protection law. It is important to recall that the primary emphasis of the Directive was to harmonize the different existing standards of data protection in Europe. Therefore, although the fifteen (now twenty-five) member states implemented the Directive in different ways, the national law was required to contain all the elements of the Directive. According to EU jurisprudence, in case of any discrepancy between the national law and the Directive, the European Court of Justice has the jurisdiction to force the member state to change its law to comport with the Directive. Moreover, the data protection law was binding from the day it officially became law (October 28, 1998), even if some member states had not transposed the Directive into their own legislative context by that date.

The Directive consists of seven chapters, and sets up a framework that is largely at the member state level. It is the national data protection commissioners that monitor the developments and the companies in their state, and it is only at the national level that prosecutions can occur. The only EU-level involvement is to provide the setting for the national data protection commissioners to meet (the Article 29 Working Party), and to officially determine (in conjunction with the member state representatives in the Article 31 Committee) whether a third country had "adequate" data protection laws or mechanisms to allow EU data exports to that jurisdiction. Thus, once the Commission determined that, for example, Canada met the adequacy standard, it was no longer permissible for national data protection commissioners to prevent data flows to companies located in Canada. The Canadian company could be prosecuted by Canada's data protection commissioner for violating the country's laws, but the Europeans would not be allowed to block transfers to that company, unless it were found guilty of violating Canada's privacy law. Thus, it would be wrong to assert that the European Data Protection Directive was a "power-grab" by the Commission to extend its competencies into a new area. Most of the monitoring, enforcement and personnel related to the European Data Protection Directive are at the member state level. For this reason, all the claims of "EU extraterritorial application of European law" also have less merit than the sound bites suggest: fifteen sovereign member states passed laws (that happened to be similar in content) to regulate how foreign companies must protect the data of their citizens. This was hardly the stuff of extraterritorial application of EU laws (and it was recognized as a red herring by negotiators in the US fairly early on[5]).

It is also essential to recall that in many of the fifteen member states, the incremental change in privacy protection embodied in the laws was not enormous. Therefore, there were significant benefits for businesses as a result of not having different standards, and hence record-keeping obligations.[6] Indeed, the Internal Market Directorate General cited the probusiness benefits of harmonization in its introduction of the Directive. Of course, some of the changes to national privacy laws that were required by the European Data Protection Directive were perceived to be significantly more onerous in countries like the UK, where certain provisions (discussed below) were characterized as particularly burdensome.

The Directive covers all personal data, defined as "any information relating to an . . . identifiable person . . . who can be identified, directly or indirectly, in particular by reference to . . . one or more factors specific to his physical, physiological, mental, economic, cultural, or social identity," (Article 2a) in the public and private sectors. The data controller (a "natural or legal person, public authority, agency or any other body, which . . . determines the purposes and means of the processing of personal data") is charged with complying with the national laws of the member states concerning any processing of data in those states. Any personal information, whether processed manually or automatically, is within the scope of the Directive. Thus, records in a filing cabinet are as protected as files on a computer. (Britain objected most vigorously to the inclusion of manual files, and in exchange for its abstention from, rather than vote against, the Directive, received a phase-in period of twelve years for the manual files.)

There are exemptions from the Directive: any data that are collected or processed for an activity outside the scope of community law, or operations concerning public security, defense, state security, and the activities of the state in areas of criminal law. Thus, for example, the European arrest warrant that was agreed to in December 2001 (under Justice and Home Affairs) would be exempt from the Directive. A second exemption is for personal data used in the course of a purely personal or household activity, meaning that telephone and address lists are also outside the provisions of the Directive. Posting photos of friends on a website, however, would not be exempt, the European Court of Justice ruled in November 2003.[7]

The Directive's provisions with respect to data quality are quite strict, and were the focus of some of the US criticism of the laws: the data controller must ensure that the personal data are "collected for specified, explicit and legitimate purposes," and must be "adequate, relevant and not excessive" relevant to that purpose. The data must be accurate, up to date, and erased when they are no longer necessary for the purposes for which they were collected. The member states can set up separate protocols for keeping data longer for historical, statistical, or scientific use. Functionally, examples of the data quality article in practice are that every business must be vigilant about erasing files of former employees, businesses must ensure that they make changes to the data if they are advised that they are incorrect, and businesses cannot sell names of customers to others.

Article 7 establishes how data controllers may obtain data legitimately, and what they may legitimately do with them. The data may be processed only if the subject has given his unambiguous assent, or if the data subject's "vital" interests require it. There are other caveats to the unambiguous assent provision, but these are primarily to protect the data subject. The question of whether "unambiguously given consent" requires subjects to "opt in," rather than "opt out," of data collection requests, is not settled in the Directive, and different member states could theoretically take different views on this requirement.

Article 8 prohibits the processing of so-called sensitive data, information about "racial or ethnic origin, political opinions, religious or philosophical beliefs, trade-union membership . . . health or sex life," unless explicit consent is given by the data subject. Exceptions to this article include a "foundation, association, or any other non-profit-seeking body with a political, philosophical, religious, or trade-union aim, and on condition that the processing relates solely to the members of the body . . . and are not disclosed to a third party without the consent of the data subject," as well as medical professionals bound by professional secrecy laws. Subject to appropriate safeguards, member states may also add exemptions for reasons of "substantial public interests."

The processing of any data concerning criminal convictions or security measures is allowed only by the properly designated public authority, though a member state may obtain a derogation to allow others to process these sensitive data (with "suitable safeguards") if it notifies the Commission. Only the official agency in a member state may keep a complete record of criminal convictions. Article 13 establishes the ability of member states to create what amounts to a national security exemption to the privacy right. By restricting the scope of obligations and rights in cases of national security, defense, public security, the prevention, investigation, detection, and prosecution of criminal offences, and important economic or financial interest of a member state or of the European Union, the Directive is fairly flexible with respect to the public interests that may require a curtailing of the right to privacy. Thus, for example, having personal data on passports and visas, or collecting information to thwart terrorism, falls outside the ambit of the Directive.

In Article 9, the Directive emphasizes the importance of specific exemptions for freedom of information, freedom of expression, and journalistic and artistic freedom (the First Amendment rights in the US) by requiring the member states' law to incorporate exceptions to privacy rights. There is, thus, an explicit attempt to acknowledge and arbitrate between different fundamental rights. However, as Swire and Litan (1998) argue, the language of the article "suggest[s] that free expression will prevail over privacy rights less often than would be true under the First Amendment to the US Constitution."[8]

Some of the most controversial elements of the Directive were the "notice" and "access" provisions incorporated in Articles 10–12. Multinational businesses in the EU as well as the US objected to the disclosure requirements for being overly complex and burdensome. Article 10 specifies that the data controller must give the subjects at least the following information: (1) the identity of the controller; (2) the purposes of the processing for which the data are intended; and (3) any further information such as the recipients of the data, and the existence of the right of access to, and the right to rectify, the data concerning them. Article 11 stipulates similar disclosure requirements if the data have not been collected directly from the subject, placing the burden of notification on the controller, who passes the data to a third party "at the time of undertaking the recording of personal data." These notification requirements are tempered by exemptions for any disclosures that "would involve a disproportionate effort," or are part of historical or statistical studies.

The administrative requirement to notify was coupled with the rights of access in Article 12 that many companies also thought extremely burdensome. Article 12 grants data subjects the right to review, "at reasonable intervals" and "without excessive delay or expense," the information that is being processed about them, as well as the purpose of that processing, and the recipients to whom the data are disclosed. The data subjects have the right to correct data that is incorrect, or to erase data that contravenes the requirements of the Directive, and to block transfers to third parties in such cases. The subjects are also given the right to object to the processing of data in certain circumstances, a decision that would be arbitrated by the national data authority.

The data controllers must also safeguard the confidentiality and security of the data (Articles 16 and 17), which means encrypting data sent over the Internet, as well as implementing other security measures. Moreover, the data controller must notify the relevant data authorities of exactly what data they are processing, and why (Articles 18–19). Although there are exemptions to this requirement, these are carefully circumscribed. Consequently, the notification requirement was perceived by businesses as being particularly cumbersome.

One of the most interesting elements of the Directive is the right of data subjects not to be subject to a "significant" decision based solely on their data. For example, the Directive would make it illegal for someone to be fired from a job based solely on his tardiness statistics, or to call a loan based solely on a deterioration of creditworthiness statistics. The article, thus, would presumably forbid profiling along the lines of the proposed (and then mothballed) Total Information Awareness program in the US.[9]

The most controversial aspect of the Directive was Article 25, which prevented all data flows to countries without an "adequate" level of data protection. The article stipulates that "Where the Commission finds . . . that a third country does not ensure an adequate level of protection within the meaning of paragraph 2 of this Article, Member States shall take the measures necessary to prevent any transfer of data." The article also gives the Commission the right to make an adequacy finding, following the comitology procedure outlined in Article 31.

Article 26 gives derogations to the transfer requirements detailed above, and proved to be essential in keeping data flows going during the extended negotiations on adequacy between the EU and third countries. Under Article 26(2), "Member States may authorize a transfer, or a set of transfers, of personal data to a third country which does not ensure an adequate level of protection . . . where the controller adduces adequate safeguards with respect to the protection of the privacy and fundamental rights and freedoms of individuals, and as regards the exercise of the corresponding rights" provided they notify the Commission and the other member states of their decision to send data to the non-EU country. The Commission or member states can object to the transfer, but have not done so to date. The Commission has explicitly instructed that the use of the Article 26 derogations be only an interim measure while the Commission evaluates third-country adequacy claims, or develops standard contractual clauses. These derogations should not be relied on in the medium-long term. As the Commission's Susan Binns, explained in 1998:

> Article 26 is a flexible provision, and it's Article 26, in a certain sense, which is keeping data flows moving at the moment, and data protection commissioners, when they exercise their authority in approving or supervising the transfer of data to third countries, will use all the flexibility they can under Article 26 to avoid the ultimate weapon that they have at their disposal, which is to say that a transfer may not take place. The problem with Article 26 is that it is micromanagement. It is very heavy in terms of its administrative burden both on the data protection commissioners and on companies themselves.[10]

Thus, the Commission expected every non-EU country to make an attempt to create the legislative environment that would ultimately enable the EU to make an adequacy finding.

The final provisions of the Directive, Articles 27–34, relate primarily to the institutional infrastructure that would govern the Directive. As noted above, the Commission did not emerge as the central institution for data protection, relying instead on every member state to establish an independent data authority that would meet under the auspices of the Commission as the Article 29 Working Party, and "consider items placed on its agenda by its chairman, either on his own initiative, or at the request of a representative of the supervisory authorities, or at the Commission's request." This ongoing role was essential to making the regulation appropriate to the quickly evolving technology environment.

Overview of Privacy Laws in the United States

When the Europeans had passed the European Data Protection Directive, it was apparent to policymakers on both sides of the Atlantic that the US system would most likely not be deemed adequate. This did not mean, however, that the US had no privacy protection. On the contrary, many of the laws that proved important in shaping the early European legislation and international guidelines were based on principles established in the US.

The primary reason that the US was not considered to have "adequate" protection for European data was because the US did not have a comprehensive privacy law. The US approach to privacy involved sectoral legislation, leaving some parts of the economy unprotected from privacy infringements. Moreover, as exemplified by the financial privacy laws (Gramm-Leach-Bliley) that were passed in 1999, sometimes the sectoral laws did not contain all the elements required by the European Data Protection Directive, and, thus, would not be judged adequate, even if covered by a legislative framework. The "patchwork quilt"[11] of privacy legislation in the US reflected the history of the establishment of the right to privacy in the US. This legislative history is often cited as the reason for "cultural" differences between the US and other countries and, thus, is briefly detailed below. As the legal literature on privacy in the US is enormous, this review is necessarily abbreviated, and the finer points of legal doctrine are ignored.[12]

The US Bill of Rights did not provide for a fundamental right to privacy. Thus, the right to privacy was organically created through original legal thinking and precedent. The first milestone in the foundation of the right to privacy was an 1890 Harvard Law Review article by Samuel Warren and Louis Brandeis, which created a "right to be left alone." Fearing the encroachment of advancing civilization, in this case, new advances in photography and the intrusive press, the authors posited that the individual had to be able to retreat from the world into solitude.

The foundation of a privacy law with torts was created in the 1960s, when the Warren and Brandeis formulation proved too vague. Prosser (1960) posited four different components of the right to privacy that included no intrusion into a person's private affairs, no public disclosure of embarrassing facts, no publicity that puts an individual in a false light, and no appropriation of an individual's name or likeness for one's own advantage.[13] In 1970, the Fair Credit Reporting Act incorporated some of the aspects of Prosser's rights, protecting consumers from the disclosure of inaccurate and arbitrary personal information held by consumer reporting agencies.

These aspects of the right to privacy were further explored with the widespread use of computer technology. In 1972, the Department of Health, Education and Welfare created an advisory committee to study the automated record-keeping systems maintained by government agencies. Its elaboration of the fair information practices that should be incorporated into all data systems was codified almost verbatim in the US Privacy Act of 1974. The basic principles of fair information practices have been adopted by most countries, and were the cornerstone of many of the domestic privacy laws and international regimes. The principles can be described as follows:

1. The Principle of Openness: The existence of recordkeeping systems and databanks that contain personal data must be publicly known, along with a description of the main purpose and uses of the data.
2. The Principle of Individual Participation: Individuals should have a right to view all information that is collected about them. They must also be able to correct or remove data that is not timely, accurate, relevant, or complete.
3. The Principle of Collection Limitation: There should be limits to the collection of personal data. Data should be collected by lawful and fair means, and should be collected, wherever appropriate, with the knowledge or consent of the subject.

4. The Principle of Data Quality: Personal data should be relevant to the purposes for which it is collected and used. It should be accurate, complete, and timely.
5. The Principle of Finality: There should be limits to the use and disclosure of personal data: data should be used only for purposes specified at the time of collection. Data should not be otherwise disclosed without the consent of the data subject or other legal authority.
6. The Principle of Security: Personal data should be protected by reasonable security safeguards against such risks as loss, unauthorized access, destruction, use, modification, or disclosure.
7. The Principle of Accountability: Record-keepers should be accountable for complying with fair information practices.[14]

The history of the Privacy Act of 1974 supports the view that Congress believed the computerization of *government* records was the primary threat to privacy. This view was reinforced by the Privacy Protection Act of 1980, which prevented government officials from searching for, or seizing, any work or documentary materials held by a "person reasonably believed to have a purpose to disseminate to the public a newspaper, book, broadcast, or other similar form of public communication" without probable cause. However, as commercial enterprises became more computerized, and information was more efficiently collected by the private sector, certain industries or commercial sectors became regulated by the federal government as well. The Cable Communications Act of 1984, the Video Privacy Protection Act of 1988, the Telephone Consumer Protection Act of 1991, the Health Insurance Portability and Accountability Act (HIPAA) of 1996, and the 1999 Financial Services Modernization Act (Gramm-Leach-Bliley) (see Appendix B for further information about each of these acts), all applied privacy and fair information practices to sensitive sectors. Usually, these sectors and industries were regulated because of abuse resulting from the absence of privacy regulations. Over time, as business and individuals adopted new technologies, the potential for privacy abuse in commercial settings, indicating significant deviations from the fair information practices, increased dramatically. Still, the US system had its supporters. Privacy expert Alan Westin described the US privacy laws in a 1996 testimony before the House Banking and Finance Committee:

> Privacy approaches in the US have been a product of the following, well-recognized fundamental elements in our national life:
>
> - The basic distrust of government, and emphasis on individual rights and choices on which our country was founded
> - The immense importance of the First, Fourth, and Fifth Amendments

in our Bill of Rights in framing the ways we define and implement privacy rights and information-handling, and how our courts balance those rights with other compelling social interests

- The strong states-rights component of our federal system
- The high status given to individually-generated litigation and court rulings as a powerful remedy for perceived harm
- Our selection of industry sectors for concrete and tailored legislative action and area-expert regulatory agency supervision (on privacy and many other matters), rather than adopting multi-industry or nationwide interventions
- A major popular preference for voluntary privacy policies and actions by business and nonprofit organizations over legislative solutions, unless such voluntary actions are seen as insufficient, or in need of legal reinforcement
- The powerful role of the media in the U.S. in exposing misconduct or abuses by businesses or government, and the actions that business and government leaders take to either avoid media thunderbolts, or to correct mistakes when they become public embarrassments
- The profound commitment of the American people to market-based solutions and private choices by individual consumers about alternative privacy policies, wherever these are meaningfully afforded . . .

A general sense, that if technological methods can be found to let people set their own different boundaries and balances of privacy, this would be a preferred solution, given the wide variation in privacy concerns and preferences from individual to individual that solid survey research shows to be the continuing situation in the US.[15]

To the extent that Westin's characterizations about the genesis of American privacy laws and public opinion are historically correct,[16] the advent of networked computers in the 1990s changed the advantages and effectiveness of the US sectoral privacy law system, and, in the process, affected US public opinion about it as well. In his review of the US privacy laws in international perspective, Gellman (1996) articulated why the US "patchwork quilt" of privacy regulations may be insufficient in the present and future. In addition to jurisdictional conflicts between states, there are also conflicts between sectors as businesses evolve into hybrids that are not explicitly covered in one sector. These jurisdictional problems may result in "forum shopping" and outright breaking of the law because of insufficient monitoring and enforcement.

The absence of comprehensive legislation was due to a lack of consensus on a definition, harkening back to arguments between Prosser and his critics about whether the right to privacy is a composite of other rights, or separate. As Regan (1995) argued, because the issue of privacy could be variously defined, different constituent groups had varied responses to the threats to that privacy. The right to privacy suffered not only a definitional problem, but also had to be explicitly traded off against constitutionally guaranteed, competing rights, especially the freedom of speech and the freedom of information. Thus, although Congress debated many bills to protect privacy, the protection of privacy as a public policy was very difficult because "discussion often became bogged down in court definitions."[17]

There were other political reasons why the US did not have the kind of comprehensive privacy protection as the European countries: well organized, well connected interests opposed legislation, and the beneficiaries of privacy protection were diverse and unorganized.

> Policy [in privacy] imposed costs on fairly well defined interests—government agencies, law enforcement, and intelligence officials, and employers. These interests were already organized, and had easy access to congressional committees and members of congress. In addition to possessing political access and support, and a clear sense of their own interests, they were able to redirect the definition of the issue away from the idea of privacy to other ideas, such as efficiency, crime control, and an honest work force. In the process, the politics of interests dominated. The ambiguity of the idea of privacy, and its definition as an individual right, made it relatively easy to move from the politics of ideas to the politics of interests . . . In these cases of privacy and technology, to disregard interests is to miss the essential story. Politics, in these cases, is similar to interest-group politics, with subcommittee chairs playing key roles, pro forma floor approval, and behind-the-scenes negotiations among a relatively small group of interested parties.[18]

These interested parties had stymied most legislative privacy protection proposals for many years. Regan notes that from 1965 to 1972, over two hundred and sixty bills related to privacy were introduced but only two were eventually passed.[19] "In the area of information privacy, there were more than one hundred and fifty days of hearings from 1965 to 1988, excluding those on the privacy of credit records. Almost fifteen committee or staff reports on information privacy were released during the same period."[20] The issue was clearly on the legislative agenda, but interests were able to "divide and conquer," and, thus, prevent significant privacy protection. The relatively few legislative acts that were passed before the 1990s reflected very public problems with the status quo, which were remedied in a specific piece of sectoral legislation rather than a global privacy right.

However, data privacy was important to the business community as well: the issue was significant to a growing sector, the telecommunications industry. Privacy figured prominently in the Internet and the "new economy" that promised enormous productivity increases. All industrialized countries were trying to foster this sector, but US companies had a commanding competitive advantage. For European companies, having a level playing field with the US (and other countries') multinational companies was essential to maintaining competitiveness in the sector. The European and US multinational companies impacted by the European Data Protection

Directive had fought against some of the more cumbersome aspects of the legislation (with little success) during the five year negotiations for the Directive. In lobbying the Clinton administration during the negotiations about Safe Harbor, US companies were in the spotlight, while to a large extent the European countries' business communities kept silent, preferring the US regulation to mirror their own.

As history unfolded, it became apparent that the US had underestimated the resolve of the Europeans to regulate, and missed its chance to negotiate a multilateral agreement that might have been closer to its approach to data privacy regulation. It is important to remember that "neither the 'equivalence' nor the 'adequacy' principle demands regulations in different countries that are identical in both formal and substantive terms."[21] Thus, there was nothing that would have prevented the US from using its own legal framework to create an omnibus privacy law that covered all public and private sectors. The problem was not the functional impossibility of crafting legislation, but rather a strong disinclination to bind the hands of the entire commercial sector.

The emergence of the Internet and e-commerce (after the Europeans had passed the European Data Protection Directive) became a polarizing factor between the positions of the Europeans and the US. The two governments had a completely different attitude toward regulating the Internet and the e-commerce sector: whereas the US government was extremely reluctant to regulate some of the adverse impact of the Internet for fear of killing the goose that lays the golden egg, the Europeans were not so reticent, and insisted that they have authority over cyberspace. This was true, not only in data privacy, but also for Internet content censorship and Internet taxation issues.[22]

If the differences between the EU and the US governments on whether to regulate privacy were clear cut, at the grassroots level the differences were almost nonexistent. Whereas others have argued that the differences between the EU and the US positions reflect cultural values, opinion polls refute such an interpretation of privacy regulation. Opinion polls conducted in the US show reasonably strong majorities in favor of more government regulation that are similar to European beliefs (see Tables 2.1 and 2.2 presented on pages 42–48 at the end of this chapter). For methodological reasons discussed below, these poll results probably understate the majorities in favor of greater privacy protection. The surveys presented here show three things: first, citizens in the EU and the US (as well as Canada) agreed that they should be asked before a company uses personal information, and should be consulted before that information is passed along. Second, terrorism did not make the US less supportive of privacy. The US was less willing to allow monitoring of phone calls and emails to fight international terrorism than the Europeans, and finally, the old stereotype, that the US is more sanguine about the motives of businesses while the Europeans are less worried about government, is also not borne out by these opinion polls. Even before the Bush administration's explicit approval of the use of commercial databases for government purposes, US respondents worried about businesses' handling of their private data.

One of the problems in trying to find evidence of similar attitudes toward privacy in different countries is that multinational survey data are extremely scarce. Thus, the same question is never asked in different countries (except in the Eurobarometer surveys of the fifteen member states). In Table 2.1, different surveys from Europe and the US are juxtaposed to adduce similar attitudes, but, as the wording is different, these comparisons should be used more as benchmarks than absolute statistics. However, the surveys show remarkable convergence, and go to the main point of privacy attitudes: at the mass public level, both the US and European citizens were concerned about threats to their privacy to similar degrees, and from similar sources. Moreover, both looked to government regulation to protect the individuals from privacy abuses.

In the EU, 91 percent of the respondents said they should be informed about why organizations are gathering personal data, and if they are sharing it with other organizations. In the US, 79 percent of the respondents said it is extremely important, while another 18 percent said it was somewhat important, that they control who can get information about them. Similarly, 77 percent said it was a major invasion of privacy, while another 19 percent said it was a minor invasion of privacy, to have companies selling information about their customers to other companies. Seventy-two percent of EU citizens said they would be very, or quite, worried to have personal information that could be used to send them advertising leaflets, or sold to shops, insurance companies, and public bodies.

Thirty-three percent of the US respondents said they would be willing to allow government agencies to monitor the telephone calls and emails of ordinary US citizens on a regular basis to reduce the threat of terrorism. In Europe, however, only 7 percent of respondents said everyone should agree to have their telephone calls monitored, though a further 54 percent were willing to allow some monitoring under strict supervision, but only of those suspected of terrorist activities. The differences in the number of choices make this comparison more difficult, but it is clear that terrorism in the US did not make the average US citizen more amenable to privacy intrusions. Indeed, the percentage of adults who said their right to privacy is "relatively absolute [sic]" (58 percent) was almost double the percentage of respondents who said sometimes their right to privacy must be balanced against the needs of society as a whole.

Finally, in the question of which privacy threats were most feared in the EU and the US, there were remarkable similarities: 57 percent of US citizens said they thought the biggest threat to their right to privacy came from banks and credit card companies, while only 29 percent thought it came from the federal government because it can secretly collect information about people's private lives. Furthermore, only 8 percent thought law enforcement agencies were the biggest threat. In the EU, only 35 percent of the respondents trusted credit card companies to use their personal data in a way they thought appropriate, while 72 percent thought that law enforcement ("the police") was using their data appropriately. As indicated, "the police" received the greatest percentage of trusting responses after "medical services and doctors."

One of the questions raised during the 1995–2000 debate about privacy was whether the US and EU citizens had similar views on how the threat to individual privacy should be addressed, even if they agreed on its existence. Mostly it was asserted, without consulting the available data, that the US citizens did not want the government to step in. This assertion, however, was belied by the wealth of survey data (see Table 2.1) that showed very strong majorities in favor of the government acting.

In all the US public discussions on how best to accommodate the provisions of the European Data Protection Directive that required adequate protection of personal data in third countries, it was asserted that the US public would not want government regulation, being essentially skeptical about the government. For that reason, as well as due to the inherent flexibility to change as technology changed, the US public was believed to prefer a system of business self-regulation. Most of the opinion polls conducted since 1995 on Internet data privacy, however, do not support the conclusion that the US citizens did not want government interference. Although most of the polls asking about data privacy have been sponsored by industry attempting to gather evidence that the US simply wants fair information practices,[23] even these polls show the public preferring the government to legislate. Perhaps the most accurate summary of US popular opinion regarding privacy on the Internet is that, ideally, the US citizens would have preferred self-regulation had it been effective, but most of them did not think business self-regulation *could* be effective and, therefore, supported government regulation. The best example of that position was a series of two questions on the Privacy & American Business 1998 survey listed in Table 2.1. Although 75 percent of computer users supported Clinton's position to allow industry to develop effective privacy rules and regulate only if the private sector fails, 68 percent of the same respondents believed that the private sector WOULD fail, requiring government legislation to make most businesses observe good privacy policies. Only with the assumption that US computer users expect businesses to fail do these two divergent responses from the same survey population at the same time make sense.

There are many methodological problems with the public opinion surveys on the subject of privacy, and some surveys suffer greater flaws than others.[24] The most obvious problem is that privacy hawks will opt out of every survey design simply by their desire to be left alone. Since the distribution of answers that privacy hawks might give is skewed very heavily toward the pro-privacy side, existing surveys tend to systematically understate the pro-privacy statistics.

There is also a problem with most telephone surveys: the survey design contacts only those with listed numbers, again excluding those who care so much about their privacy that they have paid to have an unlisted telephone number, or those who screen their calls with Caller ID. Even worse, some surveys have been conducted on the Internet, reaching only a self-selected few who are on the Internet, and who volunteer to participate in any survey. For example, Cranor et al. (1999) received responses from a group of Internet users who agreed to evaluate products and respond to surveys for *FamilyPC* magazine. Although the authors admit that they did not obtain a statistically representative sample of citizens, their results have been widely disseminated as showing, among other things, that "a joint program of privacy policies and privacy seals seemingly provides a comparable level of user confidence as that provided by privacy laws."

The wording of questions has been shown to systematically change the pattern of responses, especially the word "concerned" about "threats" to privacy.[25] The questions about whether US citizens are more concerned about privacy in the Internet age are subject to methodological problems with the survey question. However, questions about the best way to safeguard privacy, choosing from various alternatives, are less flawed, although, of course, they understate the responses of privacy hawks who may be more likely to support government regulation.

Given this pattern of responses to questions about government legislation in the late 1990s and early 2000, it is difficult to view comprehensive privacy legislation as a political impossibility in 1997–2003 (at least from the perspective of the voters). Indeed, seven privacy bills were introduced in 2000, including the Online Privacy Protection Act and the Internet Integrity and Critical Infrastructure Protection Act, which contained features like granting consumers access to their information, and making unauthorized access to personal information a crime.[26] The new Republican-controlled House, however, retreated from making Internet privacy a priority, and September 11 pushed the issue out of the public's eye, making self-regulation the dominant mode of privacy protection in the US.

Finally, a note about terminology is required to clear up any potential misunderstanding in the characterization of opinions about privacy. In this book, the terms privacy "hawks" and "doves" are used to differentiate between those who believe privacy considerations trump all other considerations in every case (hawks), and those who believe that though privacy is important, there may be other ways to achieve it (doves). The analogy to security hawks and doves, with both sides believing security is important but doves taking a less dogmatic approach to the problem, is more apropos than the conventional "privacy fundamentalist" label that is often found in privacy literature. The problem with the "privacy fundamentalist" label is that in the US context it has become identified with the often cited public opinion polling results done by Alan Westin. On the basis of multiyear opinion surveys, Westin categorized the US population as "privacy fundamentalists" (approximately 25 percent), "privacy pragmatists" (approximately 63 percent), and "privacy unconcerned" (approximately 12 percent).[27] Westin's results over time show that the proportions of each category have remained mostly stable, though the proportion of people concerned about privacy did rise in the 1990s. However, since responses to survey questions depend on a national legislative status quo relative to some personal ideal, one might expect cross-national variation in the privacy classification percentages. In order to avoid juxtaposing Westin's "privacy fundamentalist" notion with the "privacy is a fundamental human right" position often espoused by the European data protection Commissioners, this book uses a hawk-dove concept.

The next chapters detail the processes of negotiating the European Data Protection Directive and the Safe Harbor Agreement. Since this chapter has shown that cultural regulatory preferences were not the driving force behind the conflict, the following chapters highlight the relative influences of organized interest groups in each country. I argue that the data protection conflicts themselves, as well as the outcomes, were determined by organized interest groups' input into the policymaking process. The fact that there was a conflict at all deserves some explanation since the popular opinions on both sides of the Atlantic were broadly similar, and both the US and EU had signed multilateral agreements on data protection principles. Only by using a liberal intergovernmentalist framework to understand the genesis of each side's negotiating position can the emergence of a conflict be explained. Further, the outcome also is best explained by looking at the role of interest groups during the negotiation of the conflicts. The detailed history of the negotiations shows that in the EU businesses were not consulted at all during the drafting of the Directive, a fact that is significant when one considers that, on average 80 percent of the final Directive is in the Commission's first draft.[28] The principle designers of the Commission's first draft were national data privacy authorities, many of whom considered data privacy a fundamental human right. As lawyers dealing with privacy issues on a daily basis, their views about what should be enshrined at the EU level were broadly similar. Moreover, they were encouraged by their mandate to harmonize upward to the strictest standards, and, therefore, incorporated what might be termed a maximalist approach to writing the EU's Directive. Their views, rather than a more encompassing "European" view (including input from multinational businesses), which the EU Commission is supposed to represent, was the source of the European Directive.

Table 2.1 Public Opinion Surveys About Government Regulation of Privacy (Progovernment regulation opinion in italic type)

Equifax, 1993

My rights to privacy are adequately protected today by laws and organizational practices. Do you agree strongly, agree somewhat, disagree somewhat or disagree strongly?

Strongly or somewhat agree	40%
Strongly or somewhat disagree	*58%*
Not sure	2%

Privacy & American Business, 1997

(asked of computer users only)

Here are three ways that the government could approach Internet privacy issues. Which one of these three do you think would be best at this stage of Internet development?

A. Government should pass laws now for how personal information can be collected and used on the Internet,

B. Government should recommend privacy standards for the Internet, but not pass laws at this time,

C. Government should let groups develop voluntary privacy standards, but not take any action now unless real problems arise.

Pass laws	*58%*
Recommend privacy standards	24%
Let groups develop voluntary privacy standards	15%

Privacy & American Business, June, 1998

(asked of computer users only)

The Clinton administration has called on industry and public-interest groups to develop effective privacy rules and practices on the Internet now, and has said that government should legislate only if the private sector fails to do this. How do you feel about this position—do you strongly agree, somewhat agree, somewhat disagree, or strongly disagree?

Agree	75%
Disagree	22%

Some observers say that businesses will take up the Clinton administration's challenge to adopt good privacy standards because they know that consumers will not engage in active buying on the Internet unless privacy and security concerns are met. Other observers say that only legislation and legal enforcement will make most businesses observe good privacy policies. Do you think that business incentives will be enough or do you think that legislation will be needed?

Business incentives enough	26%
Legislation will be needed	*68%*

NPR/Kaiser Foundation, 1999

Is this loss of privacy problem with computers or the Internet [asked about in an earlier question] something the government should do something about, or shouldn't the government be involved?

Government should do something about	*65%*
Government should not be involved	34%
Don't know	1%

(continues)

Table 2.1 Continued

Business Week/Harris Interactive, 2000

Q: Here are three ways that the government could approach Internet privacy issues. Which one of these three do you think would be best at this stage of Internet development?

		March 2000	Feb. 1998
A:	*The government should pass laws now for how personal information can be collected and used on the Internet*	*57%*	*53%*
	The government should recommend privacy standards for the Internet, but not pass laws at this time	21%	23%
	The government should let groups develop voluntary privacy standards, but not take any action now unless real problems arise	15%	19%

Pew Internet & American Life Project, April 2, 2001

From what you've seen or read, do you think that existing laws protecting a person's telephone conversations are enough to protect their email and online activities as well, or do new laws need to be written just for the Internet?

Existing laws enough	14%
New laws need to be written	*62%*
Don't know/ refused	24%

Markle Foundation, 2000

Q: I'm going to read you a list of problems that some people talk about regarding the Internet. For each one, please tell me whether it would be better to have that problem addressed by the government, by private companies, or by non-profit groups that work on Internet-related issues.

Protecting the privacy of medical information on the Internet.

A:	*Government*	*57%*
	Private companies	18%
	Non-profits	16%

Percentage of adults who say "government should avoid creating new rules for the Internet because it will make the Internet less free and productive" versus "the government should develop rules to protect people when they are on the Internet, even if it requires some regulation of the Internet."

Government should develop rules	*64%*
Government should avoid creating new rules	32%

Percentage of adults who say "businesses and people on the Internet can't be trusted to regulate themselves" versus "I trust businesses and individuals on the Internet to make their own rules and follow them."

Businesses can't be trusted	*58%*
Businesses can be trusted	35%

Q: Now let me read you two short statements, and please tell me which one you favor:

(continues)

Table 2.1 Continued

Statement A: Some people say that companies on the Internet should not be allowed to collect information about where you go and what you buy on the Internet without first getting your explicit permission. They say Internet companies, left on their own, won't do enough to protect privacy, because they stand to gain from collecting and selling such information.

Statement B: Other people say that by collecting information about Internet usage, Internet companies can provide consumers with services better suited to their individual needs. They say that a government ban on collecting such information would limit the speed and growth of the Internet marketplace. Instead, they propose that consumers be given the option to check a box that would keep such information private.

If you had to choose, which would you favor, statement A or statement B?

A:	*Statement A*	*58%*
	Statement B	37%
	Neither (volunteered)	1%
	Don't know/refused	3%

Gallup Poll, June 28, 2001

Do you think the federal government should pass more laws to ensure citizen's privacy online or are the current laws sufficient?

Yes, federal government should pass more laws	*66%*
No, current laws are sufficient	33%
No answer	1%

Harris Poll, 2003

Existing laws and organizational practices provide a reasonable level of protection for consumer privacy today.

	2003	2001	2000	1999
Somewhat or Strongly Agree	44%	38%	51%	59%
Somewhat or Strongly Disagree	*53%*	*63%*	*47%*	*38%*

Public Interests Project, 2003

I'll read you a list of things that some people say the government has a responsibility to do. For each, please tell me whether you think it is something that the government should be responsible for, or not. . . . Guaranteeing a right to privacy . . .

Strongly responsible	*66%*
Somewhat responsible	23%
Somewhat not responsible	4%
Strongly not responsible	5%
Don't know/refused	2%

Table 2.2 Cross National Public Opinion Surveys About Privacy Fears

EU

Question:[a] Do you tend to agree or tend to disagree that you should be informed why organizations are gathering your personal data, and if they are sharing it with other organizations?

Tend to agree	91%
Tend to disagree	5%
Don't Know	4%

Canada

Question:[b] I should be asked for my permission before a company uses my personal information to build a profile on me for the purpose of marketing new products and services.

Agree	82%
Disagree	12%
Neither	6%

US

Question:[c] Privacy means different things to different people. I am going to read you a list of different aspects of privacy. Please tell me how important is . . . being in control of who can get information about you—is it extremely important, somewhat important, not very important or not important at all?

Extremely important	79%
Somewhat important	18%
Not very/ not important at all	4%

US

Question:[d] (Let me mention things that some people feel are interfering with personal privacy today. For each one, please tell me whether you think this is a major invasion of privacy, a minor invasion of privacy, or not really an invasion of personal privacy today.) . . . Companies selling information about their customers to other companies.

Major invasion of privacy	77%
Minor invasion of privacy	19%
Not really an invasion of privacy	3%
Not sure	1%

EU

Question:[e] The personal information that could be collected about people when they use these services could be used to send them advertising leaflets, or be sold to shops, insurance companies or given to public bodies. Would you be . . . about this?

Very or quite worried	72%
Not very/ not at all worried	28%

Hong Kong

Question:[f] If an advertiser keeps track of your visits to websites are the risks greater than benefits or the benefits greater than the risks?

Risks greater than benefits	72.4%
Risks about the same as benefits	22.2%
Benefits greater than risks	5.5%

(continues)

Table 2.2 Continued

EU

Question:[g] In light of the fight against international terrorism, do you think that people should agree to have their telephone calls monitored?

No, the right of individuals must always be respected	33%
Yes, if the monitoring only affects those suspected of terrorist activities	40%
Yes, but only if monitoring takes place under supervision of a (NATIONALITY) judge	14%
Yes, everyone should	7%
Don't Know	6%

US

Question:[h] In order to reduce the threat of terrorism, would you be willing or not willing to allow government agencies to monitor the telephone calls and e-mails of ordinary Americans on a regular basis?

Not willing	62%
Willing	33%
Don't know	5%

Canada

Question:[i] I would like to read you a list of initiatives which could be applied to all Canadians—not just newly arrived immigrants or those awaiting citizenship – and I would like you to tell me whether you would support or oppose being personally subjected to these actions. Allowing intelligence and law enforcement agents to monitor your personal private telephone conversations and e-mail without your knowledge.

Oppose	71%
Support	29%

US

Question:[j] Percentage of adults who say "my right to privacy is relatively absolute," versus, "sometimes my right to privacy must be balanced against the needs of society as a whole."

Right to privacy absolute	58%
Right to privacy must be balanced	38%

US

Question:[k] Which of these would you say is the biggest threat to your own personal right to privacy these days? Is it: banks and credit card companies, because they are collecting and selling marketing information about consumers; the federal government, because it can secretly collect information about people's private lives; or law enforcement agencies, because they are using more aggressive tactics against crime like surveillance cameras in public areas?

Banks and credit card companies, because they are collecting and selling marketing information about consumers	57%
The federal government, because it can secretly collect information about people's private lives	29%
Law enforcement agencies, because they are using more aggressive tactics against crime like surveillance cameras in public areas	8%
None of these (volunteered)	4%
Don't know	3%

(continues)

Table 2.2 Continued

EU

Question: Percentage of EU-15 population that trusts groups below to use their personal information "in a way you think appropriate":

The Police	72%
Social Security	69%
Tax Authorities	59%
Local Authorities	58%
National Authorities	55%
Banks and Financial Institutions	55%
Employers	55%
Market and Opinion Research Companies	43%
Insurance Companies	42%
Credit Card Companies	35%
Credit Reference Agencies	31%
Mail Order Companies	21%

US

Question:[l] As you may know, many sites on the Internet feature privacy statements, which describe what kind of information they collect about visitors to their site and how they use this information. How often do you read such privacy statements on sites . . . often, sometimes, hardly ever, or never?

Often	28%
Sometimes	31%
Hardly ever	29%
Never	12%
Don't know/refused	1%

Canada

Question:[m] How often do you read a company's privacy statement on their website before you consider doing transactions electronically with the company? Would you say . . .

Regularly	43%
Occasionally	37%
Never	20%
Don't Know	1%

Sources:

a. Special Eurobarometer 196. September 1–30, 2003. Sample: 16,124 randomly selected individuals throughout the EU. The percentages are for the EU-15. Individual country statistics can be found in the Eurobarometer publication.

b. Ekos, for The Public Interest Advocacy Centre. August, 2001. Sample: 1007 Canadians.

c. Harris Poll. February 12–16, 2003. Sample: 1,010 randomly selected adults.

d. Peter D. Hart Research Associates. March 16–20, 1999. Sample: Telephone survey of 1277 randomly selected adults.

e. Eurobarometer. October 18–November 22, 1996. Sample: 16,246 randomly selected adults throughout the EU. The percentages are for the EU-15. Individual country statistics can be found in the Eurobarometer publication.

f. Hong Kong. 2001 Opinion Survey Personal Data Privacy Ordinance.

g. Special Eurobarometer 196. September 1–30, 2003. Sample: 16,124 randomly selected adults throughout the EU. The percentages are for the EU-15. Individual country statistics can be found in the Eurobarometer publication.

(continues)

Table 2.2 Continued

h. CBS News/New York Times. November 25, 2002.
i. Ipsos Reid/Globe and Mail/CTV. October 5, 2001.
j. Markle Foundation. 2001.
k. Public Agenda Foundation for the National Constitution Center. July 10–24, 2002. Sample: telephone survey of 1,520 randomly selected adults.
l. Greenberg Quinlan Rosner Research for the Markle Foundation. October 2–23, 2000. Sample: 2,393 randomly selected individuals.
m. Sample: 229 Canadian Internet users who bought online. August, 2001.

■ Notes

1. For an excellent analysis of the pre-1990 worldwide privacy legislation, see Bennett, 1992.

2. Bennett in Agre and Rotenberg, 1998, p. 103.

3. However, he conceded that "at the level of the policy instruments . . . national forces surfaced and produced a significant variation." Bennett, 1992, p. 222. In this way, Bennett's conclusion is similar to Katzenstein's (1978) study of economic responses to the oil shock: a similar threat created various policy responses that were appropriate to the domestic context. More recently, the varieties of capitalism literature (Hall and Soskice, 2001; Berger and Dore, 1996) have reinforced the claim empirically that divergences can persist for a long time, unless explicit supranational convergence is required.

4. The official texts of the European Data Protection Directive (1995) and the Directive on Privacy and Electronic Communications (2002) can be found at http://europa.eu.int/comm/internal_market/privacy/law_en.htm#directive.

5. Interview with David Aaron.

6. Some US interest groups and companies (e.g., Hewlett-Packard and the American Electronics Association) have begun to lobby in favor of federal privacy legislation for a similar reason because "they'd rather have one uniform national law than risk the uncertainty of many state rules." See "Should States Regulate Privacy?" available at http://www.wired.com/news/politics/0,1283,41511,00.html.

7. For more details of the case, see http://www.goodwinprocter.com/publications/klosek_j_03_04.pdf.

8. Swire and Litan, 1998, p. 31.

9. The Total Information Awareness program was proposed by DARPA in 2002 to create a large data base with the transaction information from US citizens' medical, financial, communication, and travel data to find the "information fingerprint" of potential terrorists. Congress discontinued funding the program in 2003.

10. Press briefing. December 10, 1998, available at http://europa.eu.int/comm/internal_market/privacy/adequacy/briefing-eu-us-dialog_en.html.

11. Gellman, 1996.

12. One of the most thorough treatments of data privacy law in the US is Schwartz and Reidenberg, 1996.

13. Bennett, 1992, p. 66.

14. The fair information principles originated in the HEW committee and were used as the basis for the OECD and Council of Europe texts. The wording here is taken from the Center for Democracy and Technology's website http://www.cdt.org/privacy/guide.basic/generic.html.

15. Westin, 1996. Prepared Testimony before the House Banking and Financial Services Committee. It should be noted that Westin's unbiased expert credentials were tarnished in the eyes of some privacy advocates because of his financial interest in consulting businesses on privacy issues. See Gandy, 2003.

16. Gellman, 1996, gives a different reason for the present configuration of laws than Westin's "grassroots" explanation. Gellman's analysis is similar to Regan's (1995) analysis that well organized narrow interests drive the opposition to comprehensive privacy laws more than consumers' deregulatory preferences.

17. Regan, 1995, p. 15.

18. Ibid., p. 19.

19. Ibid., p. 7.

20. Ibid.

21. Simitis foreword to Schwartz and Reidenberg, 1996, p. ix.

22. Allen, 2002.

23. Gandy, 2003.

24. Wilson, 2000.

25. Katz and Tassone, 1990.

26. *Red Herring Magazine,* January 16, 2001.

27. Westin, 2001.

28. Hull, 1993.

3

Keeping Business Out of the Loop: Negotiating the European Data Protection Directive

It would be a mistake to think that data protection loomed large in the affairs of the European Union (EU) in the early 1990s. On the contrary, given the international and domestic pressures on the European Union at that time, it is rather remarkable that the issue made it to the table at all. The Cold War was over in Europe, and the status of East Germany and the other East Bloc countries was uncertain. The Soviet Union was in the throes of economic and political disintegration. The Gulf War demonstrated the military impotence of the Europeans, and the new wars in Yugoslavia thwarted all attempts at a coherent European diplomatic, foreign policy, and defense response. Most importantly, the European Union itself was making a dramatic leap in integration by adding to the goals of the union foreign policy, a new domestic and judicial agenda, four new members,[1] potentially another twelve new members, and monetary union. Thus, although it took two drafts and five years to negotiate the European Data Protection Directive, when seen in the context of the other business on the EU's plate, this record is hardly surprising. The fact that it made it to the top of the EU's agenda at all is an indication of how increasingly important the issue became over time. Nonetheless, it would be fair to say that the European Data Protection Directive negotiations never really took center stage internationally. This, however, changed dramatically when the extraterritorial impact of the Directive was discovered by a wider, international public in 1998.

■ The History of Data Protection Before the EU's Directive

Data privacy legislation in European countries had a twenty year history when it was taken on as a subject of European co-ordination. European countries were keenly aware of the potential of government misuse of personal data, partly because of many states' odious histories, and partly because the governments collected a significant amount of data for elaborate and complex welfare systems.

The first international organization to consider the data privacy issue area was the United Nations, which flagged the issue in a 1968 meeting marking the twentieth anniversary of the signing of the Universal Declaration of Human Rights. Responding to the question of whether limits should be placed on the uses of electronics, which may affect the rights of people, only the advanced industrialized countries thought there may be a conflict between technical progress and fundamental human rights.[2] As a result, the two international organizations that included those countries, the OECD[3] and the Council of Europe,[4] took up the call to propose solutions for the problem of protecting data privacy. The two organizations had largely overlapping membership in 1980, and each commissioned data protection expert committees to draft their proposals. These expert committees were generally lawyers familiar with the existing domestic law (to the extent that domestic laws existed), and familiar with the technologies' capabilities.[5] Following a 1977 symposium on transborder data flow and the protection of privacy, the OECD set up an ad hoc group of experts on transborder barriers and privacy protection[6] in 1978, which wrote the 1980 Guidelines Governing the Protection of Privacy and Transborder Flows of Personal Data.[7] At the same time, the Council of Europe was also examining data protection. The Council of Europe proposed the "Convention for the Protection of Individuals with Regard to Automatic Processing of Personal Data" ("Council of Europe Convention") in September 1980.[8] The OECD group of experts worked closely with the Council of Europe experts, and "every effort was made to avoid unnecessary differences between the texts produced by the two organizations."[9] The primary difference between the two organizations was that the Council of Europe's Convention established data protection principles that would be binding for the signatory states, whereas the OECD Guidelines were voluntary. Thus, the Council of Europe's Convention was somewhat less specific. However, many of the elements that would find their way into the European Data Protection Directive, including the controversial ones, were included in the OECD Guidelines (to which the US was a party) and the Council of Europe Convention. As Bennett described it, "the OECD's Guidelines represent a fundamental statement of international consensus on communications policy."[10]

It should be remembered, however, that the expert groups drawing up the OECD Guidelines and Council of Europe Convention did not include business or industry interests. Thus, a fundamental international consensus was created, establishing precedent by the privacy hawks without the presence of privacy doves at the negotiating table. During the negotiations of the OECD Guidelines, there was "some distrust in the United States of the underlying European motives, as well as a marked lack of enthusiasm for the monitoring of the compliance of the data processing and communications industries," but these differences were glossed over to create the non-binding guidelines.[11] The Reagan administration urged US companies to voluntarily comply with the OECD Guidelines, but by 1983 only 182 large multinational companies and trade associations had officially endorsed the OECD Guidelines.[12] As a result, when US companies subsequently complained about the European Data Protection Directive's approach, the European authorities correctly noted that the US had already subscribed to most of these principles in the OECD Guidelines, and that the Europeans were simply enforcing the guidelines more consistently. A cursory examination and comparison of the OECD Guidelines with the European Data Protection Directive shows that many of the elements that businesses explicitly opposed in the European Data Protection Directive, such as making all data available to the data subject, holding only a minimum of data for the purposes for which they were collected, and preventing data flows to other countries where they were not adequately protected, were included in the OECD Guidelines (see Appendix A for a comparison between some of the controversial EU text and the OECD text). It should be noted as well that an October 1998 OECD Conference of Ministers reaffirmed the objectives set forth in the guidelines.[13] Within Europe, there was widespread agreement that though the Council of Europe Convention and the OECD Guidelines were reasonably good international instruments, they lacked both specificity and enforcement, and because of these shortcomings, a new approach had to be found.[14]

■ The European Commission Acts

The issue of data protection had been the subject of debates and resolutions in the European Parliament for fourteen years before the Commission took up the call. Nugter's (1990) analysis of a 1979 European Parliament resolution on data privacy shows that some of the institutional characteristics of the later European Data Protection Directive, such as an independent data protection authority in each member state, were evident much earlier.[15] She also highlights the fact that the European Parliament consistently took a much more rigorous "fundamental human rights approach" than the Commission or the Council. Writing about a 1973 Commission Communication on Data Processing, she argues,

> it must be pointed out that the primary concern of the Council and the Commission seemed rather to be more the promotion of a European data

> processing industry than the safeguarding of individual rights. The European Parliament's primary concern, by contrast, has been the protection of the individual . . . In fact, these differing attitudes characterize the many reports, proposals and studies that were to come in the following years.[16]

Her research ended in 1990, but her conclusions about the relative positions of the Commission, Council, and Parliament remain accurate to the present.

In the late 1980s, the Commission's DG XIII (Telecommunications, Information Market and Exploitation of Research)[17] admitted that there had not been much progress in signing and ratifying the Council of Europe's Convention on Data Protection,[18] and the OECD Guidelines were "largely ignored" because of their nonobligatory character.[19] The European Commission had been asked thrice by the European Parliament (in 1976, 1979, and 1982) to propose a directive to harmonize data protection across the EU, and there was a new consensus in Europe that the time had come to act because different data laws were hampering data flows. The first question was whether to use the Council of Europe Convention as the template, or to harmonize at a higher standard. The limitations of the Council of Europe Convention were that it permitted large divergences in data protection in practice (as had been apparent between the countries that ratified the convention), did not solve the problem of flows of information to third countries that had not ratified the convention, did not provide any guidelines regarding which country had jurisdiction in the event of a dispute, and did not address liability for damages suffered by an individual.[20] The Commission had reserved the right to harmonize data protection legislation if member states did not sign and ratify the 1981 Council of Europe Convention "within a reasonable time."[21]

The European Data Protection Directive's legislative path, as determined by the subject matter (internal market), initially meant that it would be approved by the co-operation procedure.[22] Until the Treaty of European Union was ratified by all member states, and came into force on November 1, 1993, the European Data Protection Directive's legislative path was largely in the hands of the Council, although the European Parliament had the right to a second reading. After November 1, 1993, the directive became subject to the codecision procedure, granting the European Parliament more decisionmaking power.[23] The differences between the member states and the European Parliament, however, were not significant, and in practice, the change from co-operation to the codecision procedure was unimportant to the Directive's success.

The first draft of the Directive was adopted by the Commission on July 18, and published in September, 1990. The draft relied heavily on the German and French data protection laws, and, therefore, provoked only a tepid response from some of the other member states. The most reluctant were the traditionally Euro-skeptical countries like the UK that preferred the Council of Europe approach to data protection, and did not believe that harmonization at the EU level was necessary.[24] The emphasis on the German model of data protection, which featured (among other things) separate data privacy protection for the public and private sectors and "opt-in" approaches to data use permissions (the assumption of nonuse unless the individual expressly allows it), also ruffled feathers among the member states. The seven member states that had existing privacy legislation[25] wanted the EU directive to at least partially reflect their legal framework, while many agreed that the German approach was too strict in any case. Germany's disproportionate influence on the first Commission draft was due to the input of Hesse's data protection commissioner, Spiros Simitis, as the Chair of the Council of Europe's Data Protection Experts Committee and Chairman of the Commission's drafting group. The emphasis on the "fundamental human rights" aspect of data privacy that could not be traded off against other rights, such as the freedom of expression, also struck some member states, like Britain, as too broad.

The Commission's proposal justified strong data protection by tying it to the elimination of nontariff barriers as stipulated by the Single European Act: ". . . through Community action it is possible to guarantee a high level of equivalent protection in all the member states of the Community, and in so doing, remove obstacles to the establishment of the internal market."[26] Initially, at least, the emphasis on the internal market was essential because in this pre–Maastricht Treaty era, the idea of incorporating fundamentally political issues, e.g., fundamental rights, in EU legislation was controversial. Thus, it was important to highlight the internal market failures that had created the need for the Commission to step in. In 1989, the French subsidiary of an Italian company had been prohibited from transferring data to Italy because of insufficient data protection there, and medical information had to be removed from some records before they could be transferred to Belgium, Switzerland, and the US.[27]

In the long run, however, the emphasis on fundamental human rights came to take center stage.[28] After the Treaty on European Union (Maastricht Treaty) had been signed in 1991, it was legitimate to consider political measures, and for the advocates of data privacy, it was essential not to have harmonization at the "lowest common denominator." As Simitis indicated:

> Contrary to most other documents and nearly for the first time in the history of the Community, the Commission in its draft said that the need for the Directive is based on the need to protect human rights within the Community. This is why, when we speak of data protection within the European Union, we speak of the necessity to respect the fundamental rights of the citizens. Therefore, data protection may be a subject on

> which you can have different answers to the various problems, but it is not a subject you can bargain about.[29]

Simitis's emphasis on fundamental human rights (a "privacy hawk" position in the debates) reflected the French and German views that had been incorporated in the Commission's first draft. There was also a strategic element to the choice of labeling data protection as a fundamental human right: the European Court of Justice (ECJ, in effect the EU's supreme court) had ruled in 1974 that the ECJ was:

> bound to draw inspiration from constitutional traditions common to the member states, and that it cannot, therefore, uphold measures which are incompatible with fundamental rights recognized and protected by the constitutions of those states. Similarly, international treaties for the protection of human rights on which the member states have collaborated, or of which they are signatories, can supply guidelines which should be followed within the framework of Community law.[30]

Although the EU did not have a bill of rights, the European Court of Justice had ruled that the EU was not in the business of taking away member state guaranteed rights. There was a legal duty not to harmonize at the lowest possible level, which would create a conflict between the member states' and EU law. "Apart from the adjustments inherent in any approximation of laws, the exercise must not have the effect of reducing the level of protection already afforded in the member states."[31] Thus, while acknowledging the Council of Europe Convention principles, the Commission's 1990 draft specifically vowed to "add to those general principles in order to provide a high level of equivalent protection."[32] Ultimately, the right to protect personal data would become enshrined in the 2000 Charter of Fundamental Rights of the European Union, which was incorporated into the Draft Treaty Establishing a Constitution of Europe in 2004 as Article 50.

The emphasis on the "fundamental human right" designation of privacy inherent in the European approach was important because it meant that privacy automatically trumped other rights, and could not be traded off (e.g., for economic benefits) the way that privacy pragmatists in the US assumed. Except where privacy was in conflict with other fundamental rights, like freedom of the press or freedom of information, Europeans asserted that privacy protection was essential, even if it came at an economic cost.

The case of the European Data Protection Directive is fully consistent with studies that show that approximately 80 percent of a piece of EU legislation is contained in the Commission's first draft.[33] Although the European Parliament made more than two hundred amendments to the Commission's first draft, ninety-four of which were accepted by the

Commission and the Council, these changes did not fundamentally revise most of the principles contained in the first draft. Often, the changes were in the nature of clarifications, or refinement of details that had been too broad or ambiguous for the European Parliament. In looking at the changes that were made, it is important to keep in mind that these were changes at the margin of the proposal, and that the main outlines of the Directive were evident from the beginning. This is important when one considers that the European business response was emphatically opposed to several of the key provisions of the Commission's first draft. There was significant EU business opposition, but because businesses had been excluded from the drafting process and did not have input into the Commission's proposal early on, it was less successful at curtailing the Directive than the US businesses would be later in the Safe Harbor negotiations.

■ Details of the Commission's 1990 Draft

The Commission's first draft was influenced heavily by the privacy authorities who understood the existing member state legislation, the international instruments, and the technology. During the internal drafting process, only privacy experts were involved. Business interests, which might logically have been expected to be stakeholders, were excluded. According to Anthony Coad, a member of the European Direct Marketing Association, "no one [from the business community] was consulted. The team that put this directive together was entirely German. German laws are very tough and the thinking was that we should harmonize European laws to the highest standard."[34]

The Commission's 1990 draft had some elements that did not survive to the final Directive, but these were marginal changes demanded by the European Parliament rather than large concessions made to business interests. The differentiation between public and private sectors, mirroring the German legal system and the Council of Europe Convention, was removed in the second draft. There were also changes in the notification procedures and codes of conduct, which Germany thought too bureaucratized. There were attempts to exempt manual files and nonprofit organizations, such as political, philosophical, religious, cultural, and trade unions. Most of the principles and obligations contained in the first draft, however, survived to the final Directive with relatively minor changes.

The Directive applied to all files in the public and private sectors with the exception of files in the public sector where the activities of that sector do not fall within EC law, such as defense, national security, and public security. This became important in the post–September 11, 2001, environment, as more governments scrutinized existing privacy legislation to see if they had somehow contributed to the ability of terrorists to mobilize.[35] Also exempted in the original draft were files held by an individual solely for private and personal purposes, and nonprofit organizations, notably political, philosophical, religious, or cultural entities that were allowed to keep files on their members, as long as they had their members' consent and the information in the files was not communicated to third parties. These exemptions from the Directive were altered in the Commission's second draft, following concerns expressed by the European Parliament, to be exemptions from the notification procedure, not the Directive, as discussed below in Article 8 on sensitive data.

For the public sector, it was lawful to process personal data, as long as these data were necessary for the performance of the tasks of the public authority controlling the file. So, for example, it was legal for the tax authority to gather income, wealth, and salary information. The processing of such data for a purpose other than tax related issues, however, would only be legal if the individual consented to it, if the legitimate interests of the individual did not preclude such changes of purpose, if it were necessary to ward off an imminent threat to public order or serious infringement of the rights of others, or if it were effected on the basis of community law. Communicating the files from the public sector to third parties without notifying the data subject was legal only if it was necessary for the performance of the tasks of the public sector, or if someone in the private sector invoked a legitimate interest (on the condition that the interest of the data subject does not prevail). Otherwise, it was required for the public sector to create a personal data file, which was available for inspection by the individual, and for everyone who uses that individual's information to notify the supervisory authority, and indicate the purpose of the file and what it contains.

In the 1990 draft, the rules for the private sector were substantially the same, including the provision for an obligation to notify the supervisory authority. All information that did not come from sources generally accessible to the public would be required to be notified to the national supervisory authority, along with information regarding the name and address of the controller (the person who controls the data), the purpose of the file, the description of the types of data it contains, and the third parties to whom this information might be communicated. This provision of the draft, known as the "notification" provision, created a great deal of opposition by the private sector, which saw the notification requirement as overly bureaucratic and economically burdensome.

The notification provisions of the final Directive, however, do not differ significantly from the earlier draft. Article 10 of the European Data Protection Directive states that the controller must provide a data subject the identity of the controller, the purposes of the processing for which the data are intended, the recipients of the data, and the right to access and correct the data concerning the subject. Moreover, controllers are required to ensure that data is accurate, current, and deleted once the purpose for which they were collected is accomplished. In addition, data subjects have the right to obtain "at reasonable intervals and without excessive delay or expense" confirmation as to whether or not the data relating to them are being processed, and information as to the purposes of the processing, the categories of data, and the recipients to whom the data are disclosed.

The chief victory of business lobby groups was the reduction of the duty to report these activities to the supervisory authority. Article 18 of the final Directive stipulates that any controller must notify the supervisory authority before carrying out any automatic processing operation, but this requirement can be exempted or simplified under certain conditions. The new draft's exemptions to notification were due to business input, and represented an important change that was good for industry.[36] Data controllers must, however, communicate with the subject about the data, and keep the record of data collected and its purpose, despite their contention that this created a significant cost and administrative burden.

The Commission's 1990 draft already contained exceptions for the media where there might be conflicts between the right to privacy and the freedom of information or freedom of the press. The article was strengthened by European Parliament amendments to make it obligatory for member states to create exemptions for the freedom of information and of the press, but was otherwise identical to the final Directive's provision and language in Article 9. By contrast, the 1990 draft contained only a terse paragraph encouraging the business circles concerned to participate in drawing up European codes of conduct or professional ethics in respect to certain sectors on the basis of the Directive. In the final Directive, Article 27, the role of trade associations and other bodies representing other categories of controllers in drafting national codes of conduct was explicitly recognized and formalized.

Perhaps the greatest transformation was the article concerning sensitive data. The Commission's initial draft was restrictive and brief:

1. The Member States shall prohibit the automatic processing of data revealing ethnic or racial origin, political opinions, religious or philosophical beliefs or trade-union membership, and of data concerning health or sexual life, without the express and written consent, freely given, of the data subject.
2. The Member States may, on important public interest grounds, grant derogations from paragraph 1 on the basis of a law specifying the types of data which may be stored and the persons who may have access to the file and providing suitable safeguards against abuse and unauthorized access.

The 1992 revision of the provision on sensitive data expressly recognized the right of some countries to impose different standards on this issue than the EU harmonized level. Thus, while sensitive data may be collected when the subject has given his written consent, paragraph 2a qualifies, "except where the laws of the member state provide that the prohibition . . . may not be waived by the data subject giving his consent."

■ Business Response to the Commission's 1990 Draft

One of the basic questions that arose later in the transatlantic negotiations on the European Data Protection Directive was why European businesses had been unable to change some of the costly regulatory provisions entailed in the Directive. A review of business actions after the release of the 1990 draft shows that certain sectors were indeed aware of the Directive's adverse consequences on their business, but were simply too late to make significant changes, because they were responding to a draft that had been crafted primarily by privacy experts who held a "fundamental right" view of privacy.

A brief review of the EU business lobbying theory is appropriate to put businesses' options in perspective. The key element in most accounts of corporate lobbying is that the interests must be involved in the Commission's shaping of the legislative proposal in order to be effective. This involves, first, having advance information that the Commission may act on a certain issue. Thus, the most proactive firms would cultivate relationships with the permanent staff of the relevant Directorates General, which would prepare the all-important first draft. As Greenwood (1997) relates:

> It is essential for private interests seeking to be proactive to develop relationships with the relevant personnel within the appropriate division, rather than seeking out these individuals when it is too late after a proposal has already emerged. In doing so, an interest will be able to effectively input the information it needs to shape the thinking of those responsible for drafting initiatives, and perhaps even propose measures itself which might appear in an early draft.[37]

Private interests can also create the agenda by participating in the Commission's various advisory committees and working parties. The advisory committees, comprising expert committees (national officials and experts) and consultative committees (the relevant European-level aggregated interests) provide a means for private interests to shape the content to a significant degree by means of their technical expertise in an area. The Commission, as a relatively small bureaucracy, cannot possibly draft proposals by relying solely on its employees, and thus, relies heavily on others with expertise in an area before it drafts legislative acts. All together, these advisory committees bring together fifty thousand representatives of private interests and national civil services.[38]

Once the initial draft has left the Commission, interests can only react to the agenda, and only about 20 percent of the proposal changes in the subsequent decisionmaking process.[39] Because the workings of the European Parliament are more open than those of the Council of Ministers, and because the European Parliament's role has become more important in the 1990s, many private interests prefer to lobby the members of the European Parliament (MEPs) next. Like the US Congress, the European Parliament has committees that assess drafts and propose amendments. The rapporteur (an MEP selected by the committee to prepare the European Parliament's response) is often the target of lobbyists, but interests have also become important in "educating" the committees on specialized or technical matters.

In theory, the Economic and Social Committee would be the most likely place that interests would find a voice on EU matters, but in practice, the institution has a completely marginal role, and is largely ignored by the Council in its decisionmaking process. It brings together two hundred and twenty-two representatives of employers, workers, and other relevant interests, and issues a report on the Commission's draft. However, the committee does not even have the ability to hold up the process in any systematic way, and its role is too marginal to be significant for most lobbyists.

Finally, the Council of Ministers represents an access point for lobbyists, but its influence comes from its role as the final decisionmaking body. It has carved out a role as the make-or-break point for lobbyists trying to take out, or insert, last minute changes to the proposal before a common position is announced. Private interests can work either within the machinery of the Council in Brussels or at the individual member state level, where they must act through a ministry. The Council decides through a system of consensus, indicating that even when a qualified majority vote is the legally prescribed decisionmaking mechanism, in more than 80 percent of the cases, the member states continue to discuss and bargain until no member state objects to the text.[40] Thus, a private interest that can convince its Council representative to object until its interests are reflected in the text is in a relatively strong position. This, however, is rarely the case.

■ The Lobbying Against the European Data Protection Directive

Against this theoretical backdrop, it is important to recognize that business interests in data protection issues were one step behind the process all the way. The Commission had consulted experts in the area of data protection because of their longstanding expertise in this field. Simitis, in addition to having been Hesse's Data Protection Commissioner, had also been Chairman of the Data Protection Experts Committee of the Council of Europe, and was, thus, fully aware of problems with the Council of Europe's approach, and the data protection requirements that Germany would posit in order to agree to a European-level initiative. There is no record of other interests that were consulted before the draft Directive was released in mid-July 1990. The form and the timing of the initiative seem to have caught many business interests by surprise. Sources within the Commission confirm that business interests were not consulted in the preparation of the draft, or given advance notice; business and industry groups were largely unaware that the Commission was going to act on this matter, and the few that were, mistakenly believed the Directive would be appropriately responsive to their business needs.

This assumption changed after the publication of the draft. The primary groups that were impacted were the direct marketers and the financial groups. It is obvious that the direct marketing groups were not consulted by the Commission during the drafting of the Directive, because in May 1990, its industry representatives were still optimistic that the relatively liberal, self-regulatory approach the UK used in its 1984 data protection law would survive in the Commission's draft.[41] These same representatives were practically apoplectic when they were confronted with the details of the draft two months later.[42] By September, the European Direct Marketing Association was trying to raise £100,000 to defeat the European Data Protection Directive. "The European Directive would be a major blow if it went through unaltered," said direct marketing business owner Judith Donovan.[43] By February, 1991, an alliance of UK direct marketers and advertising agencies began to lobby the UK Home Office and the European Parliament to remove the draft's provision on obtaining the data subject's consent before using the data, and to exempt all manual files from the Directive.[44]

In March, 1991, UNICE, the Union of Industrial and Employers' Confederations of Europe, weighed the opposing elements of the Directive that would potentially lead to a "fortress Europe" by cutting off data flow to countries that did not have as strict data protection laws. Moreover, they feared the creation of a large bureaucracy.[45] By June, the banking sector had mobilized, and a group of European banking interests, including the Banking Federation of the EC, the European Savings Bank Group, the Association of Co-operative Banks of the EC, the European Federation of Finance House Associations (Eurofinas), the EC Mortgage Federation, the European Union of Consumer Credit Information Providers, Eurocheque

International, Eurocard International, and Visa, criticized the draft on the grounds that it would impose regulatory costs on the financial system, and ". . . would make it difficult, if not impossible, to hold information for such purposes as prevention of fraud and overindebtedness or to protect the rights of third parties."[46] US companies like American Express and Readers Digest also lobbied against the Directive, but did so behind the scenes for fear of being seen as "anti-privacy."[47] It seems clear in retrospect that specific industries belatedly lobbied to remove the expensive provisions, particularly the consent and notification elements, but were too late to have an impact on the draft. This is a marked contrast to the US business role in the Safe Harbor negotiations, as detailed in the next chapter.

■ The European Parliament's Role

On April 24, 1991, the Economic and Social Committee approved the draft. It had minor comments, such as, that allowing researchers anonymous access to data should be permitted, and that listening to or recording a private conversation without permission should be prohibited, but its contribution to the next draft was minimal.

The European Parliament considered the report of the Committee on Legal Affairs and Citizens' Rights on February 10, 1992, authored by Geoffrey Hoon, a British MEP who later became Britain's Secretary of State for Defence.

The entire European Parliament took up the Directive in December 1991. There was widespread agreement that data protection was an important single market objective, and that the Commission's draft was a good start. As the essential provisions of the Directive were based on the fundamental principles that had been identified by the Council of Europe (and ratified by several member states), and were also in several of the member states' data privacy laws, it would have been difficult to object to the substance of the Commission's draft in any case.

The main amendments that the European Parliament inserted, which restructured the entire Commission's draft, were: (1) to drop the formal distinction between the rules applying in the public sector and the rules applying in the private sector, and (2) to expand the provisions on the procedures for notification to the supervisory authority and on codes of conduct. The clarification of the procedures for notification to the supervisory authority was in response to the business lobbying that decried the excessive bureaucratization entailed in the Commission's first draft. They did not, however, go very far in allaying business concerns about notification procedures.

■ The Search for a Common Position in the Council

After the Commission unveiled its second draft in 1992, the Council of Ministers began to negotiate. The UK and Ireland continued to object to the entire process of harmonization, preferring instead to have all the EU countries ratify the Council of Europe Convention.[48] Germany, whose preferences had been so widely incorporated in the Commission's first draft, now found several problems with the Commission's changes, since they had moved the draft away from the stricter provisions of German law in a couple of areas. The distinction between public and private sector data protection had been mirrored in German law, and combining them would prove difficult to transpose. Also presenting constitutional questions for the Germans was the creation of legally independent data protection commissioners with the powers to intervene and prosecute. Finally, the concepts of notification and special protections for sensitive data were alien to the German data protection laws.

By the end of 1993, the UK, Ireland, Germany, and Denmark formed a blocking minority to any progress on EU-level data protection. The easiest concerns to address were those of the Danes: Denmark had taken up the medical research sector's concerns. The medical sector was increasingly worried that medical data that were essential for clinical trials and experiments would not be available to researchers, even in an anonymous fashion, because of the requirement that data be deleted as soon as their original collection purpose had been accomplished. Consequently, the other Council members agreed to insert a provision that expressly allowed these data to be retained for research purposes.

Since Sweden, Austria, Finland, and Norway[49] were due to join the EU on January 1, 1995, their concerns about the draft directive were also heard, even though they technically did not vote. The other Scandinavian countries had a long history of data protection, but also of open access to public documents. They were, thus, more concerned that the Directive not conflict with their historical open access to public documents and rules on freedom of expression. Once language to that effect was added, these concerns were adequately addressed.[50]

Britain and Ireland both wanted manual data exempted from the Directive. During the Greek and German Council Presidencies, the other member states agreed to a twelve year phase-in period for manual data, but were unwilling to give a permanent exemption for manual data because, "If you exempt manual data you will create a tendency to circumvent rules by using old techniques. We want to have precisely the opposite effect, of encouraging new techniques."[51] For Ireland, the phase-in compromise was sufficient to allow it to vote in favor of the Directive, but not for the UK. Germany, too, still had strong reservations about the draft, since it was less strict in several respects than Germany's existing legislation. Since the Council usually acts by consensus, remaining at the negotiating table until all the member states abandon their objections, negotiations continued even though Germany and the UK did not technically form a blocking minority.[52]

As is often the case in the EU, the country which holds the six month revolving Council Presidency has conflicting ambitions: on the one hand, it wants to advocate its preferences strongly to reach an agreement closer to its preference structure, but on the other hand, it wants to secure an agreement that can be marked as an accomplishment of its presidency. In the second half of 1994, Germany held the Council Presidency, and was, thus, in that bind. Building on the work of the Greek Presidency in this issue, Germany was able to change its position on a number of points. Some of the compromises Germany made were the exceptions to medical research, the twelve year transition period for manual data files, and the details of the application of the Directive to video and telecommunications technology.[53]

Germany had wanted the right to have higher standards in certain areas, such as the commercial use of personal data. Although ostensibly the rationale for having a harmonized data protection law in Europe was to facilitate commerce between member states, Germany received its right to have higher standards in certain areas, though not to prohibit transfers.

An informal political agreement on the common position was noted in a Council meeting on December 8, 1994.[54] There were other compromises by the member states to make the agreement possible: France had wanted exemptions for the processing of images or sounds on the grounds that technological advances might soon make these provisions obsolete. The final text granted exemptions for the processing of images and sounds with significance for public safety, and included a specific reference to revising the Directive later to take account of technological innovations. This was done in December 1997 with the Electronic Communications: Processing of Personal Data, Protection of Privacy Directive,[55] which was updated in July 2002 as the Directive on Privacy and Electronic Communications.[56]

The UK, however, continued to object to the Directive. Ostensibly, its dissent was about the processing of manual data, but the bigger problem was the harmonization of data privacy laws in Europe to a higher-than-UK standard, and significant opposition by UK businesses. Its objections, coming after the informal agreement on a common position in the Council had already been established, were not regarded as serious by the other member states.

> Throughout those first few weeks of 1995 the UK government had made strenuous efforts to convince their European partners to go back on the agreement reached on 8 December. These efforts were unsuccessful and the actual text of the directive was not discussed further . . . Delegations

> which acted earlier, before the deal had effectively been struck–the Danes being a good example–left the negotiating table a great deal happier.[57]

Having been isolated in its preference for data protection standards more in line with its 1984 data protection law, the UK abstained from the Directive. It would have been difficult to vote against the Directive, since the UK had a data protection law on its books,[58] but by abstaining, the UK was signaling to its business groups that it had formally opposed the strict provisions.

On February 6, 1995, the Council informally adopted a common position on the European Data Protection Directive. After checking the translation of certain texts, the Common Position was formally announced on February 20.[59] The Common Position was reviewed and approved by the European Parliament for the second reading on June 15, 1995. Following the incorporation of seven relatively minor amendments in the draft,[60] the EU's Budget Council passed the European Data Protection Directive on July 24, 1995. On October 24, 1995, the presidents of the Council and the European Parliament signed the Directive, giving the member states three years to transpose the Directive into their own law.

One footnote on the Directive's negotiations should be noted: the European Data Protection Directive was singled out by the Council of Ministers' legal service as an example of member states incorporating statements in the Council minutes appended to the legislative text that contradict or add to the enacting terms of the legislation. Citing the thirty-one statements in the minutes for the 1995 Common Position on data protection, the memo considered the number of statements excessive, because the ECJ does not give any weight to statements when interpreting the legislation. "Since the Court is not bound by such statements, they may involve the Council in liability, should they come to the knowledge of third parties for breach of the principle of legitimate expectations,"[61] the legal service wrote, noting also that these statements were an impediment to the greater transparency of Council decisionmaking. Moreover, the memo warned that "it is clear that, in the absence of agreement to incorporate [statements'] substance into the enacting terms, statements contradicting or adding to the enacting terms of legislation must absolutely not be made." As one such example, it quoted the European Data Protection Directive's Article 32, which required Britain to bring manual processing into compliance with the Directive after the twelve year period. To the Council minutes' statement, "Article 32 of the Directive contains an obligation on controllers to take, at the end of the twelve-year period . . . all reasonable steps relating to the requirements of Articles 6, 7, and 8" the member states had added (presumably to appease Britain) "that do not prove impossible or involve a disproportionate effort in terms of costs," thereby contradicting an ironclad obligation in the text. From this anecdote, it is clear that the other member states went to great lengths to get Britain on board (to the point of giving Britain an informal opt-out on the issue of manual file processing), but ultimately failed to get a consensus on the Directive.

International Impact

As this history of the Directive indicates, the international impact of the Directive was a secondary consideration, but one that would assume increasing importance. Although the EU began by harmonizing its member states' data protection laws (to the extent that they existed), the focus on the "fundamental human rights" aspect of data protection, coupled with the need to ensure that the Directive would not create "data havens" through which the Europeans' data could be churned, created a consensus among the European policymakers that the EU had to lead the way internationally. The missionary zeal of the EU was confirmed in the Conclusions of the Presidency from the June 1994 Corfu summit:

> The European Council, like the Commission, considers that the Community and its Member States do however have an important role to play in backing up this development by giving political impetus, creating a clear and stable regulatory framework (notably as regards access to markets, compatibility between networks, intellectual property rights, data protection and copyright) and by setting an example in areas which come under their aegis.[62]

If the Europeans were self-consciously aiming to set an international standard (arguably based on standards the US had already committed to in the OECD Guidelines), the US was at a structural disadvantage, since it did not have a competing data protection regime that would make an international standard. Other countries had laws incorporating the OECD principles, but the US model, based on a sectoral approach, was internationally rare.

Thus, in the early 1990s, when the issue of international "models" of data protection implicitly arose at the US and EU levels, the US did not really have a horse to race. "It is almost presumptuous for an American to suggest the need for international privacy regulation, because the United States is now significantly behind much of the Western industrialized world in addressing private sector privacy issues."[63]

Some of the provisions of the European Data Protection Directive had been explicitly considered by the Congress before. Notably, the landmark 1974 Privacy Act had created a temporary institution akin to the European Data Protection Commissioners. The Privacy Protection Study Commission's 1977 report recommended the establishment of an independent privacy agency, but Congress did not act.[64] In 1994, Senator Paul

Simon tried to attach an amendment to establish a Privacy Protection Commission to the Consumer Reporting Reform Act, but the amendment was tabled by a vote of 77 to 21 after minimal debate.[65] President Bill Clinton established the position of privacy czar in 1998 to centralize the Federal Government's privacy issues in one place, but to limited effect. Thus, it would be incorrect to assume that the European preference for comprehensive privacy legislation was so outlandish that it could never have been adopted in the US. However, as Chapter 4 will show, the idea of proposing comprehensive privacy legislation was rejected out of hand, creating a diplomatic stand-off in the late 1990s between the US and the EU.

■ Notes

1. Ultimately, only three new members joined: Norway voted to remain outside the EU.
2. Hondius, 1980, p. 90; Drake, 1993.
3. The Organization for Economic Cooperation and Development was founded in 1948 as the Organization for European Economic Coordination, designed to administer the US Marshall Plan aid to Europe. It now comprises thirty member countries. In 1980, the member states were Australia, *Austria, Belgium*, Canada, *Denmark*, Finland, *France, Germany, Greece, Iceland, Ireland, Italy*, Japan, *Luxembourg, the Netherlands*, New Zealand, *Norway, Portugal, Spain, Sweden, Switzerland, Turkey, the United Kingdom,* and the US. [Italics signify overlapping membership with the Council of Europe in 1980.]
4. The Treaty of London, which established the Council of Europe, was signed by ten states on May 5, 1949. It now comprises forty-five members. In 1980, the member states were *Austria*, *Belgium*, Cyprus, Denmark, *France*, *Germany*, *Greece*, *Iceland, Ireland, Italy*, Liechtenstein, *Luxembourg*, Malta, *Netherlands*, *Norway*, *Portugal, Spain, Sweden, Switzerland, Turkey,* and *the United Kingdom.* [Italics signify overlapping membership with the OECD in 1980.]
5. Bennett, 1992, p. 136.
6. Chaired by an Australian lawyer and including a Swedish lawyer as a consultant. OECD Guidelines, 2002, p. 29.
7. The official text of the OECD Guidelines can be found at http://www.oecd.org/document/18/0,2340,en_2649_37409_1815186_1_1_1_37409,00.html.
8. Available at http://www.coe.int/T/E/Legal_affairs/Legal_co-operation/Data_protection/.
9. OECD Guidelines, 2002, p. 28.
10. Bennett, 1992, p. 138.
11. Ibid.
12. Gellman, 1996, p. 154; foreshadowing the situation of Safe Harbor compliance, however, Gellman noted that "there is little evidence that the endorsements of the OECD *Guidelines* by American companies resulted in changes in actual privacy practices;" p. 155.
13. OECD Guidelines, 2002, p. 60.
14. Platten, 1996; Brühann. 1999.
15. Nugter, 1990, p. 32.

16. Ibid., p. 29.

17. In March 2000, after the Prodi reforms, data protection became part of the DG for the Internal Market.

18. Papapavlou, 1992.

19. Brühann, 1999, p. 11.

20. Ibid., p. 32.

21. Commission, 1990, p. 3.

22. The EU's website describes the co-operation procedure as follows: This legislative procedure requires two readings in Parliament and in the Council. The first reading, for which the EC Treaty does not impose time limits, is similar to the simple consultation. It ends with a common position of the Council adopted by a qualified majority. At the second reading, both Parliament and the Council have three months to decide. The deadlines can be extended of a month by mutual agreement between Parliament and the Council. The common position of the Council is transmitted to Parliament. The Council and the Commission fully inform Parliament of their respective positions. Parliament can approve the common position by a simple majority vote, reject the common position by an absolute majority (whereupon the Commission decides whether or not to withdraw the proposal), amend the common position by an absolute majority (whereupon the Commission has one month to re-examine its proposal in the light of Parliament's amendments and the Council adopts the proposal as re-examined by the Commission by a qualified majority (unanimously if it modifies it), and takes a decision unanimously on amendments not accepted by the Commission. If the Council does not act within the time, the proposal is lost), or does not decide within its time limits (in which the Council's common position is adopted). available at http://www.europa.eu.int/prelex/apcnet.cfm?CL=en#.

23. The EU's website describes the post-Amsterdam codecision procedure (which is a simplified version of the codecision procedure between November 1, 1993 and April 30, 1999) as follows: In this procedure, Parliament shares the legislative power with the Council. The codecision procedure can comprise up to three readings in Parliament and in the Council, and require a Conciliation Committee in the event of disagreement between the two institutions. This Committee is composed of the members of the Council or their representatives and as many representatives of Parliament. The Commission is involved and takes all the necessary initiatives. The proposal is sent formally to European Parliament and to the Council. For the first reading, the procedure is identical to the others. After opinion of Parliament in first reading:

- If Parliament does not propose any amendments, the Council may adopt the proposed act.
- If the Council approves all the amendments of Parliament, the Council may adopt the proposed act thus amended.
- Otherwise, the Council shall adopt a common position.

In second reading, Parliament may:

- Approve the common position by a simple majority and the act shall be deemed to have been adopted in accordance to the common position.
- Not decide within the time allowed and the act shall be deemed to have been adopted in accordance to the common position.
- Reject the common position of the Council and the proposed act shall be deemed not to have been adopted.

- Amend the common position by an absolute majority and the Commission has to deliver an opinion on the amendments adopted by Parliament. The opinion can be accompanied by an amended proposal.

In that case, the Council either:

- Approves all the amendments proposed by Parliament and the act is deemed to have been adopted in the form of the common position thus amended.
- Does not approve all the amendments proposed by Parliament and the Council convenes the Conciliation Committee in agreement with Parliament.

The Committee has six weeks to reach an agreement on a joint text. If it succeeds, this joint text has to be approved by the Council (qualified majority) and Parliament (absolute majority) within a further six weeks; otherwise the proposal is deemed not to have been adopted. If the Conciliation Committee does not approve a joint text, the proposal act is deemed not to have been adopted. available at http://www.europa.eu.int/prelex/apcnet.cfm?CL=en#.

24. Pearce and Platten, 1998, p. 533.
25. Denmark, France, Germany, Ireland, Luxembourg, the Netherlands, and the UK had privacy laws. Spain had ratified the Council of Europe Convention, but had no domestic legislation, and the Netherlands had not ratified the Council of Europe Convention.
26. Commission, 1990, p. 5.
27. Cate, 1995, pp. 438–439.
28. Simitis, 1995, p. 447.
29. Cate, 1995, p. 439.
30. j Nold KG v Commission, 1974, case 4/73, cited in Kuper, 1998, p. 10.
31. Commission, 1990, p. 17.
32. Ibid.
33. Hull, 1993, p. 83.
34. The *New York Times,* April 11, 1991.
35. *Handelsblatt,* English Version, September 19, 2001.
36. Author's interview with anonymous Commission official, May 28, 2003.
37. Greenwood, 1997, p. 35. Also see Hull. 1993.
38. Greenwood, 1997, p. 41.
39. Hull, 1993, p. 83.
40. Heisenberg, 2005.
41. *Marketing,* May 31, 1990.
42. *Marketing,* July 12, 1990.
43. *Marketing,* September 13, 1990.
44. *Marketing,* February 14, 1991.
45. *Tech Europe,* March 1, 1991.
46. *Tech Europe,* June 1, 1991.
47. *New York Times,* April 11, 1991.
48. Brühann, 1999, p. 16.
49. Norway ultimately did not join the EU in 1994 after the referendum for accession failed.
50. Platten, 1996, p. 31.
51. *Financial Times,* December 5, 1994.
52. Heisenberg, 2005.

53. Author's interview with Brühann; Brühann, 1999, p. 17.

54. *Tech Europe,* January 7, 1995.

55. Directive 97/66/EC of the European Parliament and of the Council of 15 December 1997, concerning the processing of personal data and the protection of privacy in the telecommunications sector. Official Journal L 024, 30/01/1998 P. 0001 - 0008 available at http://europa.eu.int/smartapi/cgi/sga_doc?smartapi!celexapi!prod!CELEXnumdoc&lg=en&numdoc=31997L0066&model=guichett.

56. Directive 2002/58/EC of the European Parliament and of the Council of 12 July 2002, concerning the processing of personal data and the protection of privacy in the electronic communications sector (Directive on privacy and electronic communications). Official Journal L 201, 31/07/2002 P. 0037 - 0047 available at http://europa.eu.int/smartapi/cgi/sga_doc?smartapi!celexapi!prod!CELEXnumdoc&lg=en&numdoc=32002L0058&model=guichett.

57. Platten, 1996, pp. 31–32.

58. Author's interview with Simitis.

59. Common Position (EC) No 1/95 adopted by the Council on February 20, 1995, with a view to adopting Directive 95/. . ./EC of the European Parliament and of the Council of . . . on the protection of individuals with regard to the processing of personal data and on the free movement of such data. Official Journal C 093, 13/04/1995 p. 0001 available at http://europa.eu.int/smartapi/cgi/sga_doc?smartapi!celexplus!prod!JO_RefPub&lg=EN&serie_jo=C&an_jo=1995&nu_jo=093&pg_jo=001.

60. According to the record available at http://wwwdb.europarl.eu.int/oeil/oeil_viewdnl.ProcedureView?lang=2&procid=59 [author's translation], the Commission accepted the seven amendments voted by the European Parliament in the second reading and modified its proposal accordingly. The amendments in question concerned:

- One specific reference concerning the secrecy of affairs as motive which permits limiting the right of a person to recognize the logic under which the automatic treatment of his data is handled.
- The recognition that, for equal treatment, there must be several co-responsible people who decide together the treatment and the means to make effective.
- Exemptions and derogations: those cannot be taken by the member states except for measures which are necessary to reconcile the right to privacy with the right to freedom of expression.
- Transfers which were judicially obligatory due to an important public interest.
- The competences given the Commission: the introduction of a reference regarding a modus vivendi between the European Parliament/Council/Commission from December 20, 1994, and replacing the regulatory committee IIIa with a Management Committee IIb.

61. Council Legal Service, 1995.

62. Conclusions of the Presidency available at http://ue.eu.int/en/Info/eurocouncil/index.html.

63. Gellman, 1996, p. 129.

64. Ibid.

65. Ibid.

4

Keeping Privacy Advocates Out of the Loop: Negotiating the Safe Harbor Agreement

With the entry into force of the European Data Protection Directive on October 24, 1995, the member states had three years to transpose the Directive into their own law. There was no doubt that the Directive contained elements, especially Articles 25 and 26, that would impact non-EU countries as well, but in 1995 and 1996, there was no hint that these implications had reached the top of the agenda of the EU's largest trading partner. Businesses, especially those in the high tech industry, and large multinational corporations that transferred data between the EU and the US, were mobilized, but the US government was not engaged.

This chapter details the diplomacy leading to the Safe Harbor Agreement in 2000. The Safe Harbor Agreement was hailed by many as the emergence of a new system of hybrid regulation, and a prototype for other transatlantic regulatory disputes.[1] Understanding the provenance of Safe Harbor, therefore, has larger implications than simply understanding the US response to the European Data Protection Directive.

Although many believe that the Safe Harbor regime reflected historical and cultural differences between the Europeans' progovernment and the US probusiness inclinations, opinion surveys show that there were fewer differences at the mass public level than the outcome would suggest. Opinion polls, as discussed in Chapter 2, showed that significant majorities in both the EU and the US wanted government legislation to protect their privacy online.

When one examines the origins of US policy, however, there are large differences in the degree of access that business and industry groups had to the policymaking process. In Europe, as detailed in Chapter 3, business interests were not consulted at all before the Commission's 1990 draft, and were able to make only marginal changes to the Directive when they were consulted in the subsequent years. By contrast, the US business groups themselves drafted the 1997 US position on e-commerce, and had significant input into the Safe Harbor Agreement. Thus, this chapter shows that the degree of access of business groups to decisionmakers was the essential element determining the outcome of Safe Harbor.

■ What Is Safe Harbor?

This section presents the features of Safe Harbor, which went into effect on November 1, 2000. The Safe Harbor Agreement permitted companies, which agreed to abide by certain rules, to send data to and from EU countries without fear of violating the European Data Protection Directive. This is often described as a hybrid self-regulatory system because it involves both industry self-regulation and some government enforcement.

The Department of Commerce is responsible for operating the system. The companies that sign up with the Department of Commerce warrant to the agency that they will abide by the Safe Harbor principles in their dealings with Europeans' personal data. Companies may also sign up with a trustmark "privacy seal" program, like BBBOnline or TRUSTe, which oversee a website's privacy policy, and provide an alternative dispute resolution mechanism for consumer complaints for a price ranging from $850–$90,000 per year.[2] These privacy seal programs are not required, but companies not opting for independent verification are obligated to conduct effective self-verification.

The enforcement of the Safe Harbor Agreement is largely complaint driven. Initially, complaints are handled by an alternative dispute resolution (ADR) mechanism, either the privacy seals programs or the EU data protection authorities. If the Safe Harbor companies fail to comply with the ADR's ruling, then the Federal Trade Commission (FTC) or the Department of Transportation (depending on which agency has oversight of the sector) can impose fines, thereby forcing them to comply. Serious cases of noncompliance can result in the companies' being struck from the Safe Harbor, and stopping data flows to and from the EU.

The companies that sign the Safe Harbor Agreement agree to the following provisions for their European data:[3]

- Notice: They will notify customers how they will use their personal data, and before they transfer it to another organization, or it is used for a purpose other than that for which it was collected.
- Choice: They will allow customers to opt out before sending their data to a third party or use it for a different purpose.
- Onward Transfer: They may only transfer data to another company (after giving notice and choice) if that company is in Safe Harbor, or has some other adequacy finding.

- Security: They must take reasonable precautions to protect the data from loss, misuse, and unauthorized access, disclosure, alteration, and destruction.
- Data Integrity: They should take reasonable steps to ensure that data is reliable for its intended use, accurate, complete, and current.
- Access: They must ensure that individuals have access to the information that the companies have about them, and be able to correct, amend, or delete information that is inaccurate, except in cases where the burden or expense of providing access would be disproportionate to the risks to the individual's privacy, or where the rights of persons other than the individual would be violated.
- Enforcement: They must provide readily available and affordable independent recourse for individuals who believe their privacy has been violated, investigation of each individual's complaints and disputes, and award damages where appropriate.

The Safe Harbor Principles were available to any companies that wished to use them. For those that did not want to, Article 26(4) of the European Data Protection Directive made a provision for the standard contractual clauses that could be used. These standard contractual clauses were unavailable until December 2001, and most companies had expected them to be more onerous to comply with than the Safe Harbor Principles, making them an unattractive alternative.

It is important, however, to observe that although the privacy concerns of the public had been prevalent even in the pre-Internet age, the emergence of the Internet created immense concern for greater privacy invasion. The Internet revolution was still in its infancy in 1995, when the European Data Protection Directive was completed, and thus, although technologically sophisticated people could anticipate the potential impact of the new technology, regulating data privacy on the Internet was hardly a mainstream concern. The established multinational bricks-and-mortar businesses, with their large human resource databases transferring mundane (yet essential) personal data between subsidiaries were concerned, but they did not constitute a critical mass to mobilize the federal government into taking one position or another regarding the European Data Protection Directive. For one thing, they already had to meet the differential, and sometimes conflicting, national data protection laws; consequently, a harmonization of their European obligations did actually present a benefit to many of these firms, to the extent that they did not already subscribe to the highest standard. Had data protection had implications only for these firms, it is quite possible there would have been much less controversy. But by 1996, the Internet and e-commerce were beginning to make their public appearance, and from that point on, the Europeans and

US lawmakers had fundamentally different preferences and interests regarding data privacy.

The Internet, which had been developing for thirty years as a US defense and research tool, suddenly burst into public view when it was privatized by the US government on April 30, 1995.[4] Two years earlier, in April 1993, there had been only sixty-two web servers in the world, but with the release of Mosaic in November 1993 (which became Netscape in 1994) participation on the Internet grew exponentially.[5] On February 8, 1996, Internet revolutionary, John Perry Barlow, in his "Declaration of the Independence of Cyberspace," first warned governments that they had no jurisdiction over cyberspace: "Governments of the Industrial World, you weary giants of flesh and steel, I come from Cyberspace, the new home of Mind. On behalf of the future, I ask you of the past to leave us alone. You are not welcome among us. You have no sovereignty where we gather."[6] His "hands-off" vision for the Internet did not, however, resonate in Europe.

The foregoing discussion of the Internet's evolution emphasizes the extent to which the European Union was ahead of the Internet revolution in its regulatory emphasis, and not responding to it. The development of the Internet, essentially after the Europeans had passed their privacy directive, though before the US had responded to it, created a wedge between the preferences of the EU and US governments. One of the arguments, used repeatedly in the US to justify leaving the Internet and e-commerce (including not only data privacy, but also matters of taxation or content censorship) unregulated, was the fear that any regulation would stifle technical innovation and progress, or worse, kill off the entire enterprise.

This "don't kill the goose that laid the golden egg" argument was less effective overall in Europe for several reasons. First, and most important, in most major EU member states, data protection was already in place. Perhaps the individual provisions of each state's laws varied, but the public and even businesses were accustomed to doing business in a privacy-regulated environment. Second, most of the Internet related activities and new businesses were in the US, and thus, these interests would be considered foreign, hence secondary, in any case. Although the EU aspired to develop a thriving information economy,[7] funding for Internet start-ups was minuscule in Europe compared to the US, and thus, the number of start-up companies was smaller and contributed less to the (perception of the) economies' overall well-being. Finally, the Europeans were less convinced than the US that the Internet was a revolution in the truest sense.[8] This skepticism created a political environment wherein the usual laws applied. If goods were taxed in a store, they should be taxed in cyberspace.[9] If content could be regulated in books and magazines, it could be regulated in cyberspace. As the Chairman of the Article 29 Working Party, Stefano

Rodota told members of the US House of Representatives: "Of course, the Internet revolution carries a lot of new challenges, but these normally concern the issues of applicable law and jurisdiction, rather than the content of the substantive rules, and this is the same kind of problem that does arise in many other areas of law."[10] Enforcement was less an issue of solving a technical problem than of solving a collective action problem, something the Europeans had become adept at during their forty year history of integration.

For these reasons, the Europeans did not appreciate the US treating the Internet with kid gloves. For them, if a fundamental human right was to be meaningful, it had to trump other, especially financial, considerations. The European consensus was this: the US would need to ensure that its environment was consonant with the Europeans' data protection law if Europeans' right to data protection was to be ironclad.

■ Privacy Interest Groups

Several new privacy interest groups were founded in the 1990s, joining pro-privacy publications like *Privacy Journal* (1974) and *Privacy Times* (1981), which became more politically active. In the UK, where privacy concerns had been highlighted by video surveillance and strict antiterrorism laws, Privacy International was founded in 1990. In the US, the networking of computers, and their use in new environments, created the conditions for establishing new pro-privacy interests groups. Groups like Privacy Rights Clearinghouse were founded in 1992 to "advocate for consumers' interests vis-à-vis telecommunications, energy, and the Internet." The emergence of new privacy interest groups, and grassroots efforts to enact comprehensive privacy legislation in the US, were also due to the perception that there was a "window of opportunity" to address these issues in a comprehensive way, because of the European Data Protection Directive. One of the most active and influential US interest groups was the Electronic Privacy Information Center (EPIC), a public interest research center founded in April 1994 by Marc Rotenberg and former presidential candidate John Anderson. The catalyst for the creation of EPIC was the fight against the Clinton administration's proposed adoption of a public encryption technology called the Clipper Chip,[11] but EPIC soon found itself at odds with the Clinton administration over other privacy issues, including the European Data Protection Directive and the Passenger Name Record Agreement.

Various consumer organizations added pro-privacy sections to their agenda, and began a fairly active lobbying of state legislatures and the federal government on privacy issues. Business interests, too, began to take notice of the pro-privacy momentum. Alan Westin, a privacy expert, founded the Global Business Privacy Policies Project in 1996 to represent "the most pro-active U.S. companies and industry associations on privacy issues that were trying to develop information on how U.S. firms have handled their employment and personnel data under European data protection laws; how contracts to comply with European laws have been negotiated by firms seeking transborder data transfer authorization; and how privacy might be added to existing consumer dispute resolution programs in 15–20 U.S. industries." Unlike the other pro-privacy interest groups, the business privacy groups rejected a comprehensive federal law to cover all industries and sectors, recommending self-regulation instead.

In 1999, the Global Business Dialogue on E-commerce (GBDe), comprising large multinational European, US, and Japanese firms, was founded, in part to forestall greater international regulation of e-commerce in the fields of "taxation, tariffs, intellectual property rights, encryption, authentication, data protection and liability."[12] In their first press statement, the GBDe made clear what their mission was: "governments around the world should recognize the dangers that regulation of the Internet would pose to their economies and societies.[13] In February 2000, the National Business Coalition on E-Commerce and Privacy was founded to lobby on behalf of major US businesses against privacy legislation generally, and the Safe Harbor Agreement specifically. On either side of the debate, interest groups were amassing their forces.

■ Getting the US Government's Ear

In the 1995–1997 period, a number of EU member states and Commission "ambassadors" of the European Data Protection Directive tried very hard to get the US to take seriously the implications of the European Data Protection Directive. Many thought that the threat to halt data flows embodied in Article 25 of the Directive would be finessed since the Europeans would not dare to put approximately $120 billion[14] in trade at risk. Moreover, the member states themselves had not all transposed the Directive into national law by October 24, 1998, and so, US businesses and policymakers alike hoped that this would prevent the strict application of all the Directive's provisions. The EU tried to correct this misperception whenever it could. Spiros Simitis, speaking at a conference in March 1998, stated, "the European Court in Luxembourg on numerous occasions—including recently—has held that Directives take effect on their stated date throughout the EU, whether or not the member states have enacted them into law."[15] He also "advised against attempts to influence the European Commission's interpretations of the Directive via appeals to organizations like the OECD, WTO or private standard setting bodies."[16]

In the US government, the person most concerned about the European Data Protection Directive was Barbara Wellbery, the Counselor to the Undersecretary for E-commerce in the Department of Commerce's International Trade Administration Bureau. Having read the final text of the Directive in 1995, she was incredulous at the breadth of the European law, especially its ability to order a halt to cross border data flows.[17] In 1996, Wellbery met with several European data commissioners to get a sense of the European thinking behind the sweeping Directive. Discussions in the Article 29 Working Party[18] were being initiated about how to operationalize adequacy findings, but there were no formal criteria until the Article 29 Working Party published their Department of Commerce document on applying Articles 25 and 26 of the Directive in July 1998.[19]

For their part, the Europeans, led by Ulf Brühann of the Commission, were thankful that they had a source of information in the government to consult on these issues. Wellbery was almost an exception in the government, however, in view of her willingness to spend time familiarizing herself with the European Data Protection Directive in 1996. For the most part, concerns about the Directive throughout 1996 and 1997 were voiced by US businesses, which rejected the extraterritorial application of EU law to their businesses, and were primarily concerned that the Clinton administration "fix" the Directive.[20] The only other indication of an acknowledgment of the potential problems between the EU and the US on the issue of privacy was a June 12, 1996, hearing called in the House Banking and Financial Services Committee, at which Alan Westin testified specifically on the questions of "how should the U.S. financial industry and the U.S. government approach these issues in light of the European Union's new Data Protection Directive, and are we headed on a collision course between the U.S. and European approaches to privacy protection in financial services—and many other fields?"

The EU Commission was dismayed that the implications of the European Data Protection Directive for the US and proposals for compliance were not discussed widely in the US policy circles. The Europeans pointed out that the US was as interested in privacy as the Europeans, a finding validated by an April 1997 opinion poll showing that 58 percent of computer users felt that the government should pass laws now on how personal information can be collected and used on the Internet; another 24 percent said the government should recommend privacy standards for the Internet, but not pass laws at this time; and only 15 percent felt that the government should let groups develop voluntary privacy standards for the Internet and monitor any problems, but not pass laws at this time.[21] Speaking at an October 1996 conference in Brussels attended by the EU,

US and Canadian industry, and administrators and academics, the Single Market Commissioner, Mario Monti, outlined his views on progress:

> It is already apparent that there is a shared awareness of the privacy problem. Indeed the US administration unveiled last year its National Information Infrastructure general privacy principles, as well as a specific White Paper applying those principles to the telecommunications sector. But if perceptions of the problem across the Atlantic are similar, there remain significant differences regarding solutions. In the Community the need for a legal framework of protection is not contested. In the US, despite the fact that some Internet software suppliers would be happy to see clear rules established, the mood remains markedly anti-regulation, particularly for the private sector. There is a residual faith that somehow the market will be able to resolve the problem unaided. We are therefore still some way from a global consensus, but recent developments in Canada, Australia and even Japan show that progress is being made, and that the European approach to privacy questions is growing in influence.[22]

In April 1997, the Commission laid out its ideas about e-commerce in a working paper titled "A European Initiative in Electronic Commerce."[23] On the issue of regulating e-commerce, the paper was quite explicit:

> The first objective is to build trust and confidence. For electronic commerce to develop, both consumers and businesses must be confident that their transaction will not be intercepted or modified, that the seller and the buyer are who they say they are, and that transaction mechanisms are available, legal and secure. Building such trust and confidence is the prerequisite to win over businesses and consumers to electronic commerce. Yet many remain concerned about the identity and solvency of suppliers, their actual physical location, the integrity of information, the protection of privacy and personal data.[24]

The Commission's fundamental premise for thriving e-commerce was strong regulatory protection of data privacy, almost entirely the opposite approach from the US.

On June 26, 1997, the Article 29 Working Party presented a working paper titled "First Orientations on Transfers of Personal Data to Third Countries—Possible Ways Forward In Assessing Adequacy."[25] The paper spelled out the process by which the EU would judge which countries meet the adequacy standard.

In its initial communications with the US, the European Commission had requested a new US regulatory body to monitor breaches of privacy on the Internet and act on consumer complaints, a proposal the Clinton administration rejected outright.[26] At first blush, the apparent disinterest in the developing US federal level privacy legislation was itself somewhat strange for an administration that prided itself on its knowledge of, and policy stance on, new technology (as well as knowing which way the political winds were blowing). Vice President Gore was keenly interested in technology, and the Internet in particular, and the Clinton administration proactively had begun thinking about the national information infrastructure and other technology policy issues. In 1995, Clinton had appointed Ira Magaziner the Administration's Global Electronic Commerce Advisor. Although Magaziner's previous writing[27] and policy work[28] suggested strong support for government regulated solutions to public policy problems, the driving force behind the Clinton administration's approach to these issues was the technology industry. Silicon Valley and other high tech companies had been enormous donors to Clinton's 1996 re-election campaign[29], and Clinton deferred to them on technological issues because of their political support and their specialized knowledge.

Magaziner's policy statement on electronic commerce, titled "A Framework for Global Electronic Commerce," was published on July 1, 1997. The report laid out five principles to guide government support for the evolution of electronic commerce, and made recommendations about nine key areas where international efforts were required. The themes were clear and unambiguous: the private sector should lead, and the government should stay out of its way and "recognize the unique qualities of the Internet." Point 3 in the report detailed the extent to which the government should be involved: "where governmental involvement is needed, its aim should be to support and enforce a predictable, minimalist, consistent and simple legal environment for commerce."[30] The thrust of the paper was very much proindustry, and implicitly challenged the European Data Protection Directive's requirements.

This proindustry perspective was not an accident: according to Michael Maibach, the chief lobbyist for the Intel Corporation, "virtually all the leading high-technology companies were involved in the drafting of [the Framework paper], arguing against too much regulation of the Internet. Other than its position on encryption, the paper read like a high-technology wish list."[31] Any US position on the European Data Protection Directive would inevitably have a strong proindustry bias, based simply on the sources of information that the Clinton administration was using. Although there were increasing numbers of pro-privacy interest groups that the administration could have consulted to get a different view of the costs and opportunities, there is little evidence that the White House ever called on these interests.

Beginning in October 1997, there were several informal senior level meetings between Wellbery and EU representatives, at which John Mogg, the EU Commission's Internal Market and Financial Services Director General, put the issue on the table. With only a year until the Directive would enter into force, there was still no solution to the "adequacy" problem (and there was widespread agreement that the US would most likely not obtain an adequacy finding unless new legislation were passed). In December 1997, the Department of Commerce invited the European private sector and government officials to attend a roundtable where they would discuss the Directive, and how the US should respond. Barbara Wellbery remembers that even among EU companies, there was still hope that the US would "fix" the Directive.[32] Primarily, however, the outcome was of stalling: there was no brilliant solution, but the roundtable participants agreed to use the OECD Guidelines as the fundamentals of any agreement between them, and spent the meeting articulating how these principles fit into the application of the US and EU laws. The OECD Guidelines, however, contained no provisions for enforcement or onward transfer rules, and therefore, no real progress was made at this roundtable meeting.

With the arrival of David Aaron as the Undersecretary of Commerce for International Trade in November 1997, the first formal meeting on how to respond to the European Data Protection Directive was convened in early 1998. Aaron, who had been the US Ambassador to the OECD from 1993 to 1997, was, therefore, familiar with the OECD Guidelines on the Protection of Privacy and Transborder Flows of Personal Data. He had also had experience with tax law and "safe harbor" ideas in the field of taxation, which turned out to be useful. Within the Department of Commerce, there was agreement that the existing privacy laws would most likely not create the "adequacy finding," and there was also consensus that any challenge of the European Data Protection Directive as a nontariff barrier to trade before the WTO would be struck down, since there was an explicit exception to the General Agreement on Trade in Services for "the protection of the privacy of individuals in relation to the processing and dissemination of personal data and the protection of confidentiality of individual records and accounts."[33]

It would be incorrect to assume that the US position on a response to the European Data Protection Directive was still open by the time Aaron became involved. In several of the accounts of Safe Harbor negotiations, Aaron's embrace of self-regulation is often seen solely as his personal preference (which it also was[34]) rather than the logical outcome of a certain path the Clinton administration had preordained earlier. Magaziner's Framework had become the administration's international position, and Magaziner himself had spent considerable time in Europe explaining the self-regulatory approach to unsympathetic European audiences. Thus, in the initial US interagency meetings, the consensus that the US would not pass comprehensive privacy legislation at the behest of the Europeans was hardly surprising.[35] David Aaron's testimony before Congress in 2001 made clear the terms on which he was negotiating:

> The first thing we established was that the United States was not going to negotiate a treaty or an executive agreement that would apply the EU Directive in the United States. What we were prepared to do was issue guidance to the American business community on how to conduct commercial relations with Europe. This comes under the existing authority of the Commerce Department. In the past, we have provided such guidance to help protect U.S. firms doing business in places like the Soviet Union, China, and elsewhere. The second thing we made clear is that we were not going to accept the jurisdiction of European law in the United States. Indeed, we agreed that the safe harbor would be silent on the issue of jurisdiction. We were prepared to have voluntary self-regulation within the framework of existing U.S. law. We were not going to pass new legislation.[36]

Part of this consensus was no doubt due to a certain nationalist "you can't make us" outrage among the participants, but there was also a much more realistic assessment of the administration that the Congress should be avoided at all cost. There were already legislative proposals before Congress, and the Clinton administration didn't want to alienate the parties and interests there. Moreover, the experience of having so many privacy bills stalled and killed in committees previously had led the administration to believe that a nonlegislative approach to complying with the Directive would be best. This feeling was only confirmed when the Monica Lewinsky scandal burst into public view in January 1998, and the relationship of the administration with Congress worsened over the course of the year.

One of the primary questions on procedure was whether the Department of Commerce even had the authority to negotiate a deal to allow compliance with the European Data Protection Directive. It was clear that the department could give advice, but traditionally, it did not have negotiation authority, and it certainly did not have any enforcement authority, a point that would become something of a hitch in finalizing the agreement. On the positive side, Ambassador Aaron had a reasonably free hand to negotiate with the Europeans. There was no negotiating mandate (beyond avoiding Congress) that Aaron would have to follow, and thus, Aaron was able to negotiate productively without having incompatible constituencies to appease, at least in the government.

There was, however, a great deal of lobbying from specific business interests, and it was there that Aaron had to tread a fine line. The most deeply concerned companies were those that had to carry on transactions with the EU in the normal course of business, and those that wanted to sell data lists. For the former group, the primary concern was to secure a guarantee against potential litigation, and to minimize the costs of compliance. For the second group, the primary fear was that the European Directive might lead to comprehensive privacy legislation in the US, which would likely put them out of business. Aaron tried to reassure industry leaders that efforts to comply with European rules have nothing to do with the privacy legislative debate in the US. "My point to them," he said, "is simple: This does not establish a precedent."[37] The former group lobbied Aaron for a self-regulatory response, while the data sellers urged a complete repudiation of the European Data Protection Directive as extraterritorial application of EU law, and hence a confrontation with the EU in the name of defending US sovereignty. In the Department of Commerce, the confrontational position was never seriously considered because of the enormous amount of trade that was potentially at risk if the Europeans did cut off data flows. According to administration estimates, as much as $120 billion in transatlantic trade was involved. To put this figure in context with other EU-US trade disputes, the next largest conflict, the US Foreign Sales Corporation dispute, was worth approximately $4 billion, and the Banana War, together with the hormone treated beef dispute, were worth $308 million.

In 1998, some of the earliest initial public offerings (IPO) of Internet stocks were held. When Internet companies like Globe.com opened at $9 and soared to $97, the importance of preserving status quo with respect to Internet regulation seemed to increase as well. Suddenly, the Internet had become not only the driver of the "New Economy," in which technology-induced increases in productivity fueled a high growth/low inflation economy,[38] but also a means for a sizeable investing elite to become incredibly wealthy in a very short time. In the eyes of a majority in the US Congress, it was hardly the time to put roadblocks in the way of this new development, and industry self-regulation appeared the best way to preserve the flexibility of the growing e-commerce sector.

A significant flaw in the US negotiating position, however, was that although the US government's position favored self-regulation, by early 1998 there were still no generally accepted self-regulatory mechanisms in place with which to demonstrate the effectiveness of self-regulation to the Europeans. Indeed, the earliest self-regulatory organization, TRUSTe (originally Etrust) had been formed in March 1996, but still had only a few companies affiliated with its program.[39] At a May 1998 IBM sponsored symposium on privacy, Magaziner publicly pleaded with the industry to get self-regulatory programs up and running in order to have something to show to the Europeans:

> We have indicated [to the Europeans] that we will not accept [cutting off data flows] and that the self regulatory solutions that we are looking towards, we think, ought to be acceptable to them. . . . We think that we can prevail in that discussion. But only if we have the self regulatory regimes up and going. Because the latest comments they have been mak-

> ing to us is [sic], "Magaziner, you've been talking about self regulation for a year. Fine. Where is it?" And at some point you can't fight something with nothing. So there is that. And then there is also, I think, a great deal of concern in Washington and in the Congress. There have been over 80 bills which introduced some kind of legislative approach on privacy and the Internet. And I think this is all going to come to a head some time in the coming months. And so if self regulation is going to be given a chance to work, it really needs to come forward soon. . . . Because we think that there is a window in time and that window will close. And basically, I think the privacy issue is going to be sort of one of those wedge issues. And you know, we stand at what I like to call a Robert Frost moment here where we've got two different paths we can take with respect to the Internet. Either it's going to become a regulated medium. Or the kind of philosophy we have been pushing which says it should be a market driven medium, is going to hold. And I think the privacy issue may well be the wedge issue around which that is decided. And for the good of the Internet, the good of our economies, we think it is very important that we follow the market in that approach.[40]

Magaziner's frank warning about the threat of a legislative solution if industry did not act quickly showed how politically significant the issue had become domestically. Pro-privacy interest groups had grown dramatically stronger, and were pressing for legislation waving opinion polls that showed an 80 percent majority in favor of protecting privacy on the Internet. They did not yet have as strong an access to the Clinton administration as the technology interests did, but there was a fear that a weakened president might be interested in any issue with 80 percent approval ratings.

There were those in other agencies who were increasingly skeptical that industry self-regulation was going to be sufficient to guarantee data privacy for US citizens, let alone the Europeans. In a prepared statement before a subcommittee of the House Committee on Commerce in July 1998, Federal Trade Commission (FTC) Chairman Robert Pitofsky voiced doubts about self-regulation:

> The Commission believes that self-regulation is preferred to a detailed legislative mandate because of the rapidly evolving nature of the Internet and computer technology. The Commission also recognizes that a private-sector response to consumer concerns that incorporates the widely-accepted fair information practices discussed in the Report and provides for effective enforcement mechanisms could afford consumers adequate privacy protection. However, despite the Commission's considerable efforts to encourage and facilitate an effective self-regulatory system, we have not yet seen one emerge. Our March 1998 survey of commercial Web sites and assessment of industry self-regulatory efforts revealed that, at the time of the survey, the state of self-regulation was inadequate and disappointing. Our survey found that the vast majority of Web sites fail to provide even the most basic privacy protection—notice of what information they collect and what they do with that information. Few of the sites sur-

> veyed—only 14% in the Commission's random sample of commercial Web sites—provide any notice with respect to their information practices, and fewer still—approximately 2%—provide notice by means of a comprehensive privacy policy.[41]

Even within the US federal government, there were those who were dubious that industry self-regulation was going to be well established and effective enough to meet the needs of privacy protection that the consumers wanted.

Among consumer groups both in Europe and the US there was a (well founded) fear that the Clinton administration was heeding only special interests' views on the issue of privacy. The Transatlantic Consumer Dialogue (TACD) was launched in September 1998 with more than sixty consumer representatives from the US and the EU in order to "provide a formal mechanism for EU and US consumer representatives to input into EU and US political negotiations and agreements as well as explore ways of strengthening the EU and US consumer view at the international level."[42] However, the input of the TACD was minimal, and its urging of the EU Commission to reject the Safe Harbor Agreement ("it reflects in too many ways the concerns of business and not the interests of consumers"[43]) was ignored.

After the European Data Protection Directive entered into force on October 24, 1998, many US companies were confused about the status of data flows. Many of them believed the Commission had arranged for a "standstill" in the implementation of the Directive as regarded Article 25, but Director Susan Binns rejected any such claims:

> When the Americans refer, as they tend to, to a stand-still which they claim to have negotiated for the present situation, this is a word that I am not very comfortable with and I discourage them from using, because it somehow implies that the Directive is not in force, or that it is on ice in some way. In fact, what is happening is that data blockages are being avoided by the proper use of Article 26.[44]

The pressure to find an appropriate solution continued on both sides, and both sides held fairly nonnegotiable positions.

▪ The Concept of Safe Harbor

On the European side, the problem was a "two-level games"[45] problem: not only did the Commission officials negotiate the terms for how best to meet the Directive's "adequacy" strictures, but whatever they negotiated had to be approved by the Article 31 Committee, the representatives of the member states. There were certain member states that were known to be extremely skeptical of the very notion of industry self-regulation (Germany, Austria, Spain, Italy, and, to a certain extent, France), thus, any US-EU proposal would ultimately need to pass muster with them. This led the US to adopt an inclusive strategy of "educating" the Europeans, insisting that not only the Commission but also the Article 29 working group members (the national data commissioners) be included in seminars and conferences.[46] David Aaron summarized the status quo before negotiations began in testimony before the House of Representatives:

> The Europeans had to recognize that we were trying to adapt the Directive to the most advanced information economy on earth. Accordingly, the actual provisions of the Safe Harbor had to be more flexible and address real-world information practices on a reasonable basis. Fortunately, we had the precedent of the privacy principles that we and the Europeans had agreed upon in the OECD many years ago, and this became a touchstone of the discussions. The European Commission accepted these points but had a bottom line of their own. They insisted on what they considered a high level of privacy protections for European personal data as provided by their Directive. It was their information. They had the right to control its dissemination from their point of view.[47]

The primary Commission negotiators were John Mogg, the DG of the Internal Market and Financial Services Directorate General, and Susan Binns, the Director in charge of data privacy. Both were, coincidentally, from the UK. This facilitated creative thinking because, unlike their more junior colleagues, they did not read the Directive word for word, and preferred a pragmatic solution to the US problem. Ultimately, however, they were constrained by the Directive's requirement that the representatives of the member states would make the ultimate "adequacy" finding, and thus, could not stray too far from the text.

Fairly early in the 1998 negotiations, David Aaron struck upon the idea of a "safe harbor" method of compliance with the Directive. As he recalled:

> Nobody knew how we were going to do this, and we were just sitting in John Mogg's office one day, and I had always been struck by the idea of "Safe Harbor." When I was first on Wall Street, was when I first encountered the term; it's used in this country primarily in the tax area, in which, if you do x, y, and z, you're presumed to fall under some tax regime exception or whatever it may be . . . Somehow the word stuck in the back of my head, and as we were discussing this issue, I thought . . . well if we couldn't get the country to be considered "adequate," maybe what we could get considered adequate are the companies. And that if we could set up some kind of a regime that could have an adequacy finding for a system, not for a whole country's law and regimes, and so the word just popped into my head, as describing Safe Harbor.[48]

Key to the development of Safe Harbor was the fact that Mogg and Binns were willing to entertain the possibility of making a slight alteration to the Directive, changing the stipulation in Article 25 from "data can only be transferred if the third *country* in question ensures an adequate level of protection," to a "*company . . .*" that ensures an adequate level of protection. Aaron suggested to Mogg that perhaps they could propose a series of steps or principles that companies could commit to utilizing, which would be deemed adequate for the purposes of the Directive. The Europeans were cautious and very skeptical. From an interinstitutional point of view, it was extremely delicate for the Commission to agree to the US doing less than the Directive demanded, and intuitively, the Commission understood that making a self-regulatory exception in the Directive for the US might undermine the Directive's efficacy completely. There were also fears that other countries might be attracted to this system, and Safe Harbor would set a dangerous precedent. However, as there were few alternatives that might prevent a trade conflict with the US, the Internal Market Director General Mogg of the Commission agreed to think about the concept, and began negotiations on those terms.

By the middle of 1998, the threat of US regulation had prompted action from US companies. The White House organized a two day Internet privacy summit in June 1998, which featured industry groups prominently displaying their pro-privacy views in an attempt to thwart government involvement. The White House summit itself had been subject to conflict as pro-privacy groups alleged a bias in the list of speakers and participants. A group of more than seventy leading privacy scholars, advocates, and technical experts signed an open letter to the White House challenging it to be more inclusive. Its plaintive tone is worth quoting at length:

> We support your efforts to convene a conference on [Internet privacy] issues. At the same time, we are troubled by the current planning for this event. We understand that the Department has essentially delegated to the private sector the responsibility for organizing this meeting. Planning has begun for the event, even though there is no formal announcement from the Department and no announced request for public participation. Many of the country's leading experts and advocates have not been contacted nor invited to participate. Given the enormous importance of this issue for so many people, we believe it is critical that the planning and organization of this event be as open and as inclusive as possible . . . The conference should be organized by full-time employees of the US government and decisions about participation, program, and conference activities must be made by the agency responsible for the event. This is simply a matter of fairness: If the Department of Commerce has the staff and resources to meet with and organize on behalf of industry groups, it must expend at least as much energy soliciting public opinion and making possible meaningful public input in the planning of a national conference on privacy.

> This function cannot be delegated to a particular stakeholder or group of stakeholders . . . The White House has made a commendable commitment to openness and accountability in the development of Internet policy. While we have not always agreed on the outcomes produced, the process has inspired confidence that the Administration is genuinely interested in all points of view. The current planning for the privacy conference inspires no such confidence. We believe that a fundamental change in the organization of this event must be made to address the issues we have outlined.[49]

A day before the White House summit, two new private sector self-regulatory programs were introduced with great fanfare: the Online Privacy Alliance (OPA) and BBBOnline. The OPA was a consortium of fifty companies organized to protect consumer privacy on the Internet. The OPA required its members to post its privacy policy and to obtain parents' permission before collecting information from children's sites, but the alliance lacked the ability to punish members who violated its privacy policies.[50] In its January 14, 1998, working Department of Commerce document titled "Judging Industry Self-regulation: When Does it Make a Meaningful Contribution to the Level of Data Protection in a Third Country?" the Article 29 Working Party had been quite specific about the enforcement issue of self-regulation:

> As this document will go on to argue, one important criterion for judging the value of a code is the degree to which its rules can be enforced. . . . The absence of genuinely dissuasive and punitive sanctions is therefore a major weakness in a code. Without such sanctions it is difficult to see how a good level of overall compliance could be achieved."[51]

It seemed the US and the EU were on a collision course because even the characteristics of industry self-regulation were in dispute.

In the second part of 1998, the Commerce department wrote the outlines of its Safe Harbor proposal, receiving feedback from the Commission on various elements of the document. By November 4, 1998, the first draft of Safe Harbor Agreement was sent by Aaron to industry representatives for their comments.[52]

The sixty-five responses from individuals, businesses, and interest associations to the proposals were, by and large, negative. This fact in itself is not unusual, since those that are favorably inclined toward the draft have less incentive to comment. However, a significant number of the responses dealt with the process of the discussion rather than only the content of the proposal per se. Privacy expert Robert Gellman expressed the general feeling that the process was merely going through the motions rather than encouraging true dialogue:

> The manner in which the Department is soliciting comments on the safe harbor principles leaves much to be desired. Ambassador Aaron's letter requesting comments is not visible or highlighted on the Department of Commerce webpage. The letter is not visible or highlighted on the International Trade Administration [ITA] webpage. A diligent effort to search for the document using search engines provided on the Department's website was unsuccessful. I was unable to find a press release announcing the request . . . Only by a random click on an otherwise unmarked graphic can a user find the document in question. In contrast, I note that my search through the ITA webpage readily found seven different photographs of Ambassador Aaron that were available for downloading . . . The salutation of Ambassador Aaron's letter is telling. It says "Dear Industry Representative." The letter is clearly not addressed to organizations that represent consumers, privacy advocates, Internet users, or ordinary citizens. Any observer of the process for soliciting comments could easily conclude that the Department is only interested in the views of carefully selected members of the American business community and that it has no particular interest in the views of other parts of the business community or any other segment of American society. The short time allowed for comments [15 days] does nothing to dispel that conclusion.[53]

Other groups were even less circumspect: a joint letter signed by eleven pro-privacy groups stated bluntly that, "we are very concerned at reports that you personally developed this proposal in private consultation with industry representatives. There has been no similar consultation with consumer or privacy advocates."[54] It is interesting to note that these comments were virtually identical to those of European business groups bemoaning having been left out of the Commission's consultation group in drafting the European Data Protection Directive. In either case, a significant stakeholder group was furious at having been left out of the loop on such an important issue.

Not that business or industry groups were thrilled about the Department of Commerce's Safe Harbor draft. A frequent complaint was that the proposals were sufficiently vague to give little comfort to businesses trying to comply with the Directive. Perhaps the most common industry group comment was that Safe Harbor ought to be more closely aligned with the privacy policy of the Online Privacy Alliance that had been formed earlier that year, and by November, encompassed more than seventy major US corporations. The OPA itself filed a comment indicating that "the OPA supports the concept of a safe harbor *only* to the extent that such a safe harbor is premised on and reflects the principles adopted by the Online Privacy Alliance—at least for data collected online . . . To the extent that the Department of Commerce draft Principles and the OPA Guidelines differ, we request that the OPA language be used as the standard for online data protection."[55] To a large extent, Safe Harbor already overlapped the OPA's privacy policy, perhaps more than the 1980 OECD privacy guidelines that were ostensibly the basis.

In Europe, the Article 29 Working Party urged the Commission to consider its advisory opinion on the draft, which was also not favorable:

> Considerable efforts have been made during recent months to improve the credibility and enforceability of industry self-regulation, particularly in the context of the Internet and electronic commerce. Nevertheless, the Working Party takes the view that the current patchwork of narrowly-focussed sectoral laws and voluntary self-regulation cannot at present be relied upon to provide adequate protection in all cases for personal data transferred from the European Union.[56]

In a second draft of the Safe Harbor proposals announced on April 19, 1999, David Aaron asked his "colleagues" (his new salutation) for new feedback, and presented frequently asked questions (FAQs) that would be used to interpret the agreement, as well as the negotiating document complete with the points of conflict highlighted. This time the comment period allowed was almost one month, and Aaron indicated that he hoped they could complete the agreement in time to sign it at the June 21, 1999, US-EU summit. With only seven points of disagreement on the main document, it seemed that this deadline would prove reasonable.

By this time, the pro-privacy groups had realized that the path of European Data Protection Directive compliance would not involve greater US privacy protection, and that the industry groups had effectively mastered the Department of Commerce's position in the US-EU negotiations. Although the term "regulatory capture" is too narrow to apply to the Department of Commerce's negotiation strategy, the fact that industry groups dominated the process, and that they had a significant role in writing the Safe Harbor principles, to the detriment of other groups, makes regulatory capture a useful analogy. The outlines of the deal with the EU were substantially in place, although there remained significant differences. The points of disagreement between the Department of Commerce and the Commission primarily concerned enforcement (for the Europeans) and notice provisions (for the US).

> Several aspects of enforcement and implementation on both sides need to be further examined. The final arrangement will need to ensure effective protection of individual privacy rights while at the same time ensuring a predictable framework and maximum legal certainty for U.S. organizations participating in the Safe Harbor. Discussions so far show that the final arrangement on the EU side will guarantee due process for U.S. organizations participating in the safe harbor if they are the subject of non-compliance complaints. Those organizations will also be ensured non-discriminatory treatment. On the U.S. side, clarification will be provided concerning the role of independent complaint resolution mechanisms, especially as regards complaint investigation and sanctions for non-compliance that will be sufficiently meaningful to ensure compliance.[57]

Fifty-three individuals and groups commented on the second draft of the Safe Harbor Agreement and the FAQs. Overall, the tone was considerably more favorable among the industry groups and businesses, but also considerably more negative on the part of the thirteen individuals that sent comments. Most of the pro-privacy groups that had participated in the first round of comments did not send follow-up comments in the second round, although EPIC encouraged its members to submit their own comments.

In November 1999, the negotiations had almost reached completion. Negotiations continued on the financial privacy issue in the Safe Harbor framework. US banking and financial interests had argued that the newly passed Gramm-Leach-Bliley (GLB) Act (signed into law on November 12, 1999) and the Fair Credit Reporting Act should be considered "adequate" for the European Data Protection Directive purposes, but the Commission had countered that several of the Directive's elements, e.g., notice, were not included in these bills, and thus, the acts could not be deemed adequate. It was increasingly apparent that financial privacy was holding up a resolution of Safe Harbor.

One significant change from the earlier draft was the venue for enforcement. As Aaron described in his November 1999 letter inviting comments on the latest draft of Safe Harbor:

> Over the summer, the EC proposed that all enforcement be carried out in the United States, subject to very limited exceptions. The Safe Harbor now would create not just a presumption of adequacy for companies in the Safe Harbor, but a finding of adequacy, for the Safe Harbor as such. The new approach is attractive because it gives deference to the self-regulatory process in the United States. In addition, since fewer complaints will actually be handled in Europe, national treatment and MFN should be less of an issue.[58]

The problem for Mogg and his Commission colleagues was that several member states still opposed the form of self-regulation and enforcement mechanisms that the US was advocating. Although the November draft that the Department of Commerce had sent to the Europeans contained a new frequently asked question (FAQ) section about Dispute Resolution and Enforcement, several member states remained skeptical, and were willing to scuttle the entire Safe Harbor system.[59] If Safe Harbor were to fail, they argued, standard contract clauses, which the Commission was working on, would be the alternative to stopping transatlantic data flows. Thus, a costly trade war was not the inevitable alternative to the Safe Harbor Agreement.

According to Farrell (2003), a significant turning point in reducing the member states' fundamental skepticism about self-regulation was a January 2000 seminar sponsored by the Department of Commerce to discuss enforcement issues. After meeting with representatives of the FTC and the privacy seal organizations, even the most skeptical Article 31 Committee members were willing to countenance the proposed self-regulation, enforced by alternative dispute resolution and backed up by FTC enforcement. An alternative explanation might give greater weight to the pressure felt by the Europeans to resolve the issue before Aaron left the Department of Commerce in March.

By March, 2000, it had become apparent that no agreement could be reached on financial privacy, but that the Commission had found a compromise on the other outstanding issues. The fact that David Aaron was set to leave the Department of Commerce at the month's end[60] provided a strict deadline for completing the negotiations. Rather than hold up Safe Harbor any longer, the Department of Commerce decided to separate financial privacy from the primary agreement. The March 17 version of Safe Harbor principles, with minor modifications, was given to the member states. On May 31, 2000, the member state representatives unanimously approved the Safe Harbor Agreement that the Commission had negotiated, and thereafter, the threat of commercial disruption vanished.

However, as the final points were being settled in the spring of 2000 between the EU and the US, the issue was still hotly debated in a number of forums. In February, 2000, a new coalition of business interests opposed to the Safe Harbor regime was formed, the National Business Coalition on E-Commerce and Privacy, to lobby on behalf of major US businesses (e.g., General Electric, CIGNA, MBNA America, and Fidelity Investments[61]). Since most of the businesses involved were from the financial services industry, the primary motivation was to try to force the Department of Commerce to continue negotiations with the EU until financial services were covered under Safe Harbor. Although the coalition submitted other critical comments to the March version of the Safe Harbor Agreement ("[we are] concerned about the fundamental principles embodied in the proposal and their possible implications for American competitiveness and sovereignty"[62]), it was unable to effect any changes in the Safe Harbor principles.

On the other side of the debate, the May 2000 FTC Report to Congress had a surprise recommendation: after two years of supporting (albeit with dissents) industry self-regulation on the Internet, it had broken with the administration's proself-regulatory approach, changed positions, and advocated legislating consumers' online privacy:

> The 2000 Survey [of commercial websites] . . . demonstrates that industry efforts alone have not been sufficient. Because self-regulatory initiatives to date fall far short of broad-based implementation of effective self-regulatory programs, a majority of the Commission has concluded that such efforts alone cannot ensure that the online marketplace as a whole will emulate the standards adopted by industry leaders. While there will con-

> tinue to be a major role for industry self-regulation in the future, a majority of the Commission recommends that Congress enact legislation that, in conjunction with continuing self-regulatory programs, will ensure adequate protection of consumer privacy online.[63]

Indeed, Commissioner Mozelle Thompson echoed some of the European complaints when he stated that legislation was needed to fill the holes in the "Swiss cheese" of self-regulation.[64] To some privacy advocates in the US, it was ironic that as one department of the US government was finalizing its agreement with the EU for a self-regulatory regime, another was recommending legislation to compensate for the drawbacks of the approach.

■ The European Parliament Objects

On the European side, the approval by the Article 31 Committee was not the final step in the process. Although the Directive itself did not give a formal vote to the European Parliament, it required the MEPs to review the agreement. Based on the criticisms of the Article 29 Working Party, a majority in the European Parliament felt that it was overly lenient, and did not safeguard European data protection as much as the Directive required. In June, the European Parliament released a report that urged the Commission to revise the Safe Harbor principles. The European Parliament, however, was largely impotent to force the Commission to do anything, since its role was only to review the agreement.

The focus of the European Parliament's criticism was twofold: first, it rejected the institutional competence of the Commission to negotiate, in essence, an international treaty without the European Parliament's input, and second, it decried the fact that the Commission had not sufficiently taken account of the various criticisms published by the Article 29 Working Party.[65] According to the Directive, the Article 29 Working Party could advise the Commission, but the final vote to establish "adequacy" lay with the Article 31 Committee, comprising member states' representatives.

In June 2000, the Commission had forwarded the Safe Harbor Agreement to the European Parliament, and the Committee on Citizens' Freedoms and Rights, Justice and Home Affairs released its report on June 21. The report produced by the committee was very critical of Safe Harbor, and the European Parliament tabled a resolution demanding that the Commission renegotiate the specific items that failed to convey "adequacy" in the eyes of the European Parliament.

In July, The European Parliament debated the resolution criticizing the Commission's handling of the dispute and demanding renegotiation. The nonbinding resolution of the European Parliament also criticized the

Commission, indicating that, with the "exchange of letters" between the Commission and the US Department of Commerce on the implementation of the Safe Harbor principles, both sides had come dangerously close to having negotiated an international agreement, which would legally require the assent of the European Parliament. On this basis, the European Parliament called for the Commission to renegotiate key elements of the agreement. Moreover, the resolution took issue with the fact that, although the Article 29 Working Party, which had the technical expertise (by virtue of comprising the national data commissioners), had expressed significant reservations about the elements of Safe Harbor, the Commission had nevertheless deemed the system "adequate" under the terms of the Directive. The resolution:

> . . . takes the view that, if issued and implemented by individual firms, such principles and the relevant explanations could be considered adequate protection . . . provided that the following changes are made to them:
>
> - recognition of an individual right of appeal to an independent public body instructed to consider any appeal relating to an alleged violation of the principles;
> - the obligation for participating firms to compensate for the damage, whether moral or to property, suffered by those involved, in the event of violations of the principles, and the undertaking by the firms to cancel personal data obtained or processed in an unlawful manner;
> - ease of identification of the steps to be taken to ensure data are cancelled and to obtain compensation for any damage suffered;
> - provision of a preliminary check by the Commission on the proper functioning of the system within six months of its entry into force and presentation of a report on the outcome of the check and any problems encountered to the [Article 29] Working Group . . . and the [Article 31] Committee . . . as well as to the relevant committee of the European Parliament;
>
> [The European Parliament] takes the view that the adequacy of the system cannot be confirmed and, consequently, the free movement of data cannot be authorised until all the components of the safe harbour system are operational and the United States authorities have informed the Commission that these conditions have been fulfilled.[66]

When Internal Market Commissioner Frits Bolkestein spoke against the resolution, he addressed the European Parliament's criticisms head on:

> It is not clear to me from this draft resolution whether Parliament intends to make a decision on whether or not the Commission has exceeded its authority. Hence I would ask Parliament to make itself clearer in its resolution. Naturally the Commission believes that it has used its authority correctly with regard to its proposal for a decision on the Safe Harbour,

> and I hope that Parliament sees it the same way. Parliament would put the Commission in an extremely difficult position if it were to adopt an unclear or negative resolution . . . The Member States . . . gave unanimous support to the Commission's draft decision when their opinion was sought at the end of May. Some of them had the same concerns as those that have come to the fore this evening in Parliament's draft resolution. But they were all agreed that it was time to give the system a chance. If Parliament were ultimately to support the Commission's proposal, then it would not end up out in the cold . . . To make approval of the determination of adequacy conditional on these changes is more likely to end up sinking the safe harbour than achieving hoped-for improvements. I would like to leave you in absolutely no doubt about this. The United States has no desire to revisit the discussions again and the Commission also takes the view that the talks are over.[67]

Despite his pleas for the European Parliament to reject the resolution, a majority (279 to 259 with 22 abstentions) supported the resolution to demand changes in the Safe Harbor Agreement before it was deemed adequate. Saying it was "disappointed" by the outcome, the Commission sought legal advice on the questions of whether it had overstepped its bounds, or whether the European Parliament's advisory opinion was legally relevant to the commencement of Safe Harbor.[68] After learning that the European Parliament did not intend to challenge the Commission's mandate (Bolkestein was told informally by senior figures that the European Parliament was not going to provoke an interinstitutional crisis by going to the European Court of Justice[69]), the Commission announced on July 26 that Safe Harbor would meet the EU's adequacy criteria. The Safe Harbor Agreement went into effect on November 1, 2000.

▪ Conclusion

It would be difficult to argue that the Safe Harbor Agreement was a not very creative solution to the problem posed by the European Data Protection Directive for the US. Its greatest accomplishment was that it prevented a major transatlantic trade conflict. However, it also gave lawyers a great deal to argue about, and provided a decent living for legal advisors who instruct companies regarding how to comply with its vague and occasionally ambiguous provisions. Favorable accounts of the system call it a hybrid, with new lessons for all on "how bodies such as the FTC may act as a nonprescriptive enforcer."[70] Less kind interpretations label it a fig leaf to prevent the disruption of transatlantic data flows and commerce, but with significantly less data protection than the European Data Protection Directive incorporates.

One of the claims in the debate that has been endorsed by almost all sides is that Safe Harbor is the result of a different level of faith in government regulation in Europe and the US. Because the Europeans trust government, and the US does not, the argument goes, it was almost inevitable that the US was not going to pass new comprehensive privacy legislation as the Europeans had done. A typical statement of the argument is this:

> More fundamentally, the debate has highlighted important divisions between EU and US approaches to data protection which reflect cultural and historical differences about the role of government regulation. In general there is a much greater confidence in public institutions and dependence upon administrative law in EU states than is the case in the US where there is far greater esteem for markets and technology.[71]

A close reading of the history of the negotiations, however, does not reveal significant differences at the mass public level between the US citizens' desire to have the government regulate privacy protection and the Europeans' view. Some of the relevant poll data were introduced in Chapter 2, but overall the argument that "Americans don't trust government to regulate properly" is simply not borne out by this analysis of Safe Harbor. More important were the close contacts between the technology interest groups and the negotiators on the US side. As this case highlighted, although pro-privacy interest groups mobilized quickly in the early 1990s (and partially in response to a perception that the European Data Protection Directive would create a window of opportunity in the US), they were systematically shut out of the process of informing government policy. Instead, the government sought out industry groups to understand their preferences for how to respond to the Europeans, and certainly incorporated their thinking into the Safe Harbor Agreement to a large extent. The Clinton administration's Framework for Global Electronic Commerce was essentially written by technology industry lobbyists, and provided the blueprint for the self-regulation mandate. Even when industry itself was not establishing self-regulatory mechanisms, the administration did not explore alternatives, and when Safe Harbor was negotiated, the comments and concerns of the industry were paramount. Indeed, the Department of Commerce's cover letter asking for comments on the first draft of Safe Harbor began "Dear Industry Representatives." One need only compare the OPA's privacy policy to Safe Harbor to see a great similarity between them. Thus, even though Farrell (2003) highlights the fact that Safe Harbor was a traditional government-to-government negotiation that did not involve industry ("they were never in the meeting rooms, they never participated in the drafting sessions, they were bystanders"[72]), it was clear that the government had already given industry the pride of place in setting the parameters of the US response.

The following chapter contrasts the US response to European Data Protection Directive with that of the other countries impacted.

Notes

1. Farrell, 2003.

2. It is difficult to believe that the cost of compliance with a comprehensive privacy policy legislated by the US federal government would have been greater than these fees paid to private agencies, but one of the business arguments against legislating privacy was always the fear of large costs of compliance.

3. The text of the Safe Harbor Agreement and the FAQs are available at http://europa.eu.int/smartapi/cgi/sga_doc?smartapi!celexapi!prod!CELEXnumdoc&lg=en&numdoc=32000D0520&model=guichett.

4. Abbate, 2000, p. 199.

5. Berners-Lee et al., 1994; cited in Abbate, 2000, p. 217.

6. Available at http://www.plazaone.com/mohammed_h_chang/cyberspace.html.

7. Bangemann, 1994.

8. *Financial Times,* July 6, 1996. Cowles, 2001.

9. Allen, 2002.

10. http://energycommerce.house.gov/107new/hearings/03082001Hearing49/print.html.

11. Gurak, 1997.

12. Cowles, 2001, p. 13.

13. Ibid., p. 16.

14. Press release available at http://usinfo.state.gov/topical/global/ecom/00053104.html.

15. American Institute for Contemporary German Studies, 1998, p. 1.

16. Ibid., p. 2.

17. Author's interview with Barbara Wellbery, October 25, 2002.

18. Working Party, 1997.

19. Working Party, 1998.

20. Author's interview with Barbara Wellbery, October 25, 2002.

21. Privacy and American Business, 1997. A discussion of the poll results is available at http://www.privacyexchange.org/iss/confpro/westinkeynote.html.

22. Single Market News, 1997. available at http://europa.eu.int/comm/internal_market/en/smn/smn6/s6mn25.html.

23. Commission, 1997.

24. Ibid.

25. Working Party, 1997.

26. *Vancouver Sun,* July 10, 1997.

27. Magaziner and Reich, 1982.

28. Previously, Magaziner had been in charge of the Clinton administration's unsuccessful bid to reform the US health care system.

29. In the 1995–6 electoral cycle, telecommunications companies donated $5.8 million and the computer and electronics industry donated $2.8 million in soft money to the Democratic Party. Data available at http://www.commoncause.org/laundromat/industry.cfm.

30. Clinton and Gore, 1997.

31. *New York Times,* August 4, 1997.

32. Interview with Barbara Wellbery, October 25, 2002.

33. Text available at http://www.europarl.eu.int/hearings/pdf/20000222/libe/framework/gats/default_en.pdf. One of the people I interviewed suggested that this exception had been inserted by the Europeans during the GATS negotiations "without the US negotiators seeming to understand its significance."

34. Interview with David Aaron, April 15, 2002.
35. Ibid.
36. Aaron, 2001, pp. 42–43.
37. *Financial Times,* March 16, 1999.
38. For research findings rejecting some of the claims of the "new economy" proponents, see Gordon, 2000.
39. Farrell, 2003, p. 290.
40. Magaziner, 1998.
41. Pitofsky, 1998.
42. TACD webpage available at http://www.tacd.org/about/about.html.
43. TACD Annual Report, 1999 available at http://www.tacd.org/db_files/files/files-130-filetag.pdf.
44. Binns' press conference available at http://europa.eu.int/comm/internal_market/privacy/adequacy/briefing-eu-us-dialog_en.html.
45. Putnam, 1988.
46. Farrell, 2003.
47. Aaron, 2001, pp. 42–43.
48. Aaron quoted in Farrell, 2003, p. 292.
49. Letter Regarding a Proposed White House Conference on Privacy available at http://www.epic.org/privacy/internet/daley_ltr_2_26_98.html.
50. *Atlanta Journal and Constitution,* June 23, 1998.
51. Commission, 1998, pp. 2–4.
52. Letter from David Aaron, Nov. 4, 1998, available at http://www.ita.DepartmentofCommerce.gov/td/ecom/aaron114.html.
53. Comments on the Safe Harbor proposal available at http://www.ita.DepartmentofCommerce.gov/td/ecom/comabc.html.
54. Comments on the Safe Harbor proposal available at http://www.ita.DepartmentofCommerce.gov/td/ecom/com1abc.html.
55. OPA Comment on Safe Harbor available at http://www.ita.DepartmentofCommerce.gov/td/ecom/com2abc.html [emphasis original].
56. Working Party, 1999.
57. Joint Report on Data Protection Dialogue to the EU/US Summit; June 21, 1999, available at http://www.ita.DepartmentofCommerce.gov/td/ecom/jointreport2617.html.
58. Aaron cover letter, November 15, 1999, available at http://www.ita.DepartmentofCommerce.gov/td/ecom/aaronmemo1199.html.
59. Farrell, 2003.
60. Aaron was replaced by Robert LaRussa, who was sworn in August 4, 2000.
61. The complete organization membership is available at http://www.practicalprivacy.org/nbcpe/meet_member_companies.html.
62. National Business Coalition letter to David Aaron, April 5, 2000, available at http://www.export.gov/safeharbor/Comments400/NatBusCoalonEcomComments.html.
63. Pitofsky, 2000.
64. Statement of Mozelle Thompson, May 22, 2000, available at http://www.thestandard.com/article/display/0,1151,16525,00.html.
65. See Working Party Opinions 1/99, 2/99, 4/99, 7/99, 3/2000, 4/2000 available at http://europa.eu.int/comm/internal_market/privacy/workingroup/wp1999/wpdocs99_en.htm#wp23.
66. Report on the Draft Commission Decision on the adequacy of the protection provided by the Safe Harbour Privacy Principles (C5-0280/2000 –

2000/2144(COS) available at http://europa.eu.int/comm/internal_market/privacy/docs/adequacy/0117-02_en.pdf.

67. Bolkestein's European Parliament testimony, July 3, 2000, available at http://www3.europarl.eu.int/omk/omnsapir.so/debats?FILE=00-0703&LANGUE=EN&LEVEL=DOC&GCSELECTCHAP=8&GCSELECT-PERS=94.

68. European Report, July 8, 2000. Henry Farrell argues that the EU Commission chose to interpret the Parliament's lack of procedural objection as tacit approval of the agreement (Farrell, 2002).

69. I thank Henry Farrell for pointing out these empirical details.

70. Farrell, 2003, p. 297.

71. Pearce and Platten, 1999, p. 2.

72. Commission official quoted in Farrell, 2003, p. 296.

5

The EU Standard Gains Critical Mass: International Responses

In most accounts of the European Data Protection Directive, the reaction of the US is the most important international response analyzed. Concentrating on the US is justified by the significance of bilateral trading and investment ties between the EU and the US, which are the most significant in the world by an order of magnitude. However, an exclusive focus on the US response can lead to the incorrect conclusion that the Europeans did not really set a new international standard, since the US compliance mechanism was substantially different and, arguably, simply a fig leaf to allow businesses to continue to operate on both continents.

When one examines the other countries that were impacted by Article 25 of the European Data Protection Directive, however, a different picture emerges, one that would show more obviously the international impact of the European Data Protection Directive. This chapter considers the other international responses in order to get a complete picture of the role the European Data Protection Directive has played. Almost all the countries that were concerned about the transborder effects of the Directive have passed, or are in the process of passing, comprehensive privacy legislation. Even the countries that initially tried to emulate the US Safe Harbor mechanisms (e.g., Japan and Australia) passed federal-level privacy laws that broadly comport with the European Data Protection Directive.[1]

The second part of the chapter examines the economics of the Directive: what costs of compliance were projected by businesses and the European Commission, and what costs have actually been borne by companies to date. The findings show that EU businesses tended to overestimate the costs of compliance before the Directive was passed, and that the actual costs of complying with the Directive and Safe Harbor have been negligible for most multinational companies.

The European Data Protection Directive's International Impact

It is important to recall that there are different ways in the European Data Protection Directive to legally transfer data across international borders: the Commission's preferred method was for the third country to pass comprehensive privacy legislation that the Article 29 Working Party would deem adequate, and the Article 31 Committee would then officially recognize. A second method, involving more administrative work on the part of the national data commissioners, was for the national data commissioners to allow individual transactions on the grounds that "adequate safeguards are in effect." These adequate safeguards could be the standard contractual clauses that were issued by the Commission in December 2001 or ad hoc contractual clauses the national data commissioners deem adequate. They could also be the data subject's unambiguous consent to the transfer, or Binding Corporate Rules on international data transfers, which the Article 29 Working Party drafted in 2003.[2] The key point of the second compliance mechanism was that most of these methods required the member state that allowed the data transfer to notify the Commission and the other member states of its actions, giving them the opportunity to oppose such transfers.

The Commission viewed these so-called Article 26 derogations as acceptable only as a matter of necessity, since not all states would have privacy legislation, but commerce had to continue. There was, however, an unspoken assumption that over time, more and more states would pass comprehensive privacy legislation, which would comport with the requirements of the European Data Protection Directive, and the necessity of relying on the derogations would decline. During the negotiations of the Safe Harbor Agreement, the Commission's Director of Data Protection, Susan Binns, had indicated that:

> The problem with Article 26 [derogations] is that it is micro-management. It is very heavy in terms of its administrative burden both on the data protection commissioners and on companies themselves. It means that there has to be an ad hoc solution for every ad hoc problem. It is workable but it is heavy, unnecessarily heavy, if we can identify situations in which the protection is adequate anyway. Why go into all this complication if we can identify broad areas where we can say that it a safe destination and you can transfer data into that area without going through all the micro-management of Article 26? That is the way in which the Committee has agreed that we should use Articles 25–6.[3]

There was, thus, an EU expectation that in the long run other states would pass privacy legislation to obtain the adequacy finding.

As Chapter 4 detailed, the US was unwilling to enact comprehensive privacy legislation in response to the European Data Protection Directive.

Although the US Safe Harbor Agreement did demonstrate internationally that there were other ways to comply with the European privacy law, most other countries that have sought an adequacy ruling did not follow the US path. This section examines how other countries have responded to the European Data Protection Directive's Article 25 stipulation that other countries have adequate privacy protection for Europeans' data.

For most countries, comprehensive privacy legislation was the most likely option: at the end of 1996, only six OECD countries were without the comprehensive privacy laws that applied the OECD's fair information principles to all organizations: Australia, Canada, Greece, Japan, Turkey, and the US.[4] Despite the fact that a majority of countries had some form of privacy legislation, as of October 2004, only Guernsey, the Isle of Man (both British crown dependencies), Switzerland, Canada, Argentina, and the US Safe Harbor had received an adequacy finding from the EU Commission.[5] Each of these countries (with the exception of the US) had passed, or amended, its national privacy legislation to comport with the requirements set by the European Data Protection Directive. For Switzerland, this was an obvious choice because of its close economic ties with the EU, and the fact that Switzerland incorporates most of the EU's regulation. Norway, along with other European Economic Area countries, Liechtenstein, and Iceland, as well as all the other EU accession countries,[6] was required to comply with the Directive.

Canada and Argentina

For Canada and Argentina, the choice was less obvious: Canada's largest trading partner, the US, was not going to pass comprehensive privacy legislation, and thus, restrictive privacy laws might pose trade difficulties with the US. Previously, the Canadian and the US privacy policies had been largely similar, but their response to the European Data Protection Directive was quite different.[7] Canadians worked to bridge the divide between government, industry, and consumer groups in order to come up with privacy codes and legislation. With 81 percent of Canadians believing that the government should be working with business to come up with guidelines on privacy protection for the private sector, the government felt compelled to enact legislation.[8]

The Canadian federal government introduced bill C-54 on October 1, 1998, three weeks before the entry into force of the European Data Protection Directive. The Canadian Personal Information Protection and Electronic Documents Act was finally passed on April 13, 2000, and received the Commission's adequacy finding in December 2001.

In Argentina, similar considerations were at work. Although the Argentine direct marketing association worked hard to defeat the country's strict privacy bill, and the US Council for International Business sent a letter to the US Ambassador James Walsh and to other US officials asking them to intervene,[9] the bill was enacted in November 2000. The Argentine bill closely mimicked the EU's Directive, and because of that overlap, Argentina was the first Latin American country to obtain the EU's adequacy finding. It was unlikely to be the last, however, because Chile, Brazil, and Peru all had privacy legislation passed, or pending, that reflected the EU's preferences. As one expert on Latin American privacy laws observed:

> Latin American privacy legislation has clearly been drafted to follow the EU Privacy Directive very closely. This will probably lead to a fair amount of harmonization among the data privacy legislation of different Latin American countries. It will also facilitate data flows between Latin American countries, and between Latin America and the European Union, as each will consider the other's laws to represent an adequate level of protection. U.S. companies, however, will likely face issues with respect to data flows and privacy rights in Latin America quite similar to those which they are already tackling in the European Union.[10]

Throughout the world, privacy legislation was proposed and amended to respond to technological changes and the new European Data Protection Directive. There were fewer sovereignty issues for the other countries because they were used to complying with international regimes that were not of their making. This section examines the new privacy bills and laws, and how the Article 25 implications were handled by domestic lawmakers. It is still too early to state unequivocally that even those countries reacting to the European Data Protection Directive will ultimately receive an adequacy finding from the Commission, but it is assumed that any third country writing a new piece of legislation in response to Article 25 concerns will be more likely to change that domestic legislation to address Article 29 Working Party concerns, and will be unlikely to take the confrontational approach that the US did. Conversely, the fact that data flows are far fewer between these third countries and Europe means that stalling may be the most common third country response in the event of a conflict.

■ International Responses

It was clear that countries with direct investments in the EU and those in which the EU member states invested would be the most affected by the European Data Protection Directive. The assumption made here is that investment relationships are more personal data–intensive than trading relationships, although, for the sake of completeness, the top exporters and importers are also listed. Table 5.1 shows the top six non-EU countries with the most investments in the EU, and those in which the EU invested: the

Table 5.1 The EU's Primary Economic Relationships

Extra-EU investment stocks into EU-15, 2001
(Top 6 non-EU investors in the EU, million euro)

US	596,570
Switzerland	122,684
Japan	48,789
Canada	43,986
Australia	19,531
Norway	19,412

EU-15 investment stocks in Extra-EU Countries, 2001
(Top 6 destinations for EU investments outside EU, million euro)

US	843,992
Switzerland	160,124
Canada	78,354
Brazil	74,508
Australia	36,105
Mexico	25,945

Top 5 EU Trading Partners, 2003
(million euro)

Imports		
	US	151.17
	China	95.22
	Japan	66.78
	Switzerland	55.96
	Russia	51.84
Exports		
	US	220.48
	Switzerland	68.41
	China	40.13
	Japan	40.06
	Russia	33.07

Source: Eurostat, 2004 Yearbook

US, Switzerland, Canada, Japan, Australia, Brazil, Mexico, and Norway. If one considers trading relationships as well, only the addition of Russia needs to be considered, although if outsourcing becomes an issue, then India also may become important.

It is of special relevance to know what kinds of privacy regimes are in place in these countries. Overall, one might be interested in whether these countries adopt a comprehensive legislation approach to privacy protection to meet the adequacy standard or the EU, or whether they prefer a business-self-regulatory approach, pioneered by Safe Harbor, and endorsed by the EU Commission. As of 2004, the self-regulatory approach had not been adopted by any other country. In 2000, there were several countries interested in self-regulatory approaches, but none ultimately chose to rely on that system to obtain the EU's approval. Moreover, it should be added that the EU Commission was hardly encouraging to other countries hoping to follow in the US footsteps by negotiating a Safe Harbor-like regime.

A striking feature of the international response is that, of the EU's largest economic partners, only the US, Canada, and Switzerland have adequacy findings eight years after the Directive was signed. Japan has privacy legislation, but the Working Party had, as of 2004, not expressed a public opinion on these laws. China does not have laws protecting privacy, and Russia's law is neither enforced nor does it incorporate all of the stipulations of the European Data Protection Directive. Thus, large EU economic relationships have the potential to become problematic if the EU Commission were to suddenly enforce the European Data Protection Directive to the letter of the law. In 2004, UK unions lodged a complaint against a firm outsourcing to India, saying British data were unprotected there, and therefore the transfers were illegal.

The US-EU trading and investment relationship is clearly the most important one in the world, and therefore, the US solution to meet the terms of Article 25 was an important signal to other countries. Farrell (2003) opined that a Safe Harbor-like self-regulatory regime might become an international alternative for countries loath to pass comprehensive privacy legislation. To date, however, there is little evidence that this is the preferred path of other states. Japan started to go down that path, but ended up passing a comprehensive privacy bill for the private sector (since the public sector was already covered by privacy legislation). Most other states have passed, or are in the process of trying to pass, comprehensive privacy legislation. The primary reason that many of them have not received the EU Commission's adequacy finding is that the new privacy laws do not necessarily meet all of the European Data Protection Directive's requirements. There are ongoing discussions with the Article 29 Working Party to negotiate what changes might be necessary to obtain an adequacy finding from the EU Commission. The Commission has also said that it would like to speed up the process of granting adequacy to other countries.[11]

This section examines the paths taken by several other countries in the area of data protection regimes. Although other countries, for example Japan, have set up trustmark programs, these supplement comprehensive legislation rather than set up self-regulatory mechanisms to comply with the EU Directive as the US has done.

Japan

Japan's public sector data were covered by a 1988 act that was completely overhauled in 2003 as the Act for Protection of Personal Data Held by

Administrative Organs. The act was based on the OECD principles, and imposes a duty on the controllers to safeguard the security and allow access and correction of the data. Like the European Data Protection Directive, it, too, prevents public sector data from being used for a purpose other than that for which it was collected.[12] Japan's private sector was not covered under any law, and until e-commerce privacy concerns arose in the late 1990s, the Japanese government preferred a self-regulatory approach to privacy, loosely co-ordinated through the Ministry for International Trade and Industry (MITI).[13] As informal contacts with MITI and the Article 29 Working Party developed in 1998, MITI issued Data Protection Guidelines ("MITI Guidelines on the Protection of Computer Processed Personal Data in the Private Sector") for the sectors it governed, with each sector drawing up its own guidelines. MITI also introduced a privacy trustmark administered by a joint public-private agency (the Japan Information Processing Development Center) in April 1998 that would be given to the companies that implemented the data protection guidelines, and a supervisory body to investigate complaints.[14] Although four academic privacy experts conducting an analysis for the EU found that there were serious shortcomings in the system,[15] the Commission supported these efforts, and urged other sectors to follow the lead of MITI. Until 1999, it seemed that Japan was going to follow the US lead and create a self-regulatory system similar to Safe Harbor.

However, in the summer of 1999, parliamentarians in the Diet proposed a new law on privacy, the Personal Data Protection Bill, which would be binding on both the government and the private sector. Public opinion in Japan was largely skeptical of existing privacy protections,[16] and broadly supportive of greater government initiatives in this area (only 34 percent of Japanese consumers believed that the existing laws and practices in Japan provided a reasonable level of consumer privacy[17]). The proposed bill, which was approved by the cabinet in March 2001, required both the government and private sector to follow five basic principles:

1. Specify the use of personal information, and restrict its use to the specified purpose.
2. Acquire personal information legally and in an appropriate manner.
3. Secure the accuracy and currency of personal information.
4. Ensure the security of personal information, including preventing it from being divulged.
5. Be transparent in the collection, use, and administration of personal information.[18]

The bill also prevented businesses from transferring data to third parties without the consent of the data subject.

From March 2000 until December 2002, the bill was debated in the Japanese Diet. In Japan, the opponents of the bill were not concentrated in the business sector, opposing government regulation. In fact, the business sector was remarkably quiescent, having worked with MITI and other government ministries to insert their input. The public, too, supported the bill, and pro-privacy legislation was seen as essential by the majority of the public. An October 1999 Ministry of Posts and Telecommunications public opinion survey found that 92 percent of the respondents believed that their personal information had been disclosed without their consent, and 83 percent believed that organizations and individuals who hold personal information should be regulated.[19]

The primary opposition in Japan came from the press, the media, and the academic sectors, which feared that the privacy bill was sufficiently vague to allow the government to censor journalists and academics on the pretext of the privacy law. Opponents viewed the new privacy law as the government's repeal of the freedom of expression and the freedom of the press. The proposed privacy bill had to, therefore, be withdrawn in December 2002 and redrafted to accommodate the bill's opponents.[20] In the redrafting, the five basic principles were dropped.

The privacy bill that was presented in January 2003 explicitly excluded media organizations and individual reporters in order to appease the opponents of the earlier bill. However, the new proposed bill was significantly watered down: instead of five principles, there was "one basic idea," that personal information "must be properly handled."[21] The bill was coupled with amendments to the public sector law, requiring jail time and hefty fines for officials who use information improperly, a response to several scandals involving the government's release of personal information illegally.[22] The government's August 2002 introduction of a new national registry prompted the amendments to the public sector law.

In March 2003, the government submitted to the Diet a package of five privacy related bills. The opposition tried to beef up the privacy provisions of the bill, inserting provisions to create new independent complaints' bureaus and to give individuals greater control over their data. However, the government's new bill had sufficient political backing to be passed on May 23, 2003. The provisions relating to the government took effect almost immediately, while those for the private sector were phased in over the course of two years. The bill's provisions for the private sector were very vague, and businesses were understandably nervous about what their obligations were.[23] Given that the government ministers had the authority to interpret and implement the act, businesses were reassured. Only businesses that refused to follow the ministers' orders could face up to six months in prison or a fine.

Although the government had initially proposed privacy legislation to obtain the EU's adequacy findings, the May 2003 privacy laws were unlikely to meet the Article 29 Working Party standards since they did not contain all of the EU's critical elements. In the two years leading up to the full implementation of the privacy laws on business, there continued to be an expectation that further implementation legislation would be created to meet some of the concerns of the EU. The key point to recall from this discussion of a legislative system still in flux is that it is fundamentally a legislative solution, not a self-regulatory one, to the problem of privacy protection. Initially, the European Data Protection Directive's pressure had resulted in a decentralized response. However, the fact that Japan's self-regulatory or hybrid response was likely to be inadequate to enable data flows to and from the EU and domestic pressure for greater personal data privacy protection combined to make a comprehensive legislative package more attractive in the end.

China and Hong Kong

The EU made $3.7 billion of new investments in China in 2002, and poured $17.9 billion of new investments into Hong Kong that same year.[24] These data are based on Chinese figures, which are somewhat distorted by financial incentives for FDI (foreign direct investment), but nonetheless evince the probability of a great deal of data transfer between the EU and China, and the Special Administrative Region (SAR) of Hong Kong. It is fairly inane to talk about data privacy in the context of China since the general concept of privacy is alien to the communist government's ideology and is viewed with suspicion. Although the Internet poses a challenge to the Communist People's Party's control over information, the party has successfully met the challenge thus far.[25] In senior-level discussions between the EU and China, data protection is not an issue simply because there are so many other differences to discuss. Most data transfers to and from China are conducted by the inclusion of standard contractual clauses. However, if the EU were suddenly to enforce or monitor compliance, it would be difficult to find an enforcement mechanism in this arrangement with China.

With so much more data presumably flowing into Hong Kong, it is perhaps more important to discover how Hong Kong reacted to the European Data Protection Directive. To some extent, the groundwork for privacy legislation was laid before the transfer of control from the UK to China on July 1, 1997. While writing what was essentially a separate constitution for Hong Kong (the Basic Law), the government was keen to promote privacy legislation to ensure a general level of individual privacy after the transfer. In 1996, the government passed the Personal Data (Privacy) Ordinance, which follows the 1980 OECD principles, and is applied to both the public and private sectors.[26] The ordinance, as written, meets the European Data

Protection Directive's requirements, a fact that sets it apart in Asia, and derives from Hong Kong's roots as a former territory of the UK.[27] However, because the onward transfer provisions of the ordinance have not been enacted,[28] many of the firms have outsourced to China, where there are no restrictions. Until those onward transfer provisions have been enacted, Hong Kong is unlikely to obtain an adequacy ruling. However, once fully implemented, the ordinance will likely be adequate since it was specifically written to incorporate the European Data Protection Directive at a time when Hong Kong still belonged to the UK.[29]

Australia

Australia, although less significant in terms of trade flows to and from the EU, is an important investor in the EU. Like the US, it tried to find an alternative to comprehensive privacy legislation for the private sector. However, it ultimately passed legislation to try to obtain the EU's adequacy ruling. Australia had passed a privacy law in 1988, based on the OECD principles, which incorporated eleven information privacy principles that apply to the government.[30] In December 2000, the government passed the Privacy Amendment (Private Sector) Act 2000, which extended some privacy protection to the private sector. This law went into effect in December 2001 and was extremely controversial. In June 2000, the EU made a submission to the Australian House of Representatives, saying explicitly that the new law would not meet the EU's adequacy standard.[31] The 2000 law puts in place the National Privacy Principles that companies are required to observe, although some may substitute a separate code of practice that the national privacy commissioner can approve. The act is weaker than the European Data Protection Directive in several areas,[32] for example, requiring companies to obtain consent for direct marketing only where "practicable," and allowing the onward transfer of data out of Australia if companies "reasonably believe" they are similarly protected in the third country.[33] In March 2001, the Article 29 Working Party released a report on the new Australian law, criticizing the exemptions to the bill (small firms and employee records are not covered), and suggesting that the other problems with the bill could be handled by a code of conduct enforced by the Chief Privacy Commissioner.[34] Australia's Attorney General criticized the EU report: "Many of the EC Committee's comments display an ignorance about Australia's law and practice and do not go to the substance of whether our law is fundamentally "adequate" from a trading point of view," and complained that ". . . in many ways, it goes significantly further than the US Safe Harbor Agreement, which was accepted by the EU as adequate . . . Obviously officials from Australia and the EC will continue to talk in order to address these concerns to everyone's satisfaction. However, Australia will only look at options that do not impose unnecessary burdens on business."[35] In February 2003, as several APEC[36] countries were revising their privacy laws on the basis of the European Data Protection Directive, Australia proposed an APEC-wide approach to privacy protection that would involve country self-certification rather than an adequacy test.[37] Australia's Attorney General also criticized the EU's approach in a September speech to APEC's privacy workshop:

> Australia is of the view that the regime put in place for cross-border transfers by the European Union's Data Protection Directive is overly detailed and prescriptive. It does not recognize that there may be a variety of legitimate approaches to data protection. And its imposition of centralized control by a third party is not suited to a multilateral agreement between equals.[38]

However, even as Australia's Attorney General was criticizing the EU, Australian privacy officials were working with the Article 29 Working Party, trying to get the EU's approval:

> The [Internet Privacy] Code will cover use and disclosure of sensitive information. Again, that is to comply with the EU concerns at the moment. And that's pretty much what it does. We have been in dialogue with the EEC about that and the wording that they have is the wording that is in here. They are responding to us with different wording.[39]

Although till 2004, Australia continued to try to obtain an adequacy ruling by the Commission, ultimately Australia's preferred remedy for the free flow of data is to convene a multilateral negotiation under the auspices of the WTO to create uniform and binding international regulations.

Other EU Economic Partners

Brazil was indirectly influenced by the EU in its data protection laws and practices, in the sense that it considered privacy protection to be an important element of a new democracy. In Brazil, the new constitution of 1988 created, for the first time, a citizen's right to control his own data, and the procedural points were ironed out in the 1997 Regulatory Law of the Habeas Data Proceeding. The interest in data protection surely came from the EU, but the form it took was a variant that threatened to establish a separate approach to data protection. As Guadamuz (2001) notes, however, the Latin American standard, embodied in the Brazilian law, did not meet all of the requirements of the EU adequacy standards, and thus, Brazil was forced to confront the same dilemma that the US had: how to adapt to the EU's requirements. In Argentina, Brazil, and much of southern Latin America, the EU's coveted adequacy ruling provided the impetus to amend the existing laws to conform to the EU standards:

> It may not come as a surprise that some countries in Latin America are choosing to implement a more restrictive version of data protection that resembles the levels established on the other side of the Atlantic . . . Brazil and Argentina have also decided to follow the European lead. A Data Protection legislation based on the Portuguese law is under discussion in the Brazilian Federal Parliament. Being based on the existing legislation of a EU member, it is fair to assume that it will provide more protection than the existing Habeas Data Constitutional provisions and that it will include some of the principles required for obtaining adequacy level from the EU.[40]

Indeed, Argentina became the first Latin American country to obtain the adequacy ruling.

Mexico, like many of the other Latin American countries, also had privacy provisions in its constitution (since 1917!). It was not, however, until the enactment of the E-commerce Act of 2001, which regulated privacy, digital signatures, electronic documents, and transactions, that Mexico dealt with the new technology questions. Three different draft bills have been considered in parliament in the past three years, all of them expressly patterned after the EU's Directive.[41] The most recent, the Draft Initiative Issuing the Federal Law of Protection of Personal Data, was approved in the Senate on April 30, 2002, but remained pending in the House of Representatives till the end of 2004. It contained the language of the EU Directive, and similarly prevented onward transfers to other countries that do not have adequate privacy protection.[42] It is clear that Mexico decided (like other Latin American countries) that its trading relationships with the EU warranted greater attention to information privacy matters, and the proposed draft laws demonstrate that interest.

Russia's 1991 constitution does have privacy protection, and Russia passed a federal law in 1995 on Information, Informatization, and the Protection of Information.[43] The law is based on the European Data Protection Directive, and appears fairly comprehensive on paper. It prohibits the collection, storage, and procession of personal data. However, a further bill defining the personal information subsumed under the federal law has not been passed,[44] and, more importantly, the federal law has not yet been enforced. Parts of Russia have even become international data sellers, despite specific prohibitions against these activities.[45]

The international cases briefly related above are a subset of other international cases, but they represent a fair sample of international responses to the European Data Protection Directive by the EU's trading partners. Although most other countries have not received an adequacy finding from the EU, and discussions for adequacy continue in several countries, most countries have passed restrictions on their private sectors' data collection practices based on the EU's principles. Even Australia, which (like the US) rejected the EU's overly regulatory approach, tried to establish a legislative/code of conduct combination that would ultimately obtain the EU's adequacy ruling. The most significant country still debating whether to follow the US self-regulatory approach, or to pass comprehensive privacy legislation to obtain the EU's adequacy finding, is India. As a prominent outsourcing location, firms in India control significant amounts of Europeans' data, and some European governments have expressed concern about data protection issues in the past.[46] In 2004, Labor MEPs affiliated with the trade union, Amicus, asked the European Commission to look into whether or not data protection rules were broken in the outsourcing of British businesses' functions. The Indian government had been considering amendments to its 2000 Information Technology Act, but there was widespread agreement that changes at the margin were unlikely to get an adequacy finding from the Commission. For this reason, India was also examining self-regulatory mechanisms to comply with the European Data Protection Directive. At the time of this writing, it seemed, however, that those preferring to pass a comprehensive data protection law consonant with the EU's laws were in the ascendancy. In response to the European Data Protection Directive, India's Ministry of Information Technology began working with the National Association of Software and Service Companies (Nasscom) to develop draft legislation, which they hoped the government would pass in 2004.[47] Saying specifically that the purpose of the new amendments was to "meet the adequacy norms specified by EU," Nasscom recognized that its EU outsourcing business would be at risk if it did not have adequate privacy safeguards. Although the legislative route is uncertain in every country since interest pressures can derail legislative attempts, the very fact that Nasscom was involved suggests that the industry's concerns might have been addressed in the process.

▪ The Legality of Third Country Transfers

As of 2004, however, most third country transfers were handled on the basis of the Article 26 derogations. There was an increasing awareness among all that often data were simply sent abroad illegally, without proper safeguards at all. In 2003, the Commission became concerned that EU member states were simply not enforcing the Directive's Article 25 provisions adequately. The Commission's first report in May 2003 on the implementation of the Data Protection Directive found that a ridiculously small number of Commission notifications had been lodged in the first five years of the law, ranging from 1,352 in Spain to 150 in Denmark, and that most national supervisory authorities were unable to indicate the number of processing operations that affected the international transfer of data.[48] The Commission concluded that:

> Indeed, international transfers appear to be an area where the lack of enforcement action creates [a gap between law and practice]. National authorities are supposed to notify the Commission when they authorize transfers under Article 26 (2) of the Directive. Since the Directive came into operation in 1998, the Commission has received only a very limited number of such notifications. Although there are other legal transfer routes apart from Article 26 (2), this number is derisory by comparison with what might reasonably be expected. Combined with other evidence pointing in the same direction this suggests that many unauthorised and possibly illegal transfers are being made to destinations or recipients not guaranteeing adequate protection. Yet there is little or no sign of enforcement actions by the supervisory authorities.[49]

From the Commission's point of view, since the original assumption that international transfers would be handled by bloc approvals in the form of adequacy rulings had not been borne out, it became essential to assure that the onward transfer obligations would be met rigorously. There were two reasons for this: first, it was important to establish the credibility of the regime, since privacy violations are difficult to monitor, and depend on individuals' taking their rights seriously and reporting violations. Without individuals understanding their rights, and believing that their rights' violations would be taken seriously, the entire European Data Protection regime would degrade.

Second, it was important to ensure that third countries without an adequacy finding would not be made too comfortable to continue to work towards a domestic regime that would meet the adequacy standard. If countries believed that the Article 26 provisions were not enforced, there would be very little impetus to challenge business groups interested in the status quo. Thus, the Commission, in its first report on the implementation of the Data Protection Directive, admonished the member states to be more correct in their reporting obligations. On the other hand, the Commission also included four points that would enable legal international flows to be easier to accommodate:

1. A more extensive use of findings of adequate protection in respect of third countries under Article 25(6), while maintaining, of course, an even-handed approach vis-à-vis third countries in line with the EU's WTO obligations
2. Further decisions on the basis of Article 26(4) so that economic operators have a wider choice of standard contractual clauses, to the extent possible based on clauses submitted by business representa-

tives, for example, those submitted by the International Chamber of Commerce and other business associations
3. The role of binding (intra) corporate rules (e.g., internal rules that bind a given multinational corporate group doing business in several different jurisdictions, both inside and outside the EU) in providing adequate safeguards for intragroup transfers of personal data
4. The more uniform interpretation of Article 26(1) of the Directive (permitted exceptions to the adequate protection requirement for transfers to third countries), and the national provisions implementing it.[50]

There was, clearly, a sense that if the international dimension of the Directive was not overhauled and enforced, the regime itself was at risk.

■ European Union Member States' Implementation of the Directive

There was another difficulty in getting international compliance with the regime to be taken seriously by third countries. By 2003, even the EU member states' implementation of the Directive was incomplete, giving other countries an example of how business as usual could continue in the face of unmet treaty obligations. The US had used the fact that all the member states had not implemented the Directive by October 1998 as a signal that the Directive would not be internationally binding in its Safe Harbor negotiations (see Chapter 4), but had not obtained the Commission's assent for that interpretation. Only four member states had passed their national laws implementing the Directive by the prescribed deadline. A year later, the Commission decided to take France, Germany, Ireland, Luxembourg, and the Netherlands to the European Court of Justice for failing to implement the legislation.

By December 2001, Germany, the Netherlands, and Belgium had completed their treaty obligations.[51] The ECJ issued a judgment that Luxembourg, France, and Ireland were indeed guilty of noncompliance, compelling Luxembourg to implement the Directive in 2002. Ireland passed legislation in April 2003 and, finally, on July 15, 2004, the French Law on Data Protection was amended in order to bring it in line with the requirements of the Directive.

Even within those countries that had implemented the European Data Protection Directive, there were significant divergences in the law, an obstacle to the harmonization of the privacy laws that the Directive had intended. The Commission's first report on the implementation of the Directive showed that some of the divergences resulted from the incorrect implementation of the Directive, which would require the modification of the member states' laws.[52] However, the majority of divergences resulted from the member states taking extreme positions wherever room for maneuver within the Directive allowed this. The Commission intended to look into the cases where member state laws were once again creating barriers to the free movement of personal data.

■ How Expensive Was Complying with the European Data Protection Directive?

The costs to businesses of complying with the European Data Protection Directive, in theory and in practice, were of obvious importance to the acceptance of the EU regime. Regulation always creates costs for businesses, even just administrative costs to evince compliance, and thus, businesses will resist regulation on those grounds alone.[53] However, if there must be regulatory costs, businesses prefer that all businesses, at least all of their competitors, are bound by the same regulation, making regulation a fixed cost, one of the many costs of doing business that companies routinely factor into their business model (the "level playing field" argument).

For most US and European businesses, the costs of complying with the European Data Protection Directive were of that character: an administrative cost, but one that could ultimately be passed on to the customer since all businesses would uniformly be subject to this requirement. The economics of their compliance will be discussed below.

There was, however, a subset of businesses in specific sectors for which the European Data Protection Directive spelled the end of their business model, since it prohibited, or made very difficult, the very service they provided: customer profiling and targeting. The Direct Marketing Association immediately saw the problems with the 1990 Commission draft, and was the earliest industry association to mobilize to try and defeat the Directive. Customer profiling was also an important ingredient in the new Internet advertising business model, which would sell advertising specifically based on consumers' web behavior.[54] There were other industries and businesses, like Choice Point and Nexis Lexis, which profited from the sale of customer information, that would also have a much more difficult time getting customer information. For these sectors and companies, especially those in the US, the European Data Protection Directive was a major crisis. These businesses were the minority, however. Moreover, the European businesses were experienced in doing business in a privacy protected environment since seven of the largest EU member states had had data protection laws on their books. It was perhaps more difficult and expensive, but it could be done.[55]

In terms of estimating the real cost of compliance with the European

Data Protection Directive, it is important to count only incremental costs relative to the status quo in 1995. Most of the largest EU member states, including Germany, France, and the UK, already had national data protection laws. The Commission had always insisted that its harmonization of data protection laws was actually business-friendly, since it (in theory[56]) created a unified standard for companies to follow instead of different national laws. A 1994 study about information systems of transnational corporations found that, ". . . the Information Systems managers interviewed cited problems with the variety of these data restriction laws, rather than their rigor. Current EC efforts at standardization are helping to alleviate this problem in Europe."[57] Indeed, even in the US, the American Electronics Association, the largest high tech trade association in the US, called on Congress to pass comprehensive federal privacy legislation in 2001 because "the threat of 50 different pieces of patchwork [state] regulations has motivated our state lobbyists for a single standard."[58] Certainly, from a management point of view, multinational companies would have an easier time complying with one European standard or, as the European standard was adopted by other countries, one global standard.

The European Commission requested an expert report on potential costs to business in 1994 before the Directive was passed.[59] The report's aims were to "undertake an in-depth evaluation of the potential financial impacts of the proposed European Data Protection Directive in the UK and the Netherlands," and its methodology involved detailed case studies, and a two part questionnaire. The cases selected were those that would be most likely to be affected by the new European Directive. They included a mail order company, a credit reference agency, a major bank, a small/medium sized enterprise, a major manufacturing company, a hospital, and a local authority.[60] The study group divided the costs into setup and recurring costs, and assumed companies would take advantage of some of the allowable exemptions in the Directive, for example, the "disproportionate effort" exemption from notifying data subjects that their data were transferred (Article 12). In its findings, the expert report to the Commission highlighted that "the financial impact of the Proposed Directive would be very small for the majority of organizations studied in both public and private sectors in the UK and the Netherlands," and "the financial impacts are substantially less than those initial estimates . . . in previous studies [because] . . . the study team believes that some previous respondents have exaggerated cost implications, [. . . and] changes have been made to the text of the [1990] proposed Directive which have removed some of the previously perceived problems."[61] The major cost concerns of the UK and the Dutch organizations were notification, informing data subjects, data subjects' access, data subjects' consent, and automated individual decisions.

Overall, the study found that for most organizations, "after initial adjustment, new procedures will fall within existing cost levels," although "the impact will be most significant for organizations having a large personal customer base, including banks, direct mailing organizations and some sectors of retailing."[62] Even in those sectors, however, the industry tended to overestimate the costs of compliance by 100 percent or more over the costs estimated by the expert study group. The study found even the highest costs for the credit reference agency (set-up £9.5 million and £100,000 annual costs) and the mail order company (set-up £1.6 million and £1million annually) significantly less than the organizations' estimates. The study group's report, released in late 1994, assuaged the fears of many in the Council of Ministers, and aided in finding a common position on the European Data Protection Directive.[63] Since the Directive was implemented, there have been no quantitative studies to assess the costs of compliance. A small study of firms doing business in the Netherlands and Germany found that "it was impossible for most interviewees to provide a precise indication of money spent on data protection issues," and "only one of the (German) companies had ever formally attempted to assess the cost of data protection and had not come to a satisfactory result."[64]

Although the Commission's report did not focus extensively on the issue of consumer trust, it was prescient in concluding that "the wider benefits of the proposed Directive in terms of . . . engendering consumer trust in new services in the developing information society may be substantial."[65] In 1994, it was not yet apparent how important the World Wide Web would become, especially the business-to-consumer part of e-commerce, which was in its infancy. As the commercial potential of the Internet became a reality, however, the trust issues on the consumer side assumed greater importance. More and more consumers feared for their privacy, and told pollsters that they would spend more on e-commerce if they felt their privacy was secure (e.g., a 1999 *Business Week* poll showed that 57 percent of Internet users said website policies that guarantee the security of their personal data affect their decision to make online purchases.[66]) From the business perspective, protecting privacy became not just a cost, but also a potential benefit in the e-commerce sector. The word "potential" here is significant because research has yet to validate the theory that consumers can distinguish between privacy policies that are sound and those that are less so, or that they tailor their buying behavior to buy only from privacy-protected sites.[67] More discussion about the trust-privacy-consumer spending dynamic is included in Chapter 7. For the purposes of this section, it suffices to say that privacy protection may confer a benefit to certain businesses (perhaps difficult to quantify) as well as a cost.

In the US also, there were attempts to quantify the costs of greater privacy protection. Unlike in the EU however, these studies were not commissioned by the government, trying to understand the real costs and benefits of regulation. In the US, these studies were financed by business groups hoping to forestall any movement toward greater privacy protection within the country, especially along the lines of the European Data Protection Directive. The Online Privacy Alliance released a study in 2000 claiming that US citizens would lose $17 billion per year and 320 million hours if financial services firms were not allowed to share information. The sources of information sharing benefits were defined as outsourcing to third parties, relationship pricing, and proactive offers.[68] Another survey looked at the apparel industry and projected $1 billion per year increase in costs if online retailers and catalogue companies did not have access to free flows of personal information.[69] The study that received the most press coverage in the US was by Robert Hahn in 2001. The Hahn study calculated a $36 billion cost to the US economy if privacy laws were created. Immediately, the study's methodology and conclusions were disputed by pro-privacy advocates, who documented that neither were the benefits of privacy included in the study, nor did it calculate only the incremental costs of adapting to new privacy laws from the basis of existing state laws.[70] The study was also criticized on the grounds that the survey participants had no real incentives to estimate realistic figures, and that the study did not factor in the cost reductions as privacy practices and systems became standardized.

Perhaps the most credible assessment of the costs to US firms in complying with the European Data Protection Directive came from Swire and Litan in 1998. In their book, the authors note that quantitative estimates were impossible to make since US firms will have differentially adapted to the European strict privacy standards. Those companies that already did business in Germany and France would have set up their operations already to be compliant with the data protection laws.[71] Thus, as the authors point out, there was no easy way to estimate the costs in dollars because of the different status quos of the US companies. "Dr. Litan and I concluded after substantial effort that we could not create a useful estimate of the likely costs of complying with the European Union Data Protection Directive."[72]

There was also the possibility that the entire business environment might change. Thus, although privacy protection might generate costs for new companies entering these European markets, as the rest of the world adopted EU-like privacy laws, the costs of setting up systems that treat data in a privacy protected manner would become, not the cost of doing business in Europe, but simply the cost of doing business internationally, routinized, and cheaper. At some point, as everyone in the world becomes part of a harmonized standard, it becomes increasingly costly not to join that standard. Indeed, there is a hint that it has already become cheaper for US multinational companies to treat all data (including US data) with the same strict privacy standard as the data of the Europeans. A random sampling of twenty-six US companies that participated in Safe Harbor found that 62 percent of them had merged all their data and utilized the EU standards on them.[73]

In the same survey, questions about the costs of complying with Safe Harbor were also asked. Forty-two percent of the companies said that there had been no change in costs, while 46 percent said that there had been a marginal increase. None of the companies interviewed said that there had been either a moderate or a significant increase in costs. Echoing some of the points made by Swire and Litan, one large computer company's contact officer said, "We were pretty much in compliance with the European data protection before Safe Harbor. We only had to review what we had, and it did not take much time to change the procedure. The cost was negligible. Indeed, we made more money due to the Safe Harbor [status] in European markets."[74]

Finally, the opinion surveys from the EU multinational companies themselves show that the fear that individuals would want to see and correct their data, thereby creating huge administrative costs, has not been borne out in the first five years of the Directive. A December 2003 survey of 3,013 data protection officers, or persons responsible for data protection issues within companies employing twenty persons and more, throughout all of the fifteen European Union member states found that 23 percent of the companies had not had a single access request in 2002, and a further 49 percent had had fewer than ten requests. Only 8 percent had had more than fifty-one requests.[75] Moreover, 96 percent had never received complaints from the people whose data were being processed.[76]

Conclusion

The international state of data protection showed that although the US has opted to create a hybrid self-regulatory system to protect the Europeans' privacy, it is the only country to have done so. Other countries, like Japan, Australia, and India, which originally thought they would try to comply with the European Data Protection Directive's onward transfer requirements through self-regulatory mechanisms, have changed their approaches, and have passed (or are in the process of passing) comprehensive privacy laws. Although comprehensive laws do not guarantee the Commission's adequacy finding, there is a well founded perception that the Article 29 Working Party is more amenable to government regulatory solutions (because of well trodden enforcement mechanisms) than to self-regulatory schemes. Consequently, the US remained an outlier by not having comprehensive privacy legislation.

It should also be noted that the catalyst for most, if not all, of the privacy legislation was the European Data Protection Directive. Although many countries referred back to the OECD Guidelines or the Council of Europe Convention when drafting their laws, the impetus for the spate of data protection laws that emerged in the 1998–2004 time frame was the European initiative. In many cases, the urgency to pass legislation was explicitly linked to the European Data Protection Directive's Article 25 provisions. Thus, it is fair to say that the EU created an international data protection regime without international negotiations or the US co-operation. Some countries that had been reluctant to pass comprehensive legislation followed the workings of the Safe Harbor arrangement closely, to see whether Safe Harbor-like arrangements would become more institutionalized, and create a "critical mass" at the international level. As the next chapter will show, however, Safe Harbor never really caught on even with a majority of US businesses, and the ongoing criticisms by the Article 29 Working Party and the European Parliament of that agreement made Safe Harbor less attractive to other countries.

As an alternative, Australia, the US, and other countries have begun calling for an international treaty on data protection, a "General Agreement on Data Protection," something akin to the WTO. However, as more and more countries pass laws consonant with the European Data Protection Directive, finding agreement on data protection significantly different from the European standard would likely be futile, because so many countries have already sunk political capital into creating a high standard of protection. The following chapter discusses the workings of Safe Harbor in the first three years, and the new challenges that arose between the US and the EU.

▪ Notes

1. It is beyond the scope of this book to detail the similarities and differences between all the national laws and the European Data Protection Directive. In this chapter, the existence of comprehensive privacy legislation is considered a binary question. Clearly, however, the fact that not all of the new national laws have received the Commission's adequacy finding likely reflects the fact that there remain significant differences in some of these bills, as well as a long lag time to go through the Article 29 Working Party review process.

2. http://europa.eu.int/comm/internal_market/privacy/docs/wpdocs/2003/wp74_en.pdf.

3. Technical briefing for journalists available at http://europa.eu.int/comm/internal_market/privacy/adequacy/briefing-eu-us-dialog_en.html.

4. Bennett, 1998, p. 113. Greece, of course, had to create comprehensive legislation to comply with the European Data Protection Directive.

5. All adequacy findings are available at http://europa.eu.int/comm/internal_market/privacy/adequacy_en.html.

6. On May 1, 2004, Hungary, the Czech Republic, Poland, the Slovak Republic, Slovenia, Malta, Cyprus, Latvia, Lithuania, and Estonia joined the EU,

and were, thus, obligated to incorporate the European Data Protection Directive into their national legislation.

7. Bennett and Raab, 1997.

8. Ekos, September 1998. Cited in a speech by John Manley, Canadian Minister of Industry, available at http://www.connect.gc.ca/en/sp/1283-e.asp.

9. "Argentine DMA to fight data threat." Precision Marketing, November 13, 2000.

10. Kenneth Slade, December, 2000, available at http://www.haledorr.com/publications/pubsdetail.asp?ID=1621112272000.

11. Commission, 2003, p. 19.

12. Privacy International. Privacy and Human Rights 2003: Country Reports available at http://www.privacyinternational.org/survey/phr2003/countries/japan.html.

13. In 2001, MITI was renamed METI, the Ministry of Economy, Trade and Industry.

14. Working Party, 1999b, p. 58.

15. Raab, Bennett, Gellman & Waters, European Commission Tender No. XV/97/18/D, Application of a Methodology Designed to Assess the Adequacy of the Level of Protection of Individuals with Regard to Processing Personal Data: Test of the Method on Several Categories of Transfer. September, 1998.

16. See Westin, 1999. Seventy-six percent of Japanese consumers said that they were worried about the potential misuse of their personal data, while only 33 percent of consumers thought that businesses handle their personal information appropriately.

17. Ibid.

18. *Daily Yomiuri,* March 28, 2001.

19. Privacy International. Privacy and Human Rights 2003: Country Reports.

20. Ibid.

21. January 29, 2003.

22. May 24, 2003.

23. Japan Economic Newswire, May 23, 2003.

24. Commission of the European Communities."A Maturing Partnership – Shared Interests and Challenges in EU-China Relations." September 10, 2003, available at http://www.europa.eu.int/comm/external_relations/china/com_03_533/com_533_en.pdf.

25. Kalathil and Boas, 2003.

26. Privacy International. Privacy and Human Rights 2003: Country Reports, Hong Kong available at http://www.privacyinternational.org/survey/phr2003/countries/hongkong.html.

27. Raymond Tang, "Personal Data Privacy: the Asian Agenda." September 12, 2003, available at http://www.pco.org.hk/english/files/infocentre/speech_20030910.pdf.

28. The substantive onward transfer provisions of the ordinance are: "A data user shall not transfer personal data to a place outside Hong Kong unless:

a) The place is specified for the purposes of this section in a notice under subsection 3.
b) The user has reasonable grounds for believing that there is in force in that place any law which is substantially similar to or serves the same purposes as this Ordinance.
c) The data subject has consented in writing to the transfer.

d) The user has reasonable grounds for believing that, in all the circumstances of the case, the transfer is for the avoidance or mitigation of adverse action against the data subject; it is not practicable to obtain the consent in writing of the data subject to that transfer; and if it was practicable to obtain such consent, the data subject would give it.
e) The data are exempt from data protection principle 3 by virtue of an exemption under Part VIII.
f) The user has taken all reasonable precautions and exercised all due diligence to ensure that the data will not, in that place, be collected, held, processed, or used in any manner which, if that place were Hong Kong, would be a contravention of a requirement under this Ordinance."

available at http://www.pco.org.hk/english/ordinance/section_41.html.

29. Raymond Tang, "A Short Paper on Implementing Data Privacy Principles: How Are Governments Making it Work in the Real World?" APEC 2003, E-Com-Merce Steering Group Data Privacy Workshop; February 13, 2003, available at http://www.pco.org.hk/english/infocentre/apec_feb03.html.

30. Privacy International. Privacy and Human Rights 2003: Country Reports, Commonwealth of Australia available at http://www.privacyinternational.org/survey/phr2003/countries/australia.html.

31. Available at http://www.aar.com.au/privacy/over/chron.html.

32. These and other examples are available at http://www.privacyinternational.org/survey/phr2003/countries/australia.html.

33. Ibid.

34. http://www.aar.com.au/privacy/over/data.html.

35. Attorney General of Australia. March 26, 2001, available at http://www.ag.gov.au/www/attorneygeneralHome.nsf/Web+Pages/8C9464056CE8169CCA256B5A001318DF?OpenDocument.

36. Asia-Pacific Economic Co-operation; established in 1989, APEC decisions are reached by consensus, and commitments are undertaken on a voluntary basis. APEC's twenty-one member economies are Australia; Brunei; Dar as Salaam; Canada; Chile; The People's Republic of China; Hong Kong, China; Indonesia; Japan; Republic of Korea; Malaysia; Mexico; New Zealand; Papua New Guinea; Peru; The Republic of the Philippines; The Russian Federation; Singapore; Chinese Taipei; Thailand; The United States of America; and Vietnam. Several APEC economies have adopted privacy legislation that is based on the European Data Protection Directive.

37. http://203.127.220.67/apec/documents_reports/electronic_commerce_steering_group/2003.html#DPW.

38. Opening Address, APEC Privacy Workshop, September 13, 2003, available at http://www.ag.gov.au/www/attorneygeneralHome.nsf/Alldocs/RWPDD66625688FF5CACCA256DA300079BC5?OpenDocument&highlight=data%20protection.

39. Duncan Giles, IIA Privacy Taskforce, August 16, 2001, available at http://www.ag.gov.au/www/attorneygeneralHome.nsf/Alldocs/9E9E9875C0853A88CA256B640013A0FF?OpenDocument&highlight=data%20protection.

40. Guadamuz, 2001.

41. Privacy International Country Report for Mexico, 2004, available at http://www.privacyinternational.org/article.shtml?cmd[347]=x-347-83805.

42. Ibid.

43. Privacy International. Privacy and Human Rights 2003: Country Reports,

Russian Federation available at http://www.privacyinternational.org/survey/phr2003/countries/russianfederation.html.

44. Ibid.

45. Ibid.

46. *Economic Times of India,* October 10, 2003.

47. *CIO Magazine.* September 1, 2003, available at http://www.cio.com/archive/090103/tl_data.html and Computer Weekly.com, June 13, 2003. Available at http://www.computerweekly.com/Article122612.html.

48. Commission of the European Communities. 2003.

49. Ibid., p. 19.

50. Ibid.

51. This, and the following information about the status of implementation in the EU can be found at http://europa.eu.int/comm/internal_market/privacy/law/implementation_en.htm#ireland.

52. Commission of the European Communities, 2003.

53. Vogel, 1996.

54. Gauthronet and Nathan, 1998.

55. *Marketing,* March 28, 1991.

56. The Commission's first report on the implementation found that, because some member states had not implemented the Directive correctly, there continued to exist divergences. However, the Commission was confident that these problems would be corrected in the short run. http://europa.eu.int/eur-lex/pri/en/dpi/rpt/doc/2003/com2003_0265en01.doc.

57. Cummings and Guynes, 1994.

58. NewsFactor Network. January 18, 2001, available at http://www.newsfactor.com/perl/story/6828.html.

59. Bainbridge et al., 1994.

60. Ibid., p. 8.

61. Ibid., p. 73.

62. Ibid., p. 73.

63. Platten, 1996, p. 31.

64. Walczuch and Steeghs, 2001, p. 154.

65. Bainbridge et al., 1994, p. 74.

66. *Business Week* online, March 16, 1999, available at http://www.businessweek.com/1998/11/b3569104.html.

67. Fogg et al., 2002.

68. Glassman, 2000.

69. Turner, 2001.

70. Swire, 2001.

71. Swire and Litan, 1998, pp. 41–45.

72. Swire, 2001.

73. Author's interviews with the Contact Officers listed in the Safe Harbor application of twenty-six randomly chosen companies.

74. Author's interview with a large computer company's Safe Harbor contact officer, July 29, 2002.

75. Eurobarometer, 147 available at http://europa.eu.int/comm/public_opinion/flash/fl147–data–protect.pdf. The wording of the question was "Approximate number of access requests received by your company during the year 2002?" Never received any: 23%; Less than 10: 49%; Between 10 and 50: 14%; Between 51 and 100: 5%; Between 101 and 500: 2%; More than 501: 1%; Don't know/no answer: 6%.

76. Ibid.

6

Implementing the Safe Harbor Agreement: How Well Does It Work?

The Safe Harbor Agreement, which had been negotiated from 1998 to 2000, came into force on November 1, 2000. With the agreement in place, US firms with data from Europeans could shield themselves from the threat of a European member state's data privacy authority halting data flows to them. The procedure for a US company was relatively simple: sign up at the Department of Commerce, make legal representations about how European data would be treated within the company, and acknowledge an alternative dispute resolution (ADR) mechanism, such as TRUSTe or BBBOnline.[1] To negotiators on both sides of the Atlantic, the Safe Harbor Agreement was a compromise that they thought would be attractive to US companies because of its self-regulatory characteristics. There was an implicit expectation that several hundred companies would sign up within the first couple of months. In October 2000 the Department of Commerce had predicted that a hundred US companies would sign up for Safe Harbor during its first month, with up to a thousand joining within a year.[2]

The reality, however, was considerably different: within the first five months, only thirty companies had signed up, and most of these were small. By February 2001 there were only 154 "Safe Harborites," and as of October 2004, only 589 companies had joined. The actual turnout was a mere fraction of the potential total, and a setback to the regime. There were several theories about why the number was so small.

In the beginning of 2001, there was still significant ignorance about the European Data Protection Directive and its requirements, as well as what Safe Harbor promised. A case in point was a hearing before a subcommittee of the House Energy and Commerce Committee when the new Republican chairman, Cliff Stearns, questioned whether the Safe Harbor self-regulatory agreement offered companies real legal protection from Europe's privacy laws. "The Safe Harbor raises a whole host of issues in and of itself. For instance, the legal status of the Safe Harbor is highly questionable."[3] The

UK's Deputy Information Commissioner tried to clarify the Safe Harbor Agreement for the committee:

> It is up to the U.S. . . . to take people onto the safe harbor list. And if they are taken onto the list, then we and all of the other EU member states have to recognize them as providing adequate protection. We have no choice in that, and this is a common standard. The area where penalties would come in is if a U.S. business is not in a safe harbor, has made no arrangements for adequacy, has no contract or other arrangements, and is transferring data in breach of the law.[4]

If even the political elite did not understand the fundamentals of Safe Harbor, it was clear that it would be even more difficult to get the businesses to sign up. Moreover, following the March 8, 2001, hearings, the Republican Congress called on the new Bush administration to renegotiate the Safe Harbor Agreement. In opening the hearings titled "the EU Data Protection Directive and its Implications for the US Privacy Debate," Cliff Stearns declared:

> The subcommittee, as part of its trade jurisdiction, will begin to examine legal and regulatory measures that may impede the growth of e-commerce globally. I rely on the words of one of our witnesses in highlighting the significance of our inquiry today when he said, "The EU privacy directive is probably the most important law by which the EU is writing the rules of cyberspace." Mr. Winer is not alone in his concern. Many large transnational and even U.S. businesses with modest international operations have expressed the same concerns to me and other members in private . . . I am not convinced, nor is corporate U.S. America, that the safe harbor provisions negotiated by Ambassador Aaron in the previous administration will help mitigate the concern over regressive effects [on international commerce].[5]

The new administration's chief complaint about the Safe Harbor Agreement was that it did not include financial services firms, which were now bound by the Gramm-Leach-Bliley Act. Instead of allowing financial firms to meet Europe's adequacy finding by allowing them into Safe Harbor, in early 2001 the Commission released the "standard contractual clauses" language that would be applicable to firms in the financial services' sector. The standard contractual clauses had been presented for comment in September 2000, but the Bush administration's Treasury and Commerce Undersecretaries complained that:

> While revisions and improvements have been made since the standard contract clauses were presented for comment in September 2000, the revision process has not been transparent to those seeking participation. We urge the Commission to provide more time for an open exchange of views with the private sector, impacted countries, and other stakeholders.[6]

The language of their complaint is virtually identical to the complaints of pro-privacy groups during the Safe Harbor negotiations:

> Any observer of the process for soliciting comments could easily conclude that the Department is only interested in the views of carefully selected members of the American business community and that it has no particular interest in the views of other parts of the business community or any other segment of American society. The short time allowed for comments does nothing to dispel that conclusion.[7]

As with the other negotiations, excluded groups challenged the process. Nominally, the process was inclusive of all views, but in practice, access to decisionmakers was the key to success.

The March 2001 Commerce and Treasury Departments' joint letter to the Commission criticized the model contracts:

> We believe there is a serious danger the adoption of the standard clauses as drafted will create a *de facto* standard that would raise the bar for U.S. and foreign firms that might be covered by other agreements . . . [imposing] unduly burdensome requirements that are incompatible with real-world operations.[8]

The letter requested a delay in the implementation of the Directive (which the EU Commission immediately rejected in a reply to the Undersecretaries: "you will understand for your part that we cannot put everything on hold to take account of U.S. domestic constraints"[9]). The Commission's spokesperson Jonathan Todd reacted to the letter with exasperation: "The US administration's letter appears to be based on a total, complete and utter absence of understanding of what the Commission is doing . . . We are aiming to make life easier for companies transferring data from the EU to countries outside the EU by clarifying the provisions in contracts which would best ensure adequate protection of personal data."[10] However, for many businesses waiting to decide how best to comply with the European Data Protection Directive, the prospect of the Bush administration renegotiating substantial parts of (or the entire) Safe Harbor Agreement, or perhaps obtaining a delay in the implementation of the European Data Protection Directive, was a significant disincentive to join immediately.

Another theory for why there was such a lackluster response to Safe Harbor was that businesses were concerned that joining Safe Harbor might, in essence, single them out for scrutiny by the European Data Privacy Commissioners. For many companies, it was simply a prudent business decision to wait to see what would happen to the first Harborites, and whether their data practices would be scrutinized more carefully than those of the nonHarborites. The first large company to join Safe Harbor was Hewlett-Packard, in March 2001, and by May it had been joined by Intel and Microsoft, thus lending some legitimacy (or at least visibility) to the regime. The fact that these large Safe Harborites were not targeted by the Commission for their data transfers (Microsoft's .NET Passport system problems[11] with the European data protection authorities were unrelated to its Safe Harbor status, as were its antitrust problems in the EU) should have encouraged other companies to join.

Finally, a third theory suggested that many businesses would join once the language of the standard contractual clauses had been sorted out, since many wanted to make sure that the model contracts were not a better way to comply with the Directive. When the standard contractual clauses were approved in June 2001, they were generally considered to be more onerous to comply with than Safe Harbor. One might, consequently, have expected companies to start joining Safe Harbor, but the pace of applications did not pick up.

On the pro-privacy side of the argument, EPIC and other pro-privacy groups pointed to the lack of enthusiasm by US companies to sign up for Safe Harbor as evidence that it did not meet the needs of businesses or consumers. In a legal analysis of the agreement, privacy advocate Joel Reidenberg suggested that there were several significant flaws in the legal architecture, especially the enforcement portions, on which the Europeans had placed significant value.[12]

Others questioned the rate of compliance by Safe Harbor companies themselves. Most Safe Harbor companies (85 percent) used "in-house" verification, while only 15 percent used third party services to verify that they were complying with the regime.[13] Moreover, an August 2001 study by Andersen Consulting found that none of the seventy-five US multinational companies it had studied met all of the Safe Harbor criteria, and only 5 percent of the companies had established mechanisms for assuring compliance with the Safe Harbor principles and for providing recourse to individuals whose privacy is breached.[14]

The Commission discovered similar problems with compliance. In anticipation of the European Parliament–mandated report on the functioning of Safe Harbor, the Commission released a staff working paper in February 2002 on the rates of compliance. The key features of that report were that less than half of the 129 companies that had signed up to Safe Harbor had complied with all of the agreement's provisions.[15] Only TRUSTe had received consumer complaints, twenty-seven, all of which had been adjudicated without any enforcement becoming necessary. However, the Commission found that "a substantial number of organizations that [are] self certified do not meet the requirement [of having a statement about a privacy policy that is readily apparent], and less than half the organizations post privacy policies that reflect all seven Safe Harbor principles."[16] True to its internal market orientation, the Commission expressed its satisfaction with the level of compliance with Safe Harbor, calling the compliance issues "teething problems," and lauding the Department of Commerce for its readiness to address the US companies' compliance problems. The fact that the Commission did not effect enforcement measures to get greater compliance by Safe Harbor companies only reinforced a generalized perception among US businesses that the Safe Harbor system was primarily a political means to avoid a trade war, rather than an effective privacy guard for Europeans' data.

The Commission's working paper also detailed the progress of the privacy seal programs, such as TRUSTe: as of December 7, 2001, there were six approved privacy seal programs, which enrolled fifty-four (42 percent) of the 129 Safe Harborites.[17] The Commission's paper faulted the seal programs for not posting statements announcing their intention to enforce Safe Harbor on their websites. It also voiced reservations about the self-regulatory features of the agreement:

> A substantial number of organizations that have adhered to the Safe Harbor are not observing the expected degree of transparency as regards their overall commitment or the contents of their privacy policies. Transparency is a vital feature in self-regulatory systems and it is necessary that organizations improve their practices in this regard, failing which the credibility of the arrangement as a whole risks being weakened.[18]

In March 2002, the Article 29 Working Party members visited Washington to gather their own information on the functioning of Safe Harbor. Their view was less positive than the Commission's had been, and in its working document on the functioning of Safe Harbor, the members requested information on the following points:

- Arrangements to increase transparency in respect of the signatory organizations, especially if a declaration of adherence to the Safe Harbor is not accompanied by appropriate privacy policies
- The possibility to provide for additional verification mechanisms in respect of the procedure for adhering to the agreement, compliance of Harborites' conduct with their privacy policies, and the possible loss of Safe Harbor benefits
- The initiatives to be adopted in order to enhance knowledge of the prerequisites for adherence to the Safe Harbor, also by means of short, easily understandable documents, and the possible integration of the Safe Harbor Workbook
- The measures to be adopted in order to refine dispute resolution mechanisms, enhance uniformity and publicity of the relevant criteria, increase transparency of the outcome of those disputes, and streamline their publication mechanisms

- The difficulties that may arise from the existence of multiple privacy policies declared by the same operator
- The priority criteria and possible additional initiatives undertaken by the competent US bodies, and the arrangements for renewed cooperation between the European data protection panel, dispute resolution bodies, and the Federal Trade Commission[19]

There is no evidence that any of these topics was taken up by the Commission in private, and a formal study of Safe Harbor by independent experts for the Commission did not address these criticisms directly.[20] The 2004 study found a number of problems in the implementation of Safe Harbor, including nontransparency of privacy protection policies, the inability to assess the rigor of in-house verification, and the difficulty of sorting data categories. The report did not make concrete policy suggestions, but suggested bookkeeping changes that would make data gathering more effective, and would make noncompliance with Safe Harbor easier to detect.[21] The report did identify various "implementation deficiency trends" including:

- Corporate policies were often hard to find
- Self-certification despite nonexistent, or publicly unavailable, policies
- Use of unclear terms or incorrect definition
- Lack of transparency regarding third party disclosure and choice
- Ambiguous and contradictory policies (or parts of policies)
- False, misleading, or irrelevant statements in certification statements or policies
- Certain companies implemented the Safe Harbor principles in part only
- Limited number of companies agreed to reverse effect of breach
- Fifteen [of the forty-one randomly sampled] organizations/companies represented that they had enrolled in a privacy program, while the explanation they provided on this point demonstrated that this was most likely not the case, as they referred to either (1) nonverifiable in-house measures, the description of which had nothing to do with a real privacy program; or (2) mere dispute resolution programs, which clearly do not fall under the category of privacy program[22]

The reaction of the Commission in its staff working paper suggested that these were minor matters that would not entail significant changes to the system. For example, in its report summarizing the study, the Commission indicated that, "While a majority of organizations do comply with the requirement of having a visible privacy policy, a substantial minority do not . . . This is a key requirement of the Safe Harbor, and its not being fully respected is a matter of concern, and needs to be corrected."[23] There was, however, little leverage the Commission could bring on this point. It called on the Department of Commerce to reverse this trend by devising guidelines on appropriate privacy policies. But beyond exhorting the EU to stress the importance of the data protection principles in meetings with their counterparts, and inviting the EU Data Protection Directors to "suspend data flows if they conclude that there is a substantial likelihood that the principles are being violated," the report did not suggest any radical changes to the agreement. This was in keeping with the privacy-dove inclination that the Commission had shown historically.

Implementation by the Member States

In 2003, the Commission was required by Article 33 to consider whether or not any modifications of the Directive itself were necessary. When the Commission released its first report on the European Data Protection Directive, it did not propose amendments, preferring to "exploit all the pragmatic possibilities at out disposal."[24] The member states and the Article 29 Working Party agreed on this recommendation, because the Directive had only recently been implemented by several member states. The Commission held a public call for comments on its data protection website, receiving a total of over ten thousand responses. Although the Commission had received very critical input by some stakeholders, including US firms, its report rejected their criticisms:

> Where amendments have been proposed by stakeholders, the aim is often the reduction of compliance burdens for data controllers. While this is a legitimate end in itself, and indeed one that the Commission espouses, the Commission believes that many of the proposals would also involve a reduction in the level of protection provided for. The Commission believes that any changes that might in due course be considered should aim to maintain the same level of protection, and must be consistent with the overall framework provided by existing international instruments.[25]

The Commission did, however, praise the tone of the business responses to its questions about the implementation of the Directive: "Both the on-line consultation and the contributions received indicated a shift in business opinions from outright hostility to data protection legislation, to constructive efforts to make the rules work in a more business-friendly and less burdensome way, an objective which the Commission shares."[26] Indeed, some veteran observers were surprised by the Commission's apparent flexibility, and its stand toward greater balancing between fundamental rights and business needs.[27]

The Commission largely agreed with businesses that divergences among member states' laws still existed, making cross border compliance more difficult than it had to be. Some of the divergences were due to the incorrect transpositions of the Directive, which the Commission pledged to eliminate. Other divergences, however, were on account of the member states taking advantage of room left in the treaty, something which the Commission chose not do anything about at that time.

One of the interesting facets of the report was the interest demonstrated by some member states to have the Commission take more of a centralizing role.[28] When the original data protection law was written, member states had been very cautious about giving the Commission a significant role, citing subsidiarity, the idea that policy should be handled by the lowest competent authority. Over time, there seems to have been an acknowledgment that the Commission should take more of a leading role in data protection.[29] There was also a hint that some member states (Sweden was on the record) agreed with business comments that the whole model should be geared more toward finding and punishing abuses of personal data, rather than monitoring data collection per se.

The report created a work plan for the Article 29 Working Party for 2004, and in 2005, the Commission pledged to review the results of the work plan and to decide whether or not to amend the Directive.

▪ Why Did Businesses' Self-Regulatory Programs Not Work?

For some groups, the optimism of the Commission, that the problems of Safe Harbor were mere teething troubles, was misplaced. They pointed to other, more fundamental, problems with the system. The lack of factual knowledge about the uses of personal information and the technologies undermined the market principles on which the self-regulatory system was based. The ability of the average user to differentiate on-line privacy codes, to discriminate between companies, and thus, to bring market forces to bear on companies with lax privacy policies was simply not empirically verifiable. According to the proponents of self-regulation, one of the aims of self-regulation was to allow companies to compete on the basis of privacy policies that would evolve to the appropriate level of privacy protection demanded by the market through competition. In the words of one witness before the House, "First, do not hinder self-regulation efforts of industry to give consumers informed choice. By and large, industry has done a good job. If a company decides to share information in a perceived detrimental way, the market is pretty quick to act."[30]

There are two problems with this neoliberal economic analysis of privacy protection: first, optimum natural markets rely on buyers and sellers having "complete and symmetrical information," and a choice whether or not to participate in the market. (Thus, for example, health care would not be a natural market since the buyers of health care are not indifferent as to whether or not to buy.) Also, there must be a choice of similar services with different privacy policies to choose from, rather than a monopolistic or oligopolistic market structure. For example, if one didn't like the privacy policies of Amazon.com, one could shop from another on-line book seller who had stricter policies. Most on-line businesses have never found it worthwhile to compete on the basis of privacy policies for the reasons described below.

There was also a huge information asymmetry between the data collectors and the data subjects about how to participate in the market for privacy protection, and ignorance about the value of personal information. The information that the average user discloses has more value than is known to the data subject. Without the awareness that there is value inherent in the personal information one is giving away, no coherent "shopping" of privacy policies can occur, and the businesses themselves have no incentive to compete on privacy. Moreover, the current "opt-out" system assigns the value of information to the businesses rather than the individuals. Thus, those who expect markets to equilibrate at the appropriate level of privacy speak of a scenario wherein market participants understand both the value of their data and the differences among privacy policies. That is far off, at this point. Consumer WebWatch, a subsidiary of the nonprofit Consumer Reports founded in 2002 to monitor consumers' web usage, found that, when asked about their web usage,

> Consumers have strong opinions about what information Web sites should provide on practices and policies, but that doesn't mean that users are always aggressive in seeking out this information. For example, . . . just 35 percent report reading the privacy policies on most sites . . . Although users may not always be diligent in reading this type of key information, they are consistent in their demands that the Web sites make the information easily available when they do want to read through the policies and practices.[31]

The study focused on the factors that contribute to a website's credibility. The results demonstrated that even less attention to privacy policies is paid in actual—rather than self-reported—web surfing behavior, leading the authors to conclude:

> Consider how having a privacy-policy statement affects the perceived credibility of a Web site. Previous research (the various studies that focused on Interpretation) found that people claim to assign more credibility to sites that have a privacy policy. This makes sense. But what if people don't notice the privacy policy? . . . Any site with a privacy policy that does not get noticed gets no credibility boost from having the privacy policy. Our research shows how this plays out in real Web sites: Fewer than 1 percent of the comments about the 100 Web sites mentioned anything about a privacy policy. This element was rarely noticed and, as a result, had almost no real impact on the credibility assessments people made.[32]

Privacy policies are usually long, subject to change without notice, and difficult to use for comparison shopping. Even educated consumers have trouble understanding the policies in toto, and deciding which the tighter privacy protecting policy is. A 2000 analysis of ten major web privacy policies found the majority are written for college level, or higher reading levels, whereas most US citizens read at a tenth grade or lower level.[33] A 2003 study by the Annenberg Foundation found that a minority (47 percent) of adults who use the Internet at home say website privacy policies are easy to understand, but of those who say they are confident of their understanding of privacy policies, 66 percent also believe (incorrectly) that sites with a privacy policy will not share their personal data.

Ideally, the seal programs, like TRUSTe or BBBOnline, would serve as a "minimum" standard, signaling to consumers a uniform set of data handling procedures that the website is legally bound to follow. However, these trustmark programs do not establish an absolute standard, but rather require only that websites follow the procedures they announce in their privacy policy. To quote TRUSTe's[35] website:

> All Web sites that display our trustmark must disclose their personal information collection and privacy practices in a straightforward privacy statement, generally a link from the home page. More than one trustmark may be displayed if personal information privacy practices vary within the site. When you see our TRUSTe seal, you can be assured that the Web site will disclose:
>
> - What personal information is being gathered about you
> - How the information will be used
> - Who the information will be shared with, if anyone
> - Choices available to you regarding how collected information is used
> - Safeguards in place to protect your information from loss, misuse, or alteration
> - How you can update or correct inaccuracies in your information[36]

The trustmark system places the burden of investigation and understanding privacy policy differences back squarely onto the consumer, while research has shown that consumers are not able to assume that burden to any real extent. Thus, the market mechanism is significantly flawed when it comes to privacy protection because the theoretical assumptions for optimum outcomes are simply not met.

One of the largest open questions about Safe Harbor is its efficacy, and how to measure it. There is widespread agreement about the facts: there have been relatively few European consumer complaints to the Alternative Dispute Resolution Mechanisms, and all have been resolved without incident. Although there have been prosecutions and fines of both European and US firms for violations of the European Data Protection Directive or the Safe Harbor Agreement (the largest fine to date was an 840,000 penalty against Spanish telecommunications firm Telefonica in 2001[37]), the number of investigated violations is smaller than one would expect, given the volume of data flows.

There is less agreement about why there have been so few complaints. The optimists conclude that business self-regulation is as effective as government regulation in ensuring compliance with a set of rules concerning personal data. Critics contend, however, that Europeans do not have sufficient information or awareness about these issues,[38] and need to be educated about their rights before a determination about the success of industry self-regulation can be made. The evidence seems to favor those that believe insufficient knowledge is the cause of the absence of complaints. The British Home Secretary, David Blunkett, noted the irony in the public's skeptical reaction to proposals for a national identification card, which would have strict data protection safeguards compared with that to shopping loyalty cards, which have much more data and can be used in almost any way the companies like.[39]

A further problem in comparing the success of self-regulation to comprehensive government regulation is that even in the EU, where data privacy policies are prescribed by law, they are seemingly not implemented better than in the US.[40] Unsurprisingly, legislation without sufficient monitoring and enforcement in the EU did not provide better protection of privacy. The national data authorities complained about lack of resources,[41] but as of 2004, none of the member states had significantly increased the funding of these autonomous agencies.

Finally, it is worth noting that when one compares industry self-regulation to government regulation in this context, it is comparing apples to oranges. The entire EU system is based on the fact that data subjects are not required to monitor their data: the data are protected by the government, whether the data subjects are aware of it or not. In the US, by contrast, data privacy requires that individuals constantly monitor the businesses they transact with and ensure that these data are not transferred, to the extent that is preventable. Thus, even when public opinion survey data show similar levels of awareness about data protection in the EU and the US, the individual's data privacy in still safeguarded in the EU, but not in the US.[42]

■ Conclusion

The agreement on Safe Harbor between the EU and the US did not end discussion on the European Data Protection Directive. As this chapter shows, the EU's approach to data protection remained very much in the international limelight, and continued to have its share of detractors. The evolution from 2000 to 2004 of the Commission's stance on data protection seems to have been one of softening a bit in light of "events on the ground." The privacy "doves" were in the ascendancy within the EU, and so the Commission pledged to make adequacy findings easier, and to approve more codes of conduct to facilitate the onward transfer obligations of the Directive. The Commission began to accommodate the US as privacy legislation clashed with first commercial, and then security concerns. It even moved the data protection unit from the Internal Market DG to the Commission's Justice, Freedom and Security Department in March 2005. It also began to encourage others to "exploit all the pragmatic possibilities" the Directive allowed. Often, the Article 29 Working Party was far less liberal in its interpretation of a privacy issue, and the European Parliament usually backed the Article 29 Working Party's interpretation. However, since all the power in this issue area is either at the Council (Article 31) level or the Commission, and the Article 29 Working Party and European Parliament's roles are only advisory, the gradual softening of the EU's position over time has made agreements possible.

The softening of the EU on rigid interpretations of the European Data Protection Directive was also, of course, due to the changing international environment. With transatlantic relations at a new low in 2002–2003 because of the Iraq war, the Commission was anxious to take any other potentially divisive issues off the table. Moreover, the burst of the dot-com bubble in 2001 took the pressure off the regulatory differences in this sector. Thus, although the Commission opined that many international transfers are taking place in contravention of the Directive, there were no new proposals to curb these abuses. The status quo was quite stable.

■ Notes

1. It was not necessary to have a privacy seal program as ADR mechanism; companies could agree to be bound by the EU Data Protection Authorities.

2. European Parliament question to Bolkestein available at http://europa.eu.int/eur-lex/en/archive/2001/ce35020011211en.html.

3. http://energycommerce.house.gov/107new/hearings/03082001Hearing49/print.html.

4. Ibid.

5. http://energycommerce.house.gov/107new/hearings/03082001Hearing49/print.html.

6. Letter to the Commission available at http://www.treasury.gov/press/releases/po116.html.

7. Comments on the Safe Harbor proposal available at http://www.ita.doc.gov/td/ecom/comabc.html.

8. March 23, 2001. Letter to the Commission available at http://www.treasury.gov/press/releases/po116.html.

9. Commission reply to Undersecretaries Hammond and Carreau available at http://europa.eu.int/comm/internal_market/privacy/docs/clausexchange/replyustreasury_en.pdf.

10. *Financial Times,* March 29, 2001.

11. Reuters, May 26, 2002; the Commission launched an investigation of .NET Passport in May 2002 to ensure all parts of the program (which collects personal information) were compatible with the European Data Protection Directive available at http://www.reuters.com/newsArticle.jhtml;jsessionid=TP3LXFNBEWOBWCRBAELCFEY?type=topNews&storyID=1012050. Microsoft changed parts of the .NET Passport system and the Commission ended its inquiry in 2003.

12. Reidenberg, 2001.

13. Dhont et al., 2004.

14. http://www.ecommercetimes.com/perl/story/12875.html.

15. Europemedia.net; February 21, 2002, available at http://www.europemedia.net/shownews.asp?ArticleID=8608.

16. http://europa.eu.int/comm/internal_market/privacy/docs/adequacy/sec-2002-196/sec-2002-196_en.pdf.

17. Ibid.

18. Ibid., pp. 10–11.

19. Article 29 Data Protection Working Party. 2002 available at http://europa.eu.int/comm/internal_market/privacy/docs/wpdocs/2002/wp62_en.pdf.

20. Dhont et al., 2004.

21. Ibid., pp. 45–47.

22. Ibid., pp. 62–77.

23. Commission, 2004.

24. Wellbery, 2002.

25. Commission, 2003; "First report on the implementation of the Data Protection Directive (95/46/EC)" available at http://europa.eu.int/eur-lex/pri/en/dpi/rpt/doc/2003/com2003_0265en01.doc.

26. Commission, May 16, 2003; "Data Protection: Commission Report Shows that EU Law is Achieving its Main Aims," DN: IP/03/697.

27. Wellbery, 2002.

28. For example, proposed amendments by Austria, Finland, Sweden, and the UK suggested the Commission be the locus of information about which third countries have been deemed as having inadequate protection. See http://www.dca.gov.uk/ccpd/dpdamend.htm#part6.

29. Wellbery, 2002.

30. Whitener, 2003.

31. Princeton Survey Research Associates, 2002, p. 2.

32. Fogg et al., 2002, p. 86.

33. *USA Today,* "Privacy isn't public knowledge: Online policies spread confusion with legal jargon." May 1, 2000.

34. Annenberg, 2003.

35. TRUSTe is the independent web seal program most often used by Safe Harbor companies.

36. TRUSTe. "So, What Does TRUSTe's Trustmark Mean To You?" available at http://www.truste.com/consumers/users_how.html.

37. "Data Fines Fall Mainly in Spain," available at http://www.osborneclarke.com/publications/text/datafines.html.

38. Reidenberg, 2001.

39. The *Guardian,* November 18, 2004.

40. Looking at website privacy policies, Consumers International (2001) found similar levels of data protection, meaning that European enforcement of data protection laws is still rather lax. Data privacy, however, goes beyond the Internet, and information practices overall are still much looser in the US.

41. Commission, 2003.

42. I thank Abe Newman for making this point clearer.

7

New Controversies Test the EU Privacy Standard

The US-EU dispute about the European Data Protection Directive might have been only a historical footnote, were it not for its ongoing impact on significant transatlantic and technological developments. Although the Clinton administration had been able to find a solution to the problem of applying privacy laws to commercial transactions, thereby maintaining the flow of information, the directive proved to be an obstacle in the Bush administration's plan to fight terrorism by using private commercial data flows to profile individuals. Unlike the US, the EU prevented businesses from transferring personal data to other businesses or governments without express consent by the individual, thereby preventing government agencies on either side of the Atlantic from collecting and filtering public,[1] commercial, and financial data, and profiling EU individuals. As this chapter will detail, this particular conflict revolved around airline passenger information, and was resolved with a one-off agreement stating that the US handling of the EU's data would be deemed adequate. However, the different approaches to the use of commercial data by government are likely to create other conflicts over time, and thus, the directive is a potential source of ongoing conflict between the US and the EU.

Another source of potential conflict is the advance of technology. Whereas the US is more willing to adopt new technology and then address potential problems, the EU Directive gives the Data Protection Authorities in each member state the responsibility to think proactively about privacy threats entailed in new technology, and to regulate the technology before privacy abuses occur. The directive, by creating the institutions of independent data privacy "agencies," therefore, has created a level of oversight of new technology that is unmatched by the US, wherein privacy lobbying groups are not as well positioned to regulate. An example of the EU's proactive stance is on the new technology called Radio Frequency Identification (RFID), the details of which are described below. It is unclear whether US citizens will ultimately have radically different ideas about how the RFID tag technology's use on consumer applications will be permitted. There is, however, more governmental scrutiny of the technology by the Europeans, and European companies assume that they will be bound by the European Data Protection Directive when they employ the RFID technology on individuals.[2] One example of the difference in approach is the issue of RFID-encoded passports, which the International Civil Aviation Organization (ICAO, an agency of the UN) mandated, and the US hoped to begin producing in 2006. The US State Department sent out requests for proposals for the new passports with the RFID signal unencrypted. This means that, unless additional privacy shields such as aluminum covers or other RFID-disabling devices are included in the final new passport design, anyone with an RFID scanner who can get within 30 feet of an American passport can "read" all of the data on the passport.[3] By contast, the Europeans (who will ultimately also comply with the RFID passports) will be required by the Directive to encrypt the passport data to ensure they are not stolen. Therefore, some of the ongoing importance of the European Data Protection Directive is to limit the applications of new technologies that would reduce Europeans' data privacy. As a result, the EU may find itself at odds with the US government or companies in the future.

■ The Passenger Name Record Conflict

The first concrete transatlantic conflict over data privacy did not actually involve Safe Harbor or data flows between businesses. Instead, the conflict resulted from the US government forcing firms to violate the European Data Protection Directive by requiring all airlines to collect, transfer (to the Department of Homeland Security), and retain thirty-nine data items on each passenger. As the US government began to plan its war against terrorism, the use of commercial information to profile potential terrorists, or to match known terrorist identities, started to become more acceptable to the Bush administration.[4] The government increasingly demanded the use of domestic commercial data to thwart terrorists.[5] Arguing that some privacy rights had to be weighed against greater societal security, the Bush administration sought authorization to collect and store US citizens' commercial data. Moreover, there was a perception in some parts of the US government that as security concerns became more important in the wake of the September 11 attacks, personal information privacy could legitimately be traded off for greater public safety. It is important to note, however, the assumption by the Bush administration that most US citizens would be willing to relinquish more privacy for security was not borne out by opinion surveys, specifically on this point. A CBS/*New York Times* poll conducted on November 25, 2002, found that 62 percent of the respondents answered "not willing" to the question, "In order to reduce the threat of terrorism, would you be willing or not willing to allow government agencies to monitor the telephone calls and e-mails of ordinary Americans on a regular basis?" It was, however, the international provisions in the Aviation and Transportation Security Act that caused the fracas with the European Union, where the right to data privacy in the commercial realm was legally protected.

The case of the Passenger Name Record (PNR) conflict between the US and the EU clearly demonstrated that power disparities had forced the EU to accede to an agreement that did not reflect many of its fundamental demands. Even the language of negotiation was brusque on the US side. The US disbelief that an agreement assuring the privacy of Passenger Name Record data transfers was actually legally necessary showed how ridiculous it considered the EU's position. Moreover, the threats that the US government made as incentives for EU airline compliance were credible and severe, attested to by the near-universal compliance with the US demands. Unlike the Safe Harbor negotiations, where the US and the EU had been on equal footing, and interests had played a major role in determining the outcome, the Passenger Name Record negotiations were government-to-government negotiations, framed as security issues rather than economic issues. Moreover, unlike the Safe Harbor negotiations, in the Passenger Name Record conflict, the US government had a legal basis for its position, a law demanding the data, which strengthened the US negotiation stance.

The source of the Passenger Name Record conflict was one of the provisions of the Aviation and Transportation Security Act passed on November 19, 2001, by the US Congress in the wake of the September 11 terrorist attacks in the US. The act required all airlines passing through the US to collect passenger information, and to pass those data along to the US Customs and Border Protection Bureau.[6] If the airlines did not comply, they would be subject to fines of $6,000 per passenger, or could lose their landing rights.[7] The passenger data demanded included the information usually contained in passports (name, age, country of origin, height and weight, race, etc.) as well as new information stipulated by the Customs and Border Protection Bureau, such as where the passenger would stay on arrival, his or her country of residence, and visa information.[8] The entire Passenger Name Record would also include the details of the purchase, such as email addresses, credit card numbers, telephone numbers, dietary preferences, and some catchall categories like "general remarks." The act required all of the Passenger Name Record information to be submitted by the airlines to the Customs and Border Protection Bureau, upon request, within fifteen minutes of takeoff. These data would then be part of the 1999 Computer

Assisted Passenger Prescreening System (CAPPS) that would screen for potential terrorist risks. In 2003, a revised system (CAPPS II) was proposed, which would be administered by the US government rather than the airlines, a change welcomed by the airlines. CAPPS II, however, never made it off the drawing board because of the negative publicity it received in the US, though a system substantially similar (dubbed "Secure Flight") was being tested by two airlines as of 2005. The hope of all of these systems was that they would provide enough information to distinguish known terrorists from many innocent passengers with similar names.

From the perspective of the European Data Protection Directive, the fact that these data were collected for a commercial purpose (flying abroad), and only subsequently exploited for national security information, created the problem for the EU.[9] Hypothetically, if the data had been collected only for security purposes, they likely would have fallen under the security exemptions that the national privacy laws have created for security and policing issues.[10]

The EU Commission, exercising its prerogatives under the "external relations" article in the European Data Protection Directive, entered into bilateral talks with the Bush administration about this problem in December 2001. According to Chris Patton, the Commissioner for External Affairs of the EU, it was difficult at first to get the Bush administration to take the privacy issue seriously: "in recent weeks [the European Commission] undertook difficult discussions to overcome a stalemate created by the United States initially taking our concerns lightly and not responding to our questions."[11] The Article 29 Working Party issued an opinion on the Passenger Name Record problems in October 2002,[12] highlighting the many parts of the US demands that conflicted with EU data protection laws, and explicitly noting the fact that transfers to government agencies were not covered under the Safe Harbor Agreement. It was only after the Commission's notification to European airline companies in November 2002 that relaying information to the US might put them in contravention of their data protection obligations, that the US government took the problem seriously in December 2002. As a result of the US-EU discussions, the Customs and Border Protection Bureau agreed to hold off enforcing the act until February 5, 2003, and to apply no penalties until March 5, 2003, for any EU airlines asserting that they are bound by the European Data Protection Directive and their national privacy laws.[13]

On February 17 and 18, 2003, the US and the EU met in Brussels to negotiate a solution to the conflict. The Director General for External Relations, Guy Legras, and the Deputy US Customs Commissioner, Douglas Browning, issued a joint statement at the conclusion of the meeting outlining some points of agreement, but failed to reach a fully satisfactory solution for the problem. Included in the statement was the allowance that national data commissioners did not have to begin enforcement actions against domestic airlines complying with the US Passenger Name Record requirements, and that sensitive data (as defined by European Data Protection Directive Article 8) would be handled separately by certain methods to be determined at a later stage. Moreover, US customs would pass along the data to other law enforcement agencies only for the purpose of combating terrorism (rather than, for example, to the Immigration and Naturalization Service for the purpose of finding illegal aliens who are not potential terrorists). Finally, the US "took note" of the fact that the EU Commission believed a multilateral agreement was necessary in the long run, and that the proper venue for any future agreement on Passenger Name Record would be the ICAO.[14]

The US-EU negotiations about the TSA obligations were conducted in a very different transatlantic atmosphere than the Safe Harbor negotiations had been. This was partly due to the fact that most European airlines were already complying with the US demands, undermining the EU's negotiating position, and making the EU's data protection demands seem frivolous and moot. However, the Department of Homeland Security's diplomatic approach was far more unilateralist than that of the Department of Commerce's had been in the Safe Harbor negotiations. This was partially due to the change in administration as well. In March 2003, Commissioner Bolkestein expressed his frustration with the Bush administration's style:

> I strongly agree with Members who expressed the view [in the European Parliament] on Monday that the American way of proceeding by unilateral action and threats of penalties is unacceptable. But not having discussions with the American side would have left them with the data and no means for the European Union side to influence their handling of it.[15]

Bolkestein conceded that as of March 5, most European airlines were sending data to the Customs and Border Protection Bureau and there were no restrictions on that data's use:

> It is not simply a question of letting the data be transferred or preventing this, much of it is flowing anyway. Therefore it seems to me that the suggestion which has been made that we should take the airlines to the European Court of Justice is not a very productive suggestion. It is happening now . . . [The airlines] know that the American side is serious about imposing penalties, including some that could put their transatlantic traffic at risk. The counterbalancing threat—namely that the Commission would start infringement proceedings, legal action for breaches of the data protection rules—was a serious concern for the airlines. However, some of them have said that is not life-threatening, whereas the American threats are.[16]

As of October 2003 only Alitalia and Austrian Airlines were refusing to submit the Passenger Name Record information to the US; all other European airlines were complying with the Department of Homeland Security's demands.[17]

As the US-EU discussions continued over the summer of 2003, the EU obtained some concessions from the US, such as the use of the Chief Privacy Officer in the Department of Homeland Security to appeal Europeans' data protection infringements, a shorter period of data retention (from 50 years to 6–7 years), and the commitment not to electronically share Passenger Name Record data with other US agencies, except on a case-by-case basis.[18] On June 13, 2003, the Article 29 Working Party submitted the second of three opinions[19] on whether there would be any hope of achieving an adequacy ruling for the Passenger Name Record problem, but expressed its pessimism toward the existence of a basis for such a ruling, even with concessions by the US. Moreover, there remained important outstanding issues that were irresolvable:

1. Purpose limitation: the US did not want to limit their use of Passenger Name Record to the fight against terrorism, but wanted to cover "other serious criminal offences," and have not, so far, been prepared to narrow this further.
2. Scope of data required: the US required thirty-nine different Passenger Name Record elements, which is hard to regard as proportionate to the purpose.
3. The still very long data storage periods (6–7 years).
4. The fact that US undertakings are insufficiently legally binding, hence our insistence, if rights are not actionable before US courts, on independent extra-judicial redress mechanisms.[20]

In September 2003, Commissioner Bolkestein admitted to the European Parliament that,

> it must be said that some real improvements in the way the US process PNR data have been made but unfortunately not to the point where the Commission can regard the requirements of "adequate protection" to have been met.[21]

By October 2003, the EU and the US had set themselves a year-end deadline for the resolution of the dispute. The Internal Market Commissioner, Bolkestein, once again found himself in the position between the European Parliament and the US. The US was refusing to make any further changes to the agreement. The European Parliament issued a resolution pressing the Commission to begin negotiating the points raised by the Article 29 Working Party, and to prevent the illegal transfer of data within two months.[22] At the same time, the Commission wanted to find a realistic resolution that would not subject European airlines to exorbitant US fines, or European passengers to long delays caused by secondary interviews in the US. Moreover, as Commissioner Bolkestein pointed out, it was not only the US that wanted passenger data for security-related reasons, but Australia and Canada were also requesting it, and others were expected to follow suit, including a couple of EU member states.[23] Thus, the problem required a more multilateral approach than the bilateral approach assumed by the European Parliament. At the International Conference of Data Protection & Privacy Commissioners held in Australia in September 2003, a resolution to that effect was passed, affirming that:

> where regular international transfers of personal data are necessary [to combat terrorism and organized crime], they should take place within a framework taking data protection into account, e.g. on the basis of an international agreement stipulating adequate data protection requirements, including clear purpose limitation, adequate and non-excessive data collection, limited data retention time, information provision to data subjects, the assurance of data subject rights, and independent supervision.[24]

The hope of creating an international treaty for PNRs grew following US-EU meetings in late November 2003. The Commission was anxious to legalize the status quo (most airlines sending the information to the US in violation of the European Data Protection Directive), and the negotiation of an international treaty would circumvent the European Parliament since only the member states would be party to the agreement.[25] There were signs of a growing rift between the accommodationist stance of the EU Commission and the European Parliament, which had a majority in favor of taking a hard line with respect to the US. Commissioner Bolkestein addressed these problems in his speech to the European Parliament on December 16, 2003, while presenting the latest draft of the adequacy agreement:

> [the Article 29] Working Party, after outlining its numerous data protection concerns, recognized that "*ultimately political judgements will be needed.*" Those talks have now been completed . . . And today the Commission exercised its "political judgement" in deciding how to take matters forward. By referring to political judgement, the Working Party acknowledged that there were many considerations at stake, in addition to data protection . . . The EU cannot refuse to its ally in the fight against terrorism an arrangement that Member States would be free to make themselves . . . I do not see any solution which serves our objectives better. I see in any case no justification at all for pursuing policies which risk producing negative outcomes for passengers and negative impacts for airlines. Parliament will be consulted on both components of these proposed arrangements. I am confident that Parliament will exercise its political judgement by weighing all the different policy issues at stake.[26]

The Article 29 Working Party issued its third opinion in January 2004,[27] stating that many of the issues it had flagged in its June opinion remained unchanged in the latest draft. It was also adamant that the EU Commission obtain guarantees that Europeans' data would never be used to test the CAPPS II system:

> in light of the circumstance that the Working Party has not been informed and consulted about the ultimate CAPSS II legal framework, any use of personal data by TSA with regard to the proposed CAPPS II system or its testing should be considered excluded now and in the future from the applicable scope of the Commission's decision. In other words, the considerations made in this Opinion are based on the assumption that the Commission's decision will not be extended in future to CAPPS II . . . otherwise, far more critical remarks would have to be made already at this stage. As a result, the Working Party recommends the Commission to make clear, through a specific clause in the decision, that US authorities shall refrain from using passenger PNR data transmitted from the EU not only to implement the CAPPS II system but also to test it.[28]

In January, EU Commission spokesperson Jonathan Todd admitted that the EU Commission had already conceded this point in negotiations, and that "we are already talking with the Americans about which security measures must be met if PNR data are to be used in CAPPS II."[29] The Article 29 Working Party also questioned the lack of US movement on the other issues, such as the purpose limitation, the number of items requested, and data retention periods (see Table 7.1 for negotiating positions and concessions).

Using the Article 29 Working Party opinion as its guide, on March 18, 2004, the Committee on Citizens' Freedoms and Rights of the European Parliament approved a resolution calling on the EU Commission to reject the adequacy proposals made by the US by a vote of twenty-five to nine with three abstentions. Their resolution came a day after a meeting with Stewart Verdery, Assistant Secretary at the US Department of Homeland Security and the lead negotiator with the EU Commission, who pointed out that "air carriers were already transferring personal data and that at the moment no rules on the storage or use of data were in place. Parliament would be well advised to prefer the draft agreement the US and the Commission had reached to no agreement at all."[30] After the EU Commission presented the European Parliament with its final agreement on March 18, the Committee on Citizens' Freedoms and Rights, Justice and Home Affairs of the European Parliament voted twenty-four to eleven with two abstentions against the agreement.[31] The entire European Parliament voted 229 to 202 on March 31 to reject the proposed Passenger Name Record Agreement, and gave Commissioner Bolkestein the date of the last European Parliament plenary session, April 19, as the deadline to withdraw the agreement.[32] Before the vote, Bolkestein pleaded with the European Parliament to pass the agreement:

Table 7.1 Analysis of Negotiating Outcomes for the Passenger Name Record Dispute

Issue	US Law Requirement	Original US Demands	Prior EU Privacy Requirements	Final "Adequate" Agreement
Access to what?	Passenger Name Records	At the discretion of US Customs, includes non-US travel information. Estimated 50-60 fields of data	Must be limited to what is strictly necessary; no access to sensitive information. Mostly information available on ticket and itinerary	34 fields. Sensitive data to be filtered by an EU institution that will also grant access to EU member states.
Purpose of transfer and processing?	Ensuring aviation safety and protecting national security	Serious criminal offences	Specific and proportionate; terrorism and serious related crime	"Terrorism and related crimes" and to "other serious crimes, including organized crime, of a trans-national nature." To be used by the EU for customs and immigration.
Sharing of data?	Beginning from the Customs Service, "may be shared with other federal agencies for the purpose of protecting national security"	Shared with other federal agencies for the purpose of protecting national security, or as otherwise authorized by law	Specific, on a case-by-case basis	Shared within the Department of Homeland Security, e.g., used in the development of the TSA's CAPPS system. Otherwise still very unclear, although DHS has apparently promised "no bulk sharing with other agencies," but not legally binding.
How to access data?	"Carriers shall make passenger name record information available to the Customs Service upon request."	Online access to airline databases to "pull" whatever information they wish. Includes access to non-US related travel	Must be limited to what is strictly necessary and limited access to sensitive information. Sharing only upon consent	Tentative statements regarding 'push' possibly through a centralized EU institution. Possible reciprocity for the EU.
Automated processing and profiling?	Unclear	Data to be used within CAPPS II	Not possible unless "logic" of system is understood	Leave for future agreement; even as European passenger data records are being used to develop the system.
Retention period?	Undeclared in law	50 years	72 hours according to EU regulations, retained for 3 years for billing disputes only. At most, "a short period"; "not more than some weeks, or even months."	3.5 years
Right of redress?	None	None promised	"Provide support and help to individual data subjects in their exercise of rights" including access to data and "appropriate redress mechanisms for individuals." Called for judicial or extrajudicial (independent) redress mechanisms	CPO in DHS; possibly with EU Data Protection Authorities representing EU citizens. Not legally binding.
Compliance reviews?	None	None promised	Must be ongoing verification of compliance	Yearly with the co-operation of the EU.

Source: Privacy International, "Inadequate Adequacy." May 2004.

> The list of demands in the resolution is no doubt a very fine one, but . . . I am afraid that I have to advise the house, based on my experience of the last 12 months, that this is pie in the sky. The result of rejecting this package will not be a better package, but no package at all . . . It certainly does not lead to better data protection in the US. We would be simply throwing away all hard-won improvements . . . There are voices in Washington only too ready to say . . . "We told you that negotiating with these people was a waste of time." There is a real risk that the US will leave the negotiating table and not return.[33]

The US also put pressure on the EU Commission to ignore the European Parliament, and move as quickly as it could, because it wanted to complete the agreement before the additional distractions of the EU enlargement to twenty-five states on May 1, 2004, and the European Parliament elections in June could change the outcome. There was a feeling in Washington that the whole interinstitutional struggle in Europe was a show of wounded pride in the European Parliament that its opinions had not been considered, and that the entire dispute was more about obtaining greater power for the European Parliament in this area rather than any fundamental objections. The impression in the US was that it would be unlikely for the European Parliament to actually go to the European Court of Justice over this matter, especially since the European Parliament had had a similar reaction to the Safe Harbor Agreement, and had not done anything in that matter. The Department of Homeland Security negotiator, Mr. Verdery, went as far as to say it "does not appear that there is any consensus in the Parliament against the deal."

These assessments proved wrong, however, perhaps due to the fact that this was the second time that the European Parliament had not approved an agreement that the EU Commission had by then concluded with the US anyway. It was also probably true that the European Parliament saw in the controversy a vehicle for obtaining greater institutional power. It was certainly consistent with the European Parliament's reputation from the 1970s of actually fighting to preserve fundamental human rights.[34] The confluence of all these reasons led the European Parliament on April 21 to vote 276 to 260, with thirteen abstentions, to take legal action, and to force the EU Commission to refrain from concluding the Passenger Name Record Agreement. Before the vote, the President of the European Parliament, Pat Cox, reportedly lobbied the members of the European Parliament not to bring a suit challenging the Commission's right to make the agreement, while EU Foreign Affairs Commissioner Chris Patten told the MEPs that data transfers were going to take place anyway, since the member states themselves could authorize them. The European Parliament, however, was not swayed.

Next, the Council of Ministers tried to see if the opinions of the European Parliament would be modified after its composition changed on May 1, when the new and inexperienced parliamentarians from the ten accession countries could formally vote. By means of a request to revisit the Passenger Name Record Agreement question, the Council put the issue to all the 732 members of parliament on May 4, but was defeated 343 to 301 on a procedural vote. It was, thus, clear that there was sufficient consensus within even the newly configured parliament to resist the other EU institutions and the US.

The Commission ignored the parliamentary resolution, as it was nonbinding, and on May 28, signed the agreement with the US. The European Parliament asked the European Court of Justice on July 27 to arbitrate the conflict using a fast track procedure, but the agreement would be binding until the court renders its verdict, presumably sometime in the summer of 2005.

From the perspective of the interinstitutional conflict, the European Parliament's resort to the European Court of Justice was a time-honored way to increase its competences.[35] There is a precedent that the European Parliament could cite in its PNR court submission, as Michelle McCown described:

> In "*Chernobyl*" . . . the EP's conflict was with the Commission, which it alleged compromised its right to be consulted, and the ECJ concluded that the Commission could not always be considered to be an effective safeguard of the Parliament's rights and granted the EP a limited standing to bring actions for annulment where it could show that its prerogatives were affected. The case law does, therefore, give the EP a somewhat more restricted right than the Council and the Commission: according to the ECJ, an action brought by the EP "is admissible provided that action seeks only to safeguard its prerogatives and is founded only on submissions alleging a breach of them."[36]

Still, as the institution of comitology was structured to deliberately leave the European Parliament out of the decisionmaking process, it would be difficult for the European Parliament to succeed in challenging the Passenger Name Record Agreement. Moreover, the European Parliament was not seeking to challenge comitology per se, but arguing that the Commission had negotiated an international agreement without proper authority. Finally, as the European Court of Justice no doubt understood, giving the European Parliament a veto over Commission-negotiated agreements with the US in this issue area would be a potential recipe for enduring transatlantic conflict and a strategic court would likely want to avoid that.

However, from the perspective of data protection, the European Parliament once again demonstrated a "fundamental human rights perspective" toward the problem that was unmitigated by any power-balancing, or information-balancing perspective. This had been the hallmark of the European Parliament in the 1970s and 1980s, and its challenge to the EU Commission reflected the continuity of that tradition.

Ultimately, the CAPPS II program was shelved by the US Congress in July 2004[37] because of US privacy concerns, rendering moot the EU's worries about using EU data to test it. In its place, the Transportation Safety Administration created "Secure Flight" in September 2004 and suggested testing it with US airline passenger data.[38]

Radio Frequency Identification Tags

It is too soon to predict whether the Radio Frequency Identification (RFID) tags will become the topic of the next transatlantic dispute over privacy policies. The technology of RFID is relatively new, and its commercial applications in supply-chain management have been its dominant use to date. RFID tags are tiny microchip transmitters that emit a signal up to twenty-five feet, which can be received by special RFID receivers without requiring direct line of sight. Previously, the technology had been too expensive to manufacture in bulk, but in 1999, MIT researchers spun off a new business, Auto-ID (which merged into EPCglobal in November 2003) that used technological advances to make the microchips cheap enough to put almost anywhere.[39] The implications of the technology were that anything could be monitored and recorded, which was why the research consortium had the US Postal Service, the US Department of Defense, and a hundred corporate sponsors interested in its output in 2003 alone. The issue of RFID tags was not necessarily a US versus EU conflict: many of the foreseeable uses of the technology were simply efficiency promoting (e.g., did the wholesaler send fifteen green coats to the retailer?), without any privacy implications. Nor was the EU particularly backward in its approach to RFID. In fact, the EU was likely to use the RFID tags in its large denomination Euro notes by 2005 to thwart money laundering,[40] and in European passports and third-country visas[41] for security reasons (as security-related applications, it could be argued that both applications would be outside the scope of the European Data Protection Directive).

It is the potential commercial applications of RFID, however, that tempt retailers interested in monitoring consumer behavior, and frighten privacy advocates. In this area, the possibility of another conflict between acceptable uses may yet arise, as the European data protection laws strictly constrain these uses, while the US laws are silent. Early evidence shows similar patterns of consumer apprehension at the idea of having their shopping behavior (or other behavior) monitored in the US and the EU. Auto-ID itself conducted surveys in the US, France, Germany, the UK, and Japan to gauge consumer impressions of the new technology. According to its 2003 survey,[42] "internationally the reaction was fairly consistent, with the US, Japan and Germany more negative than UK and France."[43] Overall, most consumers didn't see benefits for themselves, and were "negative but apathetic." Ironically, the more the business applications were explained to the survey subjects, the more negative the reaction became:

> Generally, the fears that consumers have around this technology are emotional and of the unknown, "what could happen in the future?" They have little problem with what is actually being developed—but they have big problem in how it may be abused. Quelling these fears is extremely difficult because they are based on an "unknown future," are purely emotional and appear to be quite deep rooted. In this case discussing any benefits or using rational argument is largely ineffective and is perceived as "spin." Once consumers are concerned, they remain concerned, no matter what we tell them.[44]

In its first retail applications, consumers were not told of the use of the new technology,[45] and found out indirectly: after the Dutch electronics company, Phillips, announced it would ship fifteen million RFID tags to Italian retailer Benetton, consumers threatened to boycott Benetton products, and the company was compelled to hold a press conference to announce publicly that it was simply looking into the cost effectiveness of the new technology.[46] Wal-Mart, the largest retailer in the world, and British retailer Tesco installed a "smart shelf" that read RFID tags placed into Gillette razor packages to thwart shoplifting.[47] Because of the public backlash, however, Tesco, Wal-Mart, and Gillette had to withdraw their plans to use RFID technology on consumer applications.[48]

When UK retailer Marks & Spencer decided to use RFID to track inventory to a store, it first consulted privacy advocates to address their concerns. Marks & Spencer put the RFID tags on items as a separate cardboard hangtag, which the consumer would cut off and throw away, and agreed not to place the readers by the checkout, meaning that they would not record which customers bought which items. Additionally, Marks & Spencer handed out informational brochures about RFID and its use in the store. Privacy advocates criticized the fact that the tags would not be "killed" at the point of sale (a public policy objective the Auto-ID center had set in its privacy guidelines to users of its technology), but agreed that Marks & Spencer had done a reasonably good job of protecting individual privacy in this trial. Privacy groups continued to worry, however, that Marks & Spencer had set a dangerous precedent, with no guarantees that other groups would be as careful.[49]

The open question about RFID tags is whether retail stores will begin to use the technology to gather data about consumer buying behavior, or even what they do with items after the purchase. Already in the US, consumer behavior consulting firms are advertising the benefits of RFID monitoring:

> RFID would be well suited to:
>
> - Track customer routes through store
> - Track common shopper stopping points
> - Determine customer waiting durations
> - Indicate customer interactions with specific Point of Purchase displays
> - Record instances of product handling
> - Evaluate cross merchandising activities of shoppers
> - This application of RFID could significantly reduce the time and cost associated with best-of-class in-store research initiatives, which retailers and manufacturers employ to improve sales and customer satisfaction. Eventually, as RFID systems advance, a greater reliance on RFID technology for collecting more detailed shopping behaviors may ensue.[50]

If retailers do ultimately decide to monitor consumer behavior, then transatlantic differences about data privacy laws would likely come into play. At present, even the makers of the technology admit some sort of regulatory system should be set up to assuage consumer fears about the technology: the Auto-ID international survey's recommendations advocated the regulation of the privacy aspects of the technology in order to alleviate customers' suspicion: "The research made very clear that we must be able to offer consumers reassurance that the network is in some way regulated. Without a very clear statement about regulations and controls, consumer's fears of the potential abuse of the system will remain unchecked."[51]

In Europe, the data privacy laws clearly indicate that individuals must be apprised of the data collection activity, and must consent to having their data collected.[52] It is a legal question, however, if simply posting signs saying "In this store we use RFID to monitor your shopping behavior to better serve your shopping needs" would suffice, or whether an "electronic bonus card" that the customer would apply for (and sign consent) would enable stores to manage RFID monitoring in the way that bonus card shopping programs are legal in Europe. Obviously there would also be a benefit to the customer: a grocery store in Germany tested the RFID technology at the same time as marketing itself as the "grocery store of the future."[53] Each shopper would be given an RFID reader with the shopping cart, and the reader would be activated by a personal ID card (if the customer agrees to allow the collection of personal data). On the RFID screen would appear a list of items the shopper bought last time, as well as information regarding where the products can be found. As items are put in the shopping cart, they would be crossed off the list, and their prices sent to the checkout counter. If there is a credit card on file, the shopper can simply walk out the door. The grocery store indicated that its policy would be to turn off the radio tags once the customer is outside the store.

In terms of EU privacy protection, the premise presumably would be that the new technology will be available only for those who opt in, similar to the existing bonus card schemes. The biggest difference is that because all items will contain radio frequency emitters, and there will be readers at the checkout, individuals' shopping behavior will be monitored, whether or not they agree to be monitored, posing a potential problem for privacy laws. More significantly, the sharing of consumer behavior data to create large consumer profiles would be allowed in the US (under current laws), but not in the EU (without explicit consent). It is too early yet to predict whether there will be transatlantic conflicts about this issue, or whether EU companies (and foreign companies doing business in the EU) will simply learn to live without profiling their customers the way they do in the US.

Another question is whether a new technological solution can be found to prevent the monitoring of those who do not wish to be monitored.[54] New technology approved by the FDA in 2004 allowed an RFID microchip to be implanted into humans, creating the possibility of twenty-four hour monitoring.[55] In an October 2003 report on the security/privacy trade-off, the Commission singled out RFID technology for its specific regulation, if necessary: "it is important that these RFID tags are regulated by legislation addressing identity-related issues."[56] In November 2003, a coalition of privacy groups issued its recommendation for RFID policy, and why public policy should be proactive in this area before the tags become ubiquitous.[57] It is likely that the European Commission, prodded by the Article 29 Working Party, will ultimately have to issue a statement about the use of RFID technology beyond its intended supply-chain management applications. In January 2005, the Article 29 Working Party submitted a working paper on RFID, in order to "provide guidance to RFID deployers on the application of the basic principles set out in EC Directives, particularly the data protection Directive and the Directive on privacy and electronic communications and . . . to provide guidance to manufacturers of the technology (RFID tags, readers and applications) as well as RFID standardization bodies on their responsibility towards designing privacy compliant technology in order to enable deployers of the technology to carry out their obligations under the data protection Directive."[58]

In July 2004 both the FTC and the US House Committee on Energy and Commerce held a hearing on what the RFID technology future holds for commerce, security, and the consumer.[59] There, representatives from businesses stressed the nonprivacy-invasive uses the technology can be beneficial for, and opined that congressional regulation was unnecessary. Privacy advocates from EPIC and the ACLU, by contrast, stressed the need for proactive legislation precluding some of the consumer data collecting practices that RFID made possible.

Ultimately, the question about this and other new technologies would be how much the European Data Protection Directive would frame the privacy debates in the US concerning the regulation of consumers' personal data. The fact that the European Data Protection Directive was invoked in the US discussions about RFID (as well as in discussions of camera phones,[60] for example) shows that the Directive has had cross border effects in the US even if the US never fully accepts its every detail.

Conclusion

The Passenger Name Record dispute between the US and the EU exposed ongoing differences between the EU and the US approach to individual data privacy, as well as the extent to which the US could unilaterally force the EU to make concessions when the government had a unified position, unencumbered by different interests. The main difference between the Passenger Name Record and Safe Harbor Agreements was that interest groups were far less involved in the Passenger Name Record negotiations, giving the two governments a free rein to conclude an agreement. Moreover, there was greater consensus between the US and EU governments about the right of the US (and other countries wanting similar data) to use them in the fight against terrorism. The US and EU disagreed on important details, to be sure, but the fundamental right to use data to fight terrorism was not in question. This weakened the negotiating positions of the privacy hawkish institutions, the Article 29 Working Party, and the European Parliament when it came to moving the agreement closer to the European Parliament's preferences (not to mention the letter of the European Data Protection Directive). Moreover, since the European airlines were already sending the data without any safeguards at all, the Commission could credibly argue (as it did) that almost any agreement was superior to the absence of an agreement.

The lack of interest group divisions within the US position on the Passenger Name Record strengthened the US negotiating position vis-à-vis the European institutions (which were divided), and, in the final analysis, led to an agreement that was much more of a take-it-or-leave-it ultimatum than a real compromise among different preferences. The next chapter examines the consequences of these data privacy conflicts on transatlantic relations, and the emerging international regime on data protection.

■ Notes

1. The Article 29 Working Party issued an opinion on how public sector information could be reused. See Opinion 7/2003 on the reuse of public sector information and the protection of personal data. available at http://europa.eu.int/comm/internal_market/privacy/docs/wpdocs/2003/wp83_en.pdf.

2. Transcript of the FTC's RFID workshop meeting, pp. 303–304 available at http://www.ftc.gov/bcp/workshops/rfid/transcript.pdf.

3. The American Civil Liberties Union (ACLU) protested this design in its November 2004 white paper, "Naked Data: How the U.S. Ignored International Concerns and Pushed for Radio Chips in Passports Without Security" available at http://www.aclu.org/privacy/privacy.cfm?ID=17078&c=130.

4. O'Harrow, 2005.

5. In the course of testing some of the computer programs designed to profile terrorists in 2002, the US government used Mexican, Latin American, and US personal data acquired from ChoicePoint, a company that compiles information from various public and commercial sources. The Mexican and Latin American data were later found to have been illegally obtained. US domestic airline carriers such as Northwest, JetBlue, American, and United also gave passenger information to US government agencies like the FBI and the TSA to test the profiling systems.

6. FAQs about the Passenger Name Record conflict are available at http://www.europa.eu.int/rapid/start/cgi/guesten.ksh?p_action.gettxt=gt&doc=MEMO/03/53|0|RAPID&lg=EN&display=.

7. *Financial Times,* September 24, 2003.

8. *Financial Times,* February 25, 2003.

9. I thank Scott Blackmer for explaining the legal roots of the problem to me.

10. According to the Commission, some of the national laws did not implement the Directive correctly, creating divergences between European member states. Commission. 2003.

11. Patton, Remarks to the European Parliament's Committee on Citizens' Freedoms and Rights, Justice and Home Affairs, March 12, 2003, available at http://www3.europarl.eu.int/omk/omnsapir.so/cre?FILE=0312me&LANGUE=EN&LEVEL=DOC&NUMINT=3-164&LEG=L5.

12. Working Party, 2002.

13. http://www.europa.eu.int/rapid/start/cgi/guesten.ksh?p_action.gettxt=gt&doc=MEMO/03/53|0|RAPID&lg=EN&display=.

14. Joint Statement, available at http://www.europa.eu.int/comm/external_relations/us/intro/pnr.html.

15. Bolkestein's remarks to the European Parliament available at http://www3.europarl.eu.int/omk/omnsapir.so/debatsL5?FILE=20030312EN&LANGUE=EN&LEVEL=DOC&NUMINT=3-168.

16. Ibid.

17. *Financial Times,* October 18, 2003.

18. Bolkestein's Address to European Parliament Committee on Citizens' Freedoms and Rights, Justice and Home Affairs, September 9, 2003, available at

http://europa.eu.int/rapid/pressReleasesAction.do?reference=SPEECH/03/396&format=HTML&aged=0&language=EN&guiLanguage=en.

19. http://europa.eu.int/comm/internal_market/privacy/docs/wpdocs/2003/wp78_en.pdf.

20. Ibid.

21. http://europa.eu.int/rapid/pressReleasesAction.do?reference=SPEECH/03/396&format=HTML&aged=0&language=EN&guiLanguage=en.

22. http://www3.europarl.eu.int/omk/omnsapir.so/pv2?PRG=CALDOC&FILE=20031009&LANGUE=EN&TPV=PROV&LASTCHAP=16&SDOCTA=11&TXTLST=1&Type_Doc=FIRST&POS=1.

23. The Australians and Canadians received largely favorable reviews by the Article 29 Working Party for the safeguards they put in place on Passenger Name Record data. Bolkestein's Address to European Parliament Committee on Citizens' Freedoms and Rights, Justice and Home Affairs, September 9, 2003, available at http://www.europa.eu.int/rapid/start/cgi/guesten.ksh?p_action.gettxt=gt&doc=SPEECH/03/396|0|RAPID&lg=FI&display=.

24. Resolution concerning the Transfer of Passengers' Data available at http://www.privacyconference2003.org/resolutions/RESOLUTION_CONCERNING_THE_T.DOC.

25. *Financial Times,* November 23, 2003.

26. Speech by Bolkestein to European Parliament Committee on Citizens' Freedoms and Rights, Justice and Home Affairs, December 16, 2003 available at http://europa.eu.int/rapid/pressReleasesAction.do?reference=SPEECH/03/613&format=HTML&aged=0&language=EN&guiLanguage=fr.

27. http://europa.eu.int/comm/internal_market/privacy/docs/wpdocs/2004/wp87_en.pdf.

28. Ibid., p. 5.

29. http://www.edri.org/cgi-bin/index?id=000100000123.

30. European Parliament Press Service; March 18, 2004 available at http://www2.europarl.eu.int/omk/sipade2?PUBREF=-//EP//TEXT+PRESS+NR-20040318-1+0+DOC+XML+V0//EN&LEVEL=2&NAV=S.

31. Technically, the European Parliament committee was voting on whether the draft agreement was ready to be sent to the Council of Ministers for final approval.

32. A second European Parliament committee, the Committee on Foreign Affairs, Human Rights, Common Security and Defence Policy also voted twenty-three to nineteen with one abstention on April 6 to reject the agreement.

33. http://www.eupolitix.com/EN/News/200403/303fa633-33e0-4bb0-af81-b551d5b01ebc.html.

34. Nugter, 1990.

35. McCown, 2003.

36. Ibid., p. 983.

37. http://www.cnn.com/2004/TRAVEL/07/15/passenger.background/index.html.

38. *New York Times,* September 22, 2004.

39. On November 1, 2003, EPCglobal, Inc., a joint venture between EAN International and the Uniform Code Council, Inc., was formed to carry on the research completed by the Auto-ID Center, and to work toward the development of industry accepted standards and commercial adoption. The newly formed organization took on the mission of working with end users, and hardware, software, and integration solutions providers to build the EPC Network infrastructure and support implementation.

40. eetimes, December 19, 2001, available at http://www.eetimes.com/story/OEG20011219S0016.
41. http://europa.eu.int/eur-lex/en/com/pdf/2003/com2003_0558en01.pdf.
42. http://www.autoidcenter.org/publishedresearch/cam-autoid-eb002.pdf.
43. Ibid., p. 8.
44. Ibid., p. 11.
45. RFID Journal, October 23, 2003, available at http://216.121.131.129/article/articleprint/623/-1/1/.
46. CNET news.com, April 7, 2003, available at http://news.com.com/2100-1029-995744.html.
47. The RFID tags activated a security camera every time a package of razors was picked up, and then the customer's picture was compared with the one at the checkout, alerting store security to potential shoplifters.
48. http://news.com.com/Wal-Mart+cancels+'smart+shelf'+trial/2100-1017_3-1023934.html.
49. Ecommerce, October 16, 2003, available at http://www.internetnews.com/ec-news/article.php/3093101.
50. RFID News, October 20, 2003, available at http://www.rfidnews.org/weblog/2003/10/20/sponsored-feature-a-vision-for-rfid-instore-consumer-observational-research/.
51. Ibid., p. 11.
52. See the letter from the Article 29 Working Party Chairman to the FTC Director of Consumer Protection, July 15, 2004, available at http://www.ftc.gov/os/comments/rfid-workshop/508920-0044.pdf.
53. http://www-1.ibm.com/industries/wireless/doc/content/news/pressrelease/872647104.html.
54. http://www.eweek.com/article2/0,3959,1229567,00.asp.
55. http://www.4verichip.com/nws_10132004FDA.html.
56. Commission Press Release on its report, "Security and privacy for the citizen in the Post-September 11 digital age: A prospective overview," October 6, 2003, http://europa.eu.int/rapid/start/cgi/guesten.ksh?p_action.gettxt=gt&doc=IP/03/1344%7C0%7CRAPID&lg=EN.
57. CASPIAN et al., "Position Statement on the Use of RFID Technology on Consumer Goods," available at http://www.privacyrights.org/ar/RFIDposition.html.
58. Working Party, 2005, pp. 2–3.
59. For the FTC transcripts, see http://www.ftc.gov/bcp/workshops/rfid/transcript.pdf, and for the House Hearings statements, see http://energycommerce.house.gov/108/Hearings/07142004hearing1337/hearing.html.
60. http://www.rundeep.co.uk/new/knowledge/papers_picturephone.asp.

8

Implications for the Future

One of the biggest misperceptions about the European Data Protection Directive and the Safe Harbor Agreement was that these conflicts were primarily about privacy preferences. According to conventional wisdom, the Europeans, because of the horrific legacy of past abuses in several member states, had created a privacy directive that did not balance the right to privacy against other freedoms. Consequently, the "unbalanced" nature of the European Data Protection Directive was often played up in US debates, despite the explicit exemptions for press and security freedoms, and a lack of complaints from European journalists, or other interested parties.[1] Framing the issue as privacy made it possible politically to relegate the issue to a subset of interested parties. This ensured that it would primarily be the US lawyers who would speak about the issues, and legal questions would take priority over policy questions. The transatlantic data privacy conflict, however, was about much more than privacy. It was about who owns personal information that is potentially valuable, and what anyone can do with that information. An opt-in system (wherein the default position is "no marketing") confers property rights to the individual. An opt-out system (which prescribes the default position that businesses may use the personal information unless told not to) accords property rights to businesses. As one economist stated: "the assignment of property rights could alter the distribution of net benefits, even if that assignment had no effect on efficiency."[2] The larger transatlantic conflict was which party would bear the burden of acting: would businesses have to spend money contacting individuals to obtain their approval to use their information (or to give individuals incentives to allow use of that information), or would individuals have to expend time and effort to be removed from marketing lists?[3] It was very much about money, and there was a great deal at stake for some businesses.[4]

Safe Harbor as Privacy Agreement

"We pretend to work and they pretend to pay us," was a quip in Communist East Germany before the 1989 fall of the Wall. It expressed very well a modus vivendi between workers and businesses in the attempt to keep up the appearance of a well functioning economy. The Safe Harbor Agreement had many of the same characteristics: both the EU Commission and the US Department of Commerce wanted to give the appearance of protecting Europeans' privacy, but whether or not it was actually fully protected was relatively unimportant to both. The chief goal of the Safe Harbor Agreement was to keep data flowing between the two economic regions, and that purpose was achieved.

This utilitarian characterization of Safe Harbor should not come as a surprise. In Europe, the Commission chose to house the Data Protection Group in the Internal Market Directorate General, and in the US, the chief negotiator was from the Department of Commerce. There were other parts of the Commission that might have had greater expertise over, or synergies with, data protection. Although initially data protection had to be housed in the Internal Market Directorate General because the first draft of the European Data Protection Directive originated before the Maastricht Treaty allowed political initiatives, a more logical place to lodge the Data Protection Unit in the long run might have been the Information Society Directorate General, which was set up as part of the Commission's action plan on Europe's way to the Information Society in 1994. In that Directorate General, trade-offs between the EU's development of e-commerce and strict privacy rights (to the extent that there is a trade-off, which some dispute) might have had more substantive discussions, and negotiations between the EU and the US on privacy might have been led by more people willing to listen to the recommendations of the Article 29 Working Party at the risk of a disruption of data flows.

On the US side, by having the Department of Commerce take the lead on the negotiations with the Europeans, the Clinton administration also explicitly framed the problem as a commercial dispute rather than an opportunity to build greater privacy rights in at the federal level.[5]

It was, therefore, logical that both sides in the EU-US negotiations perceived the avoidance of a costly trade war as their primary duty rather than the preservation of Europeans' (or Americans') data privacy. Safe Harbor embodies that trade calculus rather than being a privacy regime for the US. It is important to recall that other countries were more attentive to the pro-privacy arguments, and, therefore, reacted differently: Canada passed its Personal Information Protection and Electronic Documents Act (PIPEDA) in 2000, and other countries introduced comprehensive privacy legislation for the first time in response to the European Data Protection Directive.

The US was an international outlier in that it did not contemplate adding greater privacy protection.

From the beginning, the US government had refused to consider supporting a federal data protection law. Given that a significant majority of the US public told pollsters that they would like greater privacy protection from the government, especially on the Internet, why did this issue not resonate with the President and the Congress? The answer to that question is not historical and cultural aversion to regulation. The more accurate answer is that, in the US, the issue was handled exclusively by the telecommunications and high tech industry, which was a major contributor to the Clinton administration's 1996 re-election campaign. Moreover, with their specialized knowledge of the technology and its promise, the Clinton administration's impulse to allow these industries to participate in writing the rules was understandable. Add to that the fact that relations with Congress in the crucial 1998–2000 period were marred by the Monica Lewinsky scandal, and one can see why the Clinton administration's willingness to propose a major legislative initiative in the area of privacy protection was sharply curtailed.

It may, however, seem strange that a politician under siege would not want to get the attention of the public by proposing legislation that has substantial popular support. Public opinion polls showed significant majorities in favor of greater privacy protection (primarily on the Internet, the focus of most polls), and more than 50 percent of Americans favored the government to step in and regulate. In one 2001 poll, 64 percent of the respondents said, ". . . the government should develop rules to protect people when they are on the Internet, even if it requires some regulation of the Internet," and in another question, 58 percent of the respondents believed that "businesses and people on the Internet can't be trusted to regulate themselves."[6] (To put these polling numbers into context, a January 1992 poll showed that 58 percent of the respondents were somewhat, or very, dissatisfied with the quality of health care in the US generally,[7] and the Clinton administration interpreted these numbers as a huge mandate to restructure the health care industry in its first term.) If one considers the foreign pressure from the EU, one could have imagined a window of opportunity for a sweeping federal level privacy law that would preempt potentially fifty different state-level privacy laws.

Privacy, however, was not an issue that was electorally useful since, at the elite level, there were no real party differences. People would not vote based on perceptions of candidates' records on privacy because neither candidate had a lock on the public's "pro-privacy" perception. In a 2000 poll asking "Which presidential candidate, Gore or Bush, do you trust to do a better job protecting people's privacy on the Internet?" 40 percent answered Bush, while 39 percent answered Gore, with another 21 percent answering "both," "neither," or "no opinion."[8] In 2004, the question asked which candidate "would do a better job protecting ordinary citizens from government invasions of their privacy," and again the results were relatively close, with 49 percent of the respondents saying Kerry, and 40 percent saying Bush.[9] Thus, privacy legislation posed the political risk of alienating key industry sectors without much electoral benefit.

In principle, the issue became more salient following the erosion of privacy in the name of public security after the September 11 attacks on the US. With federal legislation (US Patriot Act) programs (Total Information Awareness,[10] and the Computer Assisted Passenger Prescreening System, or CAPPS II[11]), voters were increasingly confronted with the privacy issues, raising the issue's electoral visibility. Again, however, the pro-privacy coalition of legislators fighting the Bush administration's proposals was bipartisan. When the amendment to discontinue the funding for the Department of Defense's Total Information Awareness Program was attached to a defense appropriations bill, the bill was passed unanimously in the Senate. When the Senate voted to prevent the deployment of CAPPS II until the General Accounting Office made its report, the vote was taken as a voice vote.[12] On privacy issues related to security, there was a bipartisan coalition of lawmakers that confronted the more privacy invasive proposals. On commercial privacy, there was no lawmaker consensus since money and interests were involved. In those issues, grass-roots activism forced state-level action because of the lack of success at the federal level.

■ The International Privacy Regime

Personal data privacy has remained a relevant issue at the international level because there continue to be new technologies and applications that challenge existing rules and practices. External circumstances and technological advances combine to put pressure on the viability, effectiveness, and desirability of privacy laws and policies of states. However, policymakers do not react to these exogenous influences with complete policy freedom: they are constrained by existing laws, information practices, and international regimes.[13] Moreover, as Pierson (2000) argued, the constraints on policy freedom actually tighten over time since decisions made early in the evolution of new policy regimes are more significant than those made later. It becomes increasingly difficult to change the framing of the issues once an edifice of laws and practices has been created. This is why the EU's creation of an international data protection regime is important.

This book is a detailed examination of an uncommon occurrence:[14] in the 1990s, the EU was able to create an international data protection regime without multilateral negotiations or the agreement of the US, arguably the most important state in the technological world. In order to understand this state of affairs, the provenance of the European Data Protection Directive, Europe's standard, and the world's reaction to its cross border provisions were traced and analyzed. Although it is true that the parameters of the international regime were essentially created twenty years earlier in the OECD Guidelines on the Protection of Privacy and Transborder Flows of Personal Data and the Council of Europe Convention for the Protection of Individuals with Regard to Automatic Processing of Personal Data, the codification of the principles that countries had agreed to in the 1970s proved to be more contentious than would have been expected, in view of that consensus. Thus, despite the fact that Bennett (1992) shows significant convergence of domestic data protection principles in the late 1980s among OECD countries, the process of implementing them formally into legal arrangements showed a marked divergence of preferences. The process of creating formal international arrangements proved to be more difficult than Bennett's analysis suggested, and provides the basis for this book's puzzle.

The fact that an international regime for data protection was ultimately created on the model of the European Union's preferences is an important lesson in how these regimes can be established despite the lack of participation of very powerful states in the international system. In effect, this turns the original research question of regime theory, "Is a hegemon necessary to form a regime, or can it be done without a hegemon?"[15] on its head: "Can a regime be created despite the wishes of the hegemon?" With contentious debates surrounding the US role in the world, leading to very different conclusions, it is perhaps wise to sidestep the issue of hegemony generally, and focus more narrowly on the US role in the emergent information technology sector, wherein the US in 1990 arguably had a preponderance of power. Thus, one might have presumed that the US would be able to disproportionately incorporate its preferences into any regime that impacts that sector, like data protection. Ultimately, however, as this book reveals, although the US was quite successful in the negotiations of the Passenger Name Record Agreement, and in preventing many of the international data protection regime elements it opposed from being applied to its data transfers within the Safe Harbor Agreement, it was not able to prevent the EU from getting others to join its emergent international data protection regime, and from becoming relatively isolated in its position on data protection. This is a somewhat surprising result. If one had just examined the facts as they stood in 1990, predicting this particular outcome would have been unlikely.

The success of the EU in creating an international data protection regime is significant because there is evidence that the creation of an international regime in an emerging issue area like data protection "locks in" certain norms, ideas, or practices, which make it more difficult to reverse later. This suggests that negotiating at the beginning of a regime is less risky than not participating in the regime, and hoping it will fail. Thus, to the extent that data protection regimes will evolve over time, while responding to external events (e.g., terrorism) and advances in technology (e.g., RFID) there is a greater likelihood that policy makers will react by tweaking existing laws and practices to make them appropriate to the new circumstances rather than scrapping wholesale the existing legal infrastructure. Pierson calls this the "increasing returns to scale" argument in politics:

> In an increasing returns process, the probability of further steps along the same path increases with each move down that path. This is because the *relative* benefits of the current activity compared with other possible options increase over time. To put it a different way, the costs of exit—of switching to some previously plausible alternative—rise.[16]

Others[17] have noted that technological issues are particularly prone to increasing returns processes, on account of the inherent complexity and uncertainty. Pierson agrees that international technology policy should be especially prone to increasing returns arguments: "There are good reasons to think that increasing returns processes are widespread in politics, since they will be characteristic in institutional development, collective action, the exercise of authority, and the emergence of our understandings of the political world."[18] Finally, one of the salient features of the increasing returns arguments is that timing and sequence matter, "because earlier parts of the sequence matter more than later parts, an event that happens "too late" may have no effect, although it might have been of great consequence if the timing had been different."

This book takes seriously the arguments about sequence and timing in the creation of an international data privacy regime. It analyzes why the EU created the European Data Protection Directive, and how that harmonization of European laws was able to forge a de facto international privacy regime that most advanced industrialized countries except the US participated in. The analytical lens of the book supports Krasner's conception that power does matter in regimes (namely, which countries are forced to bear the costs of adapting to the regime), but elaborates the sources of that power more closely than a strictly realist account that only looks at the international level. It also shows the limitations of power by detailing the timing of the decisions. By shifting the focus to the domestic groups or institutions that create the negotiating positions of states to begin with, and noting which are helped or hindered by foreign pressure, this book reaches four main conclusions:

1. The US and the EU disagreed about personal data protection regulations, not because of fundamentally different cultural or historical approaches to regulation or commerce, but because different, and opposing, interest groups in each government were the source of the government's negotiating position.
2. Although the US was able to avoid complying with the EU's preferences for omnibus privacy legislation, other states were not able to negotiate a hybrid system because domestic business interest groups did not completely resist comprehensive privacy legislation (certainly market power played a significant role there), and because they did not have easy or exclusive access to their country's negotiators to shape their positions.
3. The EU's data protection standards have become a de facto international privacy regime for commercial data because they were the first to implement the OECD Guidelines, and thus, the standards were adopted by a critical mass of countries. Therefore, the costs of an alternative standard have risen relative to accepting the status quo, even if, hypothetically, an alternative standard were technically superior. This suggests that in the long run, it would be more difficult for the US to change the international regime, even if it had a better system.
4. The effectiveness of business self-regulatory privacy protection was not definitely confirmed or disconfirmed in the first four years of Safe Harbor, but the fact that most other countries elected not to utilize it as a significant part of their privacy protection implies that its usefulness as a regulatory device was limited.

Each of these points will be examined in turn below.

■ The Source of the Transatlantic Conflict

Imagine a completely different, counterfactual scenario about international data protection in the 1990s:

The EU Commission realized that the disruption of data flows among member states was hindering the single market, and called on business groups and data protection authorities to work together to draft legislation based on the OECD Guidelines. The legislation reflected a greater compromise on the relatively few issues that were considered antibusiness (see Chapter 3 for more details), but still considered data protection a fundamental human right, implying it could not be sold, manipulated, profiled, etc. When the US negotiators met with EU Commission officials to discuss the cross border implications, they contemplated two different ideas, a multilateral treaty that would bind all countries to a similar level of regulation, or a comprehensive privacy bill that would cover all sectors in the US not already covered by specialized sectoral privacy legislation, and thus, meet the EU's adequacy standard. In the US there was significant popular interest in greater privacy protection, meaning that a majority (60 percent and upward) of the US public favored greater privacy regulation by the government. Although some business groups, like the Direct Marketing Association, were against it since it threatened their entire business model, most businesses were weakly supportive, or neutral, because the new standard held all their competitors to the same data protection standards, and these standards were not administratively intensive.

In the counterfactual scenario above, there is no US-EU data protection conflict. The outcome gives US businesses certainty about regulatory standards throughout most of the world, and preempts potential state laws that would impose greater obligations on the businesses. The public is aware that their personal data are covered by a minimum standard, that is, they are not being sold or transferred without their consent, and learns to shop on the Internet with confidence.

Could the international data privacy issue have been so easily resolved? Critics might dismiss the version above as Panglossian, but this counterfactual scenario meets the six criteria for judging counterfactuals, as proposed by Tetlock and Belkin (1996).[19] The public, in both the US and the EU, had similar progovernment regulation opinions, belying explanations that put US-EU cultural differences at the root of the conflict.

The difference between this counterfactual scenario and reality was the inclusion of a limited number of participants in the formulation of each side's negotiation position. In the EU's case, the Commission only consulted privacy experts without taking serious note of the practical implications of the proposal, and the US only consulted antiregulation interests. In both cases, this lack of consultation was due to the nature of the decisionmaking institution: both the EU Commission and the US Department of Commerce were bureaucratic, rather than legislative, institutions that did not have to obtain the assent of wider set of interests.

The issue of data protection is hardly the stuff of high politics. Even within the EU, the issue was negotiated out of the limelight over five years, rising to the top of the EU's agenda only after the Greek and German Presidencies in 1994 made them a legislative priority. Similarly, the potential trade problems created by the Directive were handled primarily by bureaucrats rather than heads of state. Nowhere in these pages is there evidence that the top levels of governments or heads of state were ever seriously exercised about the European Data Protection Directive. The chief negotiator of the Safe Harbor Agreement had little guidance from the Clinton White House about how to handle this commercial dispute.[20] All this is rather different from traditional treaty negotiations in which governments appoint negotiators who usually have carefully delineated instructions, and are almost always constrained, either by narrowly circumscribed positions or, more frequently, by the need to domestically ratify the treaty that they negotiate. Data protection, by contrast, was handled by technocrats and bureaucrats.

If there is a downside to the "politics of bureaucrats" that the US-EU negotiations represented, it is that the policies are affected by organized or specialized interests to a much greater extent than most treaty negotiations would be. This is partly due to the nature of highly specialized and often technical or arcane details around which the negotiations revolve. It is also partly due to the invisibility of the negotiation process to the public; no specific representatives of civil society are included at the negotiation table or in a ratification vote. However, in this case, most of the downside of bureaucratic politics was the fact that the affected interests had more of a stake in the outcome, had more resources to bring to bear on decisionmakers, and had greater access to the decisionmakers than the public. This aspect of regulatory politics was noted by Olson more than thirty years ago, and remains valid in the US today.[21]

As the case study of the European Data Protection Directive reveals, however, the Olsonian account of this dynamic between lawmakers and interests is not universal. In the US, where the state is often seen as highly permeable to special interest input into legislative politics, the Olsonian explanation is highly applicable. However, in other countries where the state is able to articulate preferences independently, and speak more authoritatively for the public good, special interests have much less access and input.[22] The EU Commission asked the expert committee (in this case, the national data protection authorities) to take the leading role in drafting the Directive, while explicitly excluding business groups. Subsequently, although there was considerable lobbying by interest groups after the Commission had made its first proposal in 1990, the changes made to accommodate the business interests were minimal, and the Council of Ministers passed the Directive with only one abstention (the UK). The right to data privacy eventually became a fundamental human right at the EU level, incorporated into the EU's Charter of Fundamental Rights in 2000, and into the new EU Constitution.

In contrast to the process within the EU, the US business lobby was highly effective in preventing comprehensive privacy legislation in the US on account of its significant access to the architects of the Clinton administration's position. Comprehensive privacy legislation could have been a realistic possibility, as the Chairman of the Article 29 Working Party pointed out to members of the US House of Representatives: ". . . many highly sensitive issues and topics are being dealt with in the USA by means of legislative tools, as shown by the many laws passed in the US at the State level and by the Executive Order issued by Clinton on 8 February, 2000 to prohibit the use of genetic data for federal employees."[23] Moreover, public opinion was highly supportive of government regulation in this area. Thus, it was not a foregone conclusion that legislative solutions were impossible, but an administration policy decision to exclude that option.

That policy decision was driven almost entirely by the preferences of the technology industry. Ira Magaziner's 1997 Framework for Global Electronic Commerce paper was primarily written by technology firm lobbyists, and it provided the blueprint for the US response to the European Data Protection Directive. When industry groups did not come up with self-regulatory systems fast enough to make the Clinton administration's self-regulatory negotiation position credible in Europe, the Commerce department threatened business groups that the administration would not be able to hold off the gathering forces in favor of government regulation for very long. This had the desired effect of mobilizing the technology industry to finally create some structures that could be presented to the Europeans. Likewise, when issues like the viability and success of industry self-regulation were discussed at a White House Internet Privacy summit in June 1998, proconsumer privacy organizations had to resort to public letters expressing their frustration with the conference agenda and invited speakers, which they perceived as resolutely proindustry:

> If the Department of Commerce has the staff and resources to meet with and organize on behalf of industry groups, it must expend at least as much energy soliciting public opinion and making possible meaningful public input in the planning of a national conference on privacy. This function cannot be delegated to a particular stakeholder or group of stakeholders.[24]

In the final analysis, the lack of comprehensive privacy legislation in the US was primarily due to the influence of the technology sector in formulating the US position, and Clinton administration officials never seriously consulted pro-privacy interests in the matter. Conversely, in the EU, only pro-privacy interests were consulted in the drafting of the legislation, while proindustry views were systematically excluded. The conflict was a result of these different interests having a quasi-monopoly on the creation of the government's position.

■ Other International Reactions

The second argument of this book is that almost none of the other countries reacted by rejecting comprehensive privacy legislation. Over time, even those that initially hoped they could make do with a similar business self-regulatory system as the US, changed their policy to pass omnibus privacy legislation. The sudden interest in privacy legislation throughout the world in the late 1990s was almost exclusively due to the pressure brought about by the EU's Directive. Although popular support of greater government regulation was evident in most countries, the impetus for governments to craft or amend privacy legislation was provided by the EU's threat to halt data transfers if data privacy adequacy was not met. Moreover, in all of the countries examined, the credible threat of market exclusion from the enormous EU market drove business preferences in the same direction as popular preferences. Only in Japan, where business also held a privileged position in the decisionmaking process, did they initially propose a self-regulatory plan. By 2003, however, even the Japanese parliament had passed an omnibus privacy law, and was negotiating with the EU Commission about an adequacy ruling.

The effect of so many other countries passing privacy laws that broadly reflected the European Data Protection Directive was that it had become the de facto international standard. "The European Union's Data Protection Directive has become a benchmark by which many jurisdictions measure the adequacy of their data-transfer controls," stated an international law firm in its 2003 survey of multinational data protection laws.[25] The firm also reported that, although there was significant variation in the data protection laws within the EU as well as in other jurisdictions trying to obtain an adequacy ruling, many multinational firms were using the EU's standards on all of their data, assuming it was the gold standard that would meet the regulatory requirements of other countries.[26]

Thus, in effect, the EU did use its market power, as Shaffer (2000) suggests, to get other countries to adopt similar protections for Europeans' data, but that power was created by giving foreign businesses the incentives to align behind a common standard, rather than by the absence of regulation. This nuance is important because it separates the issue area of data protection from other areas, such as financial market regulation or accounting standards (for example), in which the EU could not force an international standard on other non-US countries. If the US had had its own comprehensive data protection standard that was different from the EU's, it would have been difficult, if not impossible, for the EU to compel other countries to adopt its standard over that of the US. As it was, however, the absence of comprehensive commercial privacy laws in the US made the EU's demands viable, and, for most countries, gave businesses the impetus to align with domestic pro-privacy consumer interests, and establish privacy legislation.

■ First Mover Advantage

Closely linked to the above point is the fact that the EU was the first large "country" to force other countries doing business with its citizens to safeguard their data, giving the EU the "first-mover advantage." From the perspective of the negotiations about an international standard, the creation of demand motivates other countries to decide whether or not to comply. If the threat of limiting market access is credible, most countries will choose to avoid noncompliance (as was the case here). However, the subsequent decision after that is whether to comply by means of negotiating a different standard, or whether to acquiesce to the standard demanded. Arguably, the decision of whether or not to negotiate a different standard is correlated with commercial power: if the other country could cause the EU commercial pain, it was in a position to negotiate an alternative proposal, but if it did not, it had less of a realistic opportunity to negotiate a different approach.[27] As this book shows, only the US was in a position to create a different approach to data protection, and one that was barely acceptable to the EU as a whole. All of the other countries ultimately tried to pass omnibus legislation to broadly comport with the requirements of the Europeans.

There are two aspects of this first-mover problem to note: first, research on product standardization has shown that the first-mover advantage can lead to the first standard being adopted as the international standard since it provides a focal point around which other businesses can plan with certainty; and second, it does not necessarily ensure the emergence of the best technological standard.[28] Once that standard has been adopted, however, even a technologically superior standard is unlikely to break the path dependency built by all the adopters of the earlier standard. Data protection legislation is not product standardization, and therefore, to some extent, the argument has less applicability because it is not integral to further products in exactly the same way as the product technologies around which the economic literature is based. However, there are certain commonalities: first, it is politically difficult to legislate; thus, to the extent that countries and politicians have invested in privacy legislation, alternative legislation would be seen as costly, as the incremental changes would not necessarily be deemed worth the political effort and capital. Moreover, after privacy is legislated to mimic the EU's Directive, companies make changes to their information technology systems and operating procedures, and governments create new institutions to deal with data protection. Changing their systems to another legislative environment would, therefore, entail costs of adoption similar to those faced by technological changes, and make most businesses less enthusiastic about the alternative. Thus, even if, as many US businesses argued, the European data privacy standards were impractical in a networked world, the fact that most of the world adopted similar legislation would make any new US standard, even a better one, extremely difficult to propagate.

■ The Efficacy of Business Self-Regulation

The fourth point this book makes is that much of the new governance literature about self-regulation being the most promising method for effectively resolving cross border regulatory differences may be wrong.[29] This case study, a single but prominent case, does not provide evidence that business self-regulation was a success, or that it proved its critics wrong and was, therefore, adopted by more states. On the contrary, even those states that were initially leaning toward business self-regulation of data protection eventually adopted government regulations.

It is important to recognize, however, that the lack of interest in other self-regulatory solutions to the EU's adequacy problems may have stemmed more from power considerations rather than the collective consensus that self-regulatory privacy protection was flawed. Indeed, the EU Commission discouraged other countries from thinking along the same lines as Safe Harbor because the US-EU agreement was so controversial within the EU institutions themselves. The European Parliament had never liked it, and the subsequent interim reports to the EU Commission about the functioning of Safe Harbor did nothing to dispel the European Parliament's initial skepticism. Thus, it was hardly surprising that the EU Commission would not want to go down that road again with another country.

There are two ways to argue about the efficacy of business self-regulation, leading to two different conclusions. To the proponents of the system, Safe Harbor was a compete success because of the virtual absence of complaints, and the successful resolution of the few that did emerge. The rate of complaints was certainly no higher than in Europe, and the US public's knowledge about privacy protections roughly mirrored that of the European Union citizens'. It was not the case that the European laws had made the European public more knowledgeable (in 2003, 68 percent of European citizens had never heard of the independent authorities that heard consumer complaints), or secure (64 percent tended to agree that they were worried about leaving personal information on the Internet) than the US. Thus, advocates of business self-regulation compared the results of the Safe Harbor Agreement to those of the European Data Protection laws, and concluded that they were equally effective.

To the detractors of the self-regulatory system, the similarity of the record of Safe Harbor and the European laws was irrelevant because of a fundamental flaw in the market mechanism per se in this issue area and the role of consumer awareness in the protection. While admitting that both the European and the US systems suffered from consumers' ignorance of their rights, the critics of self-regulation insisted that this information asymmetry fundamentally changed the market mechanism, rendering it ineffective. Consumers were ignorant of their rights or confused about the remedies, and thus, did not complain to the companies. In the EU context, consumer ignorance of rights could be ameliorated through education because the rights were similar throughout the EU. In the US, however, the consumer had to check each website each time they visited if they were to be informed,[30] and a rational consumer would not have the time (or in some cases legal education), to go through the extensive privacy notices on every page. Moreover, the privacy seal programs do not provide an absolute standard, instead verifying only that the company followed its posted privacy policies, which were often far from the EU's laws.[31] Thus, there was too much of a burden on the consumer to make self-regulation a plausibly effective regulatory mechanism. Finally, in the EU, individuals' privacy rights were protected despite their lack of awareness. This was not true in the US context.

Left underspecified in the discussion of critics and proponents of self-regulation is the issue of why consumers have been so lackadaisical about their data privacy rights. In both the US and the EU, citizens told pollsters that they are worried about data privacy, and think the government should do something about it, but in both areas citizens were also woefully under-informed about what has been done, and what they individually could do, to help protect their data privacy. This suggests fodder for both camps in the regulation dispute: the government regulation supporters insisted that this inaction meant that citizens could not absorb the information, either because not enough effort had gone into educating them, or because it was too technical for the most part, and therefore, the government should step in to protect their rights. For self-regulation proponents, the lack of consumer activism in this area reflected weaker-than-reported preferences for data protection, and therefore, a less restrictive, more individualistic framework was preferable to a general, highly restrictive one. By their logic, if data privacy was not worth anything to the individual, as demonstrated by the consumer's actions ("revealed preferences"), but was valuable to a company, then the company should be allowed to realize the economic benefits from that information.

■ Implications for the Future of Data Protection

One of the changes on the horizon is that more US businesses are expected to be amenable to federal level privacy regulation. In 1998, a significant coalition of businesses was determined to prevent privacy legislation in the US. However, the logic of their position has changed in the past six years. As discussed in Chapter 4, the greater administrative burden of proving compliance, for example, would accrue to all firms in a sector, meaning that the incentive to lobby against privacy legislation would theoretically be evenly distributed among firms in a sector and would equal the projected rise in costs. Thus, one expected to see (and indeed, did see) certain sectors, like the Direct Marketing Association and financial services, investing more money in defeating the privacy bills. However, the costs of compliance were not the reason most often cited against regulating privacy: the reason given by most businesses, regardless of sector, was that privacy legislation would stifle innovation in the newly emergent e-commerce sector. This answer was the most popular in prepared testimony by business interests before House and Senate committee hearings. It was designed to caution legislators against the unintended consequences of stricter privacy legislation.[32] It did not dwell on the distributional effects of the policy; it threatened the demise of a new and promising technology, an appeal that would resonate beyond partisan or geographic boundaries. A recent example of this answer was given by the US Electronics Association's Senior Vice President in charge of Congressional affairs:

> The role of government is to be the balance point in the middle—assuring that effective and enforceable solutions are implemented fairly, without jeopardizing the beneficial uses of this information by online companies. Caution must also be taken to assure against the adoption of burdensome regulations that could impede the continued growth of online commerce or patchwork state level solutions that are neither consonant nor enforceable across a borderless medium. The imposition of stringent privacy regulations on the Internet could severely slow down the projected e-commerce growth . . . Poorly crafted legislation will translate into higher consumer costs, fewer online services, and less free content—thus hurting the same consumers such legislation intends to benefit.[33]

In practice, however, it is difficult to find examples of the lack of privacy protection in e-commerce leading to new and innovative products. Leaving aside the question of whether or not greater privacy would actually increase the amount of e-commerce, as many studies have suggested, it is not evident that a lack of privacy protection has created more business opportunities, innovation, markets, or products. Over time, therefore, the potency of this argument has declined with a corresponding increase of popular interest in privacy legislation (as evinced by the growing number of state privacy bills).

Another factor changing the costs and benefits calculation is that the coalition against regulation has lost the financial services industry. The financial services industry, which had lobbied against the European Data Protection Directive, and stood to incur disproportionately greater costs of a European-style law,[34] is now bound by the Gramm-Leach-Bliley (GLB)

Act. Although the GLB Act is not as strict as the Europeans had wanted (it failed to obtain an adequacy ruling by the Commission), it may lend strength to financial services industry calls for a level playing field in the US. Add to that the increasing costs of identity fraud, which also disproportionately fall on financial services firms,[35] and a significant part of the coalition against federal privacy legislation is eliminated.

Finally, for most other businesses, the most compelling reason to have federal legislation, and the most prominent reason it might be passed in the next five years, is to harmonize existing state laws while preempting new ones. The threat of fifty different state standards unites two different types of businesses in favoring federal legislation: those that follow higher standards anyway, and do not want to incur the expense of ensuring compliance in separate jurisdictions, and those that want to preempt the higher set of privacy protections that states like North Dakota, California, and Minnesota have passed (in response to consumer initiatives). In the words of the American Electronics Association lobbyist: "The passage of Internet privacy legislation this past year in California and Minnesota highlights the growing need for preemption legislation. The inherent danger is both imminent and profound. Other states are now looking to make a template of these new laws—laws that are provincial in nature and unconcerned with their deleterious impact on interstate commerce."[36] There were signs, however, that there would be more state activism as the issue salience would grow and the federal level would not act. Each year between 2000 and 2003, more information privacy bills were introduced. In 2002, North Dakota consumer groups actually mobilized to hold a referendum on whether or not the state's opt-in privacy law should be overridden by federal legislation (in this case, the Gramm-Leach-Bliley Act, which incorporates an opt-out standard, but permits stricter state standards). Despite having been outspent six to one by the financial services lobby, the referendum passed with 73 percent approval.[37] The 2005 leak of more than 40,000 Americans' commercial and private data by ChoicePoint prompted renewed hearings in Congress and interest in new laws. The threat of more, and different, state-level privacy laws certainly increased businesses' willingness to contemplate federal level commercial privacy legislation.

■ Changes in the EU

In the EU, subtle changes are also afoot, especially in the Commission's attitude toward third country adequacy. Working under the assumption that a lot of data flows are transferred out of the EU in contravention of the Directive, the Commission indicated that it would like to increase the pace at which adequacy findings are made, and that it would make it easier to find industry codes of conduct, standard contractual clauses, or binding corporate rules that would render these transfers legal. Looking at the first detailed report on the implementation of the European Data Protection Directive in 2003, it was possible to discern a slight increase in the willingness of the Commission to compromise. There was a sense that the privacy hawks in the Article 29 Working Party were rejecting the good in order to wait for the perfect, and that by doing so, the EU was alienating countries trying to comply to a large extent. The Commission was concerned about the threat to the credibility of the data privacy regime if the member states and the Commission continued to look the other way in third country data transfers.

Ultimately, the international privacy regime that the EU created will likely not be as strict as it is on paper. Thus far, the experience has shown that although EU member states have been willing to fine violators of the domestic privacy laws, the enforcement of the more "administratively intensive" aspects of the laws is fairly lax. The EU has the right to amend the Directive after consultation with other interests, as is necessitated by changes in technology or practices. It would be unlikely, however, that the changes to the privacy regime would be dramatic. Many in Europe see the Directive and its adoption throughout the developed world as a reasonable success. It reflects a growing consensus among the European elite that the EU must project its values abroad, and fits with its broader global governance theme, as expressed in a section of the 2001 Commission White Paper on European Governance:

> The objectives of peace, growth, employment, and social justice pursued within the Union must also be promoted outside for them to be effectively attained at both European and global level. This responds to citizens' expectations for a powerful Union on a world stage. Successful international action reinforces European identity and the importance of shared values within the Union . . . To achieve these objectives, the Union needs to speak more with a single voice.[38]

The international privacy regime is a good example of this type of policy. However, the EU was able to achieve this outcome only because the US did not have a different privacy standard that would compete with the EU's, since the US negotiating position was captured by narrow special interests, and because the US did care whether other countries would adopt the EU standard, thereby isolating it. The final version of an international privacy regime is certainly not written yet, but it seems fair to say that the next analysis of international privacy will feature the European Data Protection Directive prominently.

■ Notes

1. See for example Westin, 1996. "Privacy approaches in the U.S. have been a product of the following: . . . the immense importance of the First [freedom of speech and press], Fourth [against unreasonable search and seizure], and Fifth Amendments [due process and right against self-incrimination] in our Bill of Rights in framing the ways we define and implement privacy rights and information-handling, and how our courts *balance* those rights with other compelling social interests."

2. Lacker, 2002, p. 10.

3. The story of the do-not-call registry is instructive in this context: businesses insisted that consumers appreciated the informational service provided by their telemarketers because the number of consumers opting out of telemarketing lists at the state level was low. Once the federal do-not-call registry was available and registered, over fifty-four million telephone numbers in three months, telemarketers challenged the list on free speech issues in court, and began to disseminate information about how much unemployment the success of this list would create. Ultimately, the telemarketing industry's terms of debate completely shifted when consumers found an effective way to prohibit marketing. This issue is also discussed in the "revealed preferences" section of this chapter.

4. The stakes may also be growing. A recent study (Odlyzko, 2003) suggests that one of the most significant economic consequences of the Internet's profiling capabilities in the long term will be differential pricing of most e-commerce goods. Already, airlines and computer retailers price differentially, depending on what they know of the buyer, and the only limiting factor to more and more price discrimination is whether it is easy to develop a secondary market for the goods involved. Thus, marketing per se may not be the only commercial value of personal information—it may go to creating different tiers of consumers, a tendency which economists would laud because of its inherent efficiencies, but which would strike many US citizens as discriminatory.

5. The Bush administration created a chief privacy officer within the DHS in 2002, the first statutory privacy officer in the federal government. (See http://www.cdt.org/testimony/20040210dempsey.shtml for the history of privacy officers within federal departments.)

6. Markle Foundation, 2001.

7. Aetna survey; January 1992 available from Powell Tate.

8. ABC News/Washington Post poll, July 24, 2000.

9. Gallup poll, March 2004.

10. For more information, see http://www.epic.org/privacy/profiling/tia/.

11. For more information, see http://www.eff.org/privacy/cappsii/.

12. Voice voting implies the issue was reasonably uncontroversial and the vote not close.

13. An excellent overview of the issues and governance regimes is Braman, 2004.

14. The EU has done extremely well in setting international product standards, according to Mattli and Büthe, 2003, because of its institutional structures that coordinate and inform more successfully than US structures. There is less evidence for EU setting other regimes, especially international regulatory regimes.

15. Keohane, 1984.

16. Pierson, 2000, p. 252.

17. Arthur, 1994; and David, 1985.

18. Pierson, 2000, p. 263.

19. Tetlock and Belkin, p. 18, describe the six criteria as follows: (1) Clarity, (2) Logical consistency and cotenability, (3) Historical consistency (minimal rewrite rule), (4) Theoretical consistency, (5) Statistical consistency, and (6) Projectability.

20. Ibid.

21. Olson, 1971.

22. The poster child for the strong state is France although recent scholarship (Levy, 1999) makes the case that even this characterization is overblown.

23. http://energycommerce.house.gov/107new/hearings/03082001Hearing49/print.html.

24. February 26, 1998; Joint Letter Regarding a Proposed White House Conference on Privacy available at http://www.epic.org/privacy/internet/daley_ltr_2_26_98.html.

25. Available at http://www.whitecase.com/article_raskopf_proliferation_of_data_privacy_laws_6_2003%20.pdf.

26. http://www.whitecase.com/article_cross_border_data_7_29_2003.html.

27. This was especially true since the adequacy ruling was not the sole means of compliance with the European Data Protection Directive. The more difficult standard contractual clauses were available to all, but were sufficiently unattractive to make this a last resort. Moreover, the EU Commission indicated to all that adequacy rulings were its preferred option.

28. For a good overview, see Paul David and Shane Greenstein, "The Economics of Compatibility Standards." *Economics of Innovation and New Technology* 1; no. 1. 1990.

29. There is emerging literature on self-regulation, especially dealing with the Internet or the information society generally (see Price and Verhulst, 2000). In this section, I reduce the discussion only to the main branch of self-regulation, business, or market self-regulation. For more on this approach, see Kamarck, 2002; Cutler et al., 1999; and Haufler, 2001.

30. Typical was this part of the Expedia.com privacy policy: "To provide and process the services you request, Expedia.com shares your personally identifiable information (PII) with our authorized service providers that perform certain services or functions on our behalf. We only share information about travel either reserved or purchased on Expedia.com. Our service providers need information about your traveler profile, as well as your credit card information, to process and confirm your travel reservation. These service providers will disclose information about your traveler profile to hotel, airline, cruise, rental car, and other travel suppliers whose products you have purchased. Like any other travel agent, this information must be shared with our travel suppliers to confirm your reservation and travel preferences. Although Expedia.com offers travel products from hotel, airline, cruise, rental car, and other travel suppliers that are reputable companies, *we have not placed limitations on these suppliers from using or disclosing your information without your permission. Therefore, we encourage you to review the information privacy practices of any travel suppliers whose products you purchase on Expedia.com.* In addition, these travel suppliers may also contact you as necessary to obtain additional information about your confirmed reservation."

31. A good example is from excerpts of the Yahoo.com privacy policy, last viewed October 21, 2004: " Yahoo! does not rent, sell, or share personal information about you with other people or nonaffiliated companies except . . . under the following circumstances:

- We provide the information to *trusted partners who work on behalf of or with Yahoo! under confidentiality agreements. These companies may use your personal information to help Yahoo! communicate with you about offers from Yahoo! and our marketing partners.* However, these companies do not have any independent right to share this information.
- We transfer information about you if Yahoo! is acquired by or merged with another company. In this event, Yahoo! will notify you before information about you is transferred and becomes subject to a different privacy policy. [But you cannot opt out.]
- Yahoo! displays targeted advertisements based on personal information. Advertisers (including ad serving companies) may assume that people who interact with, view, or click on targeted ads meet the targeting criteria—for example, women ages 18-24 from a particular geographic area.
- Yahoo! advertisers include financial service providers (such as banks, insurance agents, stock brokers, and mortgage lenders) and non-financial companies (such as stores, airlines, and software companies).
- Yahoo! works with vendors, partners, advertisers, and other service providers in different industries and categories of business. For more information regarding providers of products or services that you've requested please read our detailed reference links. [The "reference links" link has over fifty other web pages, each with its own privacy policy!]

32. I thank an anonymous reviewer for pointing out that the "stifle innovation" argument is best understood in the context of several decades of discussion of the deregulation of telecommunications that began in the 1970s, and was used by those in the US who were interested in deregulation for quite other reasons.

33. Palafoutas, 2002.

34. Studies on financial services costs: EU Commission study.

35. The FTC reported that approximately ten million consumers were the victims of identity fraud in 2002. The cost to businesses was approximately $48 billion (Federal Trade Commission, 2003).

36. Palafoutas, 2002.

37. http://www.state.nd.us/sec/Elections/2002/Primary/results/2002measure2.html.

38. Commission of the European Communities. 2001. White Paper on European Governance available at http://europa.eu.int/eur-lex/en/com/cnc/2001/com2001_0428en01.pdf.

Appendix A: Comparing the European Data Protection Directive and the OECD Guidelines

EU Data Protection Directive	OECD Guidelines
Article 2 Definitions For the purposes of this Directive: (a) 'personal data' shall mean any information relating to an identified or identifiable natural person ('data subject'); an identifiable person is one who can be identified, directly or indirectly, in particular by reference to an identification number or to one or more factors specific to his physical, physiological, mental, economic, cultural or social identity; (b) 'processing of personal data' ('processing') shall mean any operation or set of operations which is performed upon personal data, whether or not by automatic means, such as collection, recording, organization, storage, adaptation or alteration, retrieval, consultation, use, disclosure by transmission, dissemination or otherwise making available, alignment or combination, blocking, erasure or destruction; (c) 'personal data filing system' ('filing system') shall mean any structured set of personal data which are accessible according to specific criteria, whether centralized, decentralized or dispersed on a functional or geographical basis; (d) 'controller' shall mean the natural or legal person, public authority, agency or any other body which alone or jointly with others determines the purposes and means of the processing of personal data; where the purposes and means of processing are determined by national or Community laws or regulations, the controller or the specific criteria for his nomination may be designated	**Definitions** 1. For the purposes of these Guidelines: a) "data controller" means a party who, according to domestic law, is competent to decide about the contents and use of personal data regardless of whether or not such data are collected, stored, processed or disseminated by that party or by an agent on its behalf; b) "personal data" means any information relating to an identified or identifiable individual (data subject); c) "transborder flows of personal data" means movements of personal data across national borders.

EU Data Protection Directive	OECD Guidelines
by national or Community law; (e) 'processor' shall mean a natural or legal person, public authority, agency or any other body which processes personal data on behalf of the controller; (f) 'third party' shall mean any natural or legal person, public authority, agency or any other body other than the data subject, the controller, the processor and the persons who, under the direct authority of the controller or the processor, are authorized to process the data; (g) 'recipient' shall mean a natural or legal person, public authority, agency or any other body to whom data are disclosed, whether a third party or not; however, authorities which may receive data in the framework of a particular inquiry shall not be regarded as recipients; (h) 'the data subject's consent' shall mean any freely given specific and informed indication of his wishes by which the data subject signifies his agreement to personal data relating to him being processed.	
Article 3 Scope 1. This Directive shall apply to the processing of personal data wholly or partly by automatic means, and to the processing otherwise than by automatic means of personal data which form part of a filing system or are intended to form part of a filing system.	**Scope of Guidelines** 2. These Guidelines apply to personal data, whether in the public or private sectors, which, because of the manner in which they are processed, or because of their nature or the context in which they are used, pose a danger to privacy and individual liberties.
2. This Directive shall not apply to the processing of personal data: • in the course of an activity which falls outside the scope of Community law, [. . .]and in any case to processing operations concerning public security, defense, State security (including the economic well-being of the State when the processing operation relates to State security matters) and the activities of the State in areas of criminal law, • by a natural person in the course of a purely personal or household activity.	3. These Guidelines should not be interpreted as preventing: a) the application, to different categories of personal data, of different protective measures depending upon their nature and the context in which they are collected, stored, processed or disseminated; b) the exclusion from the application of the Guidelines of personal data which obviously do not contain any risk to privacy and individual liberties; or c) the application of the Guidelines only to automatic processing of personal data. 4. Exceptions to the Principles contained in Parts Two and Three of these Guidelines, including those relating to national sovereignty, national security and public policy ("ordre public"), should be: a) as few as possible, and b) made known to the public.

EU Data Protection Directive

Article 6

1. Member States shall provide that personal data must be: (a) processed fairly and lawfully; (b) collected for specified, explicit and legitimate purposes and not further processed in a way incompatible with those purposes. Further processing of data for historical, statistical or scientific purposes shall not be considered as incompatible provided that Member States provide appropriate safeguards; (c) adequate, relevant and not excessive in relation to the purposes for which they are collected and/or further processed; (d) accurate and, where necessary, kept up to date; every reasonable step must be taken to ensure that data which are inaccurate or incomplete, having regard to the purposes for which they were collected or for which they are further processed, are erased or rectified; (e) kept in a form which permits identification of data subjects for no longer than is necessary for the purposes for which the data were collected or for which they are further processed. Member States shall lay down appropriate safeguards for personal data stored for longer periods for historical, statistical or scientific use.

OECD Guidelines

Collection Limitation Principle

7. There should be limits to the collection of personal data and any such data should be obtained by lawful and fair means and, where appropriate, with the knowledge or consent of the data subject.

Data Quality Principle

8. Personal data should be relevant to the purposes for which they are to be used, and, to the extent necessary for those purposes, should be accurate, complete and kept up-to-date.

Purpose Specification Principle

9. The purposes for which personal data are collected should be specified not later than at the time of data collection and the subsequent use limited to the fulfilment of those purposes or such others as are not incompatible with those purposes and as are specified on each occasion of change of purpose.

Article 7

Member States shall provide that personal data may be processed only if:
(a) the data subject has unambiguously given his consent; or (b) processing is necessary for the performance of a contract to which the data subject is party or in order to take steps at the request of the data subject prior to entering into a contract; or (c) processing is necessary for compliance with a legal obligation to which the controller is subject; or (d) processing is necessary in order to protect the vital interests of the data subject; or (e) processing is necessary for the performance of a task carried out in the public interest or in the exercise of official authority vested in the controller or in a third party to whom the data are disclosed; or (f) processing is necessary for the purposes of the legitimate interests pursued by the controller or by the third party or parties to whom the data are disclosed, except where such interests are overridden by the interests for fundamental rights and freedoms of the data subject which require protection under Article 1(1).

Use Limitation Principle

10. Personal data should not be disclosed, made available or otherwise used for purposes other than those specified in accordance with Paragraph 9 except: a) with the consent of the data subject; or b) by the authority of law.

EU Data Protection Directive	OECD Guidelines
Article 9 Processing of personal data and freedom of expression Member States shall provide for exemptions or derogations from the provisions of this Chapter, Chapter IV and Chapter VI for the processing of personal data carried out solely for journalistic purposes or the purpose of artistic or literary expression only if they are necessary to reconcile the right to privacy with the rules governing freedom of expression.	[There is no comparable explicit exemption for the rights of freedom of expression or information.]
Article 10 Information in cases of collection of data from the data subject Member States shall provide that the controller or his representative must provide a data subject from whom data relating to himself are collected with at least the following information, except where he already has it: (a) the identity of the controller and of his representative, if any; (b) the purposes of the processing for which the data are intended; (c) any further information such as • the recipients or categories of recipients of the data, • whether replies to the questions are obligatory or voluntary, as well as the possible consequences of failure to reply, • the existence of the right of access to and the right to rectify the data concerning him in so far as such further information is necessary, having regard to the specific circumstances in which the data are collected, to guarantee fair processing in respect of the data subject.	**Openness Principle** 12. There should be a general policy of openness about developments, practices and policies with respect to personal data. Means should be readily available of establishing the existence and nature of personal data, and the main purposes of their use, as well as the identity and usual residence of the data controller.

EU Data Protection Directive

Article 12 Right of access
Member States shall guarantee every data subject the right to obtain from the controller:
(a) without constraint at reasonable intervals and without excessive delay or expense:

- confirmation as to whether or not data relating to him are being processed and information at least as to the purposes of the processing, the categories of data concerned, and the recipients or categories of recipients to whom the data are disclosed,
- communication to him in an intelligible form of the data undergoing processing and of any available information as to their source,
- knowledge of the logic involved in any automatic processing of data concerning him at least in the case of the automated decisions referred to in Article 15 (1);

(b) as appropriate the rectification, erasure or blocking of data the processing of which does not comply with the provisions of this Directive, in particular because of the incomplete or inaccurate nature of the data;
(c) notification to third parties to whom the data have been disclosed of any rectification, erasure or blocking carried out in compliance with (b), unless this proves impossible or involves a disproportionate effort.

Article 14 The data subject's right to object
Member States shall grant the data subject the right: (a) at least in the cases referred to in Article 7 (e) and (f), to object at any time on compelling legitimate grounds relating to his particular situation to the processing of data relating to him, save where otherwise provided by national legislation. Where there is a justified objection, the processing instigated by the controller may no longer involve those data; (b) to object, on request and free of charge, to the processing of personal data relating to him which the controller anticipates being processed for the purposes of direct marketing, or to be informed before personal data are disclosed for the first time to third parties or used on their behalf for the purposes of direct marketing, and to be expressly offered the right to object free of charge to such disclosures or uses. Member States shall take the necessary measures to ensure that data subjects are aware of the existence of the right referred to in the first subparagraph of (b).

OECD Guidelines

Individual Participation Principle
13. An individual should have the right: a) to obtain from a data controller, or otherwise, confirmation of whether or not the data controller has data relating to him; b) to have communicated to him, data relating to him within a reasonable time; at a charge, if any, that is not excessive; in a reasonable manner; and in a form that is readily intelligible to him; c) to be given reasons if a request made under subparagraphs *(a)* and *(b)* is denied, and to be able to challenge such denial; and d) to challenge data relating to him and, if the challenge is successful to have the data erased, rectified, completed or amended.

Accountability Principle
14. A data controller should be accountable for complying with measures which give effect to the principles stated above.

EU Data Protection Directive	OECD Guidelines
Article 18 Obligation to notify the supervisory authority 1. Member States shall provide that the controller or his representative, if any, must notify the supervisory authority referred to in Article 28 before carrying out any wholly or partly automatic processing operation or set of such operations intended to serve a single purpose or several related purposes. 2. Member States may provide for the simplification of or exemption from notification only in the following cases and under the following conditions: • where, for categories of processing operations which are unlikely, taking account of the data to be processed, to affect adversely the rights and freedoms of data subjects, they specify the purposes of the processing, the data or categories of data undergoing processing, the category or categories of data subject, the recipients or categories of recipient to whom the data are to be disclosed and the length of time the data are to be stored, and/or • where the controller, in compliance with the national law which governs him, appoints a personal data protection official, responsible in particular: for ensuring in an independent manner the internal application of the national provisions taken pursuant to this Directive; for keeping the register of processing operations carried out by the controller, containing the items of information referred to in Article 21 (2), thereby ensuring that the rights and freedoms of the data subjects are unlikely to be adversely affected by the processing operations. 3. Member States may provide that paragraph 1 does not apply to processing whose sole purpose is the keeping of a register which according to laws or regulations is intended to provide information to the public and which is open to consultation either by the public in general or by any person demonstrating a legitimate interest. 4. Member States may provide for an exemption from the obligation to notify or a simplification of the notification in the case of processing operations referred to in Article 8 (2) (d). 5. Member States may stipulate that certain or all non-automatic processing operations involving personal data shall be notified, or provide for these processing operations to be subject to simplified notification.	[There is no comparable notification policy, beyond what is stated in Section 12 (above)]

EU Data Protection Directive

Article 19 Contents of notification
1. Member States shall specify the information to be given in the notification. It shall include at least: (a) the name and address of the controller and of his representative, if any; (b) the purpose or purposes of the processing; (c) a description of the category or categories of data subject and of the data or categories of data relating to them; (d) the recipients or categories of recipient to whom the data might be disclosed; (e) proposed transfers of data to third countries; (f) a general description allowing a preliminary assessment to be made of the appropriateness of the measures taken pursuant to Article 17 to ensure security of processing.
2. Member States shall specify the procedures under which any change affecting the information referred to in paragraph 1 must be notified to the supervisory authority.

EU Data Protection Directive

Article 25 Principles

1. The Member States shall provide that the transfer to a third country of personal data which are undergoing processing or are intended for processing after transfer may take place only if, without prejudice to compliance with the national provisions adopted pursuant to the other provisions of this Directive, the third country in question ensures an adequate level of protection.
2. The adequacy of the level of protection afforded by a third country shall be assessed in the light of all the circumstances surrounding a data transfer operation or set of data transfer operations; particular consideration shall be given to the nature of the data, the purpose and duration of the proposed processing operation or operations, the country of origin and country of final destination, the rules of law, both general and sectoral, in force in the third country in question and the professional rules and security measures which are complied with in that country.
3. The Member States and the Commission shall inform each other of cases where they consider that a third country does not ensure an adequate level of protection within the meaning of paragraph 2.
4. Where the Commission finds, under the procedure provided for in Article 31 (2), that a third country does not ensure an adequate level of protection within the meaning of paragraph 2 of this Article, Member States shall take the measures necessary to prevent any transfer of data of the same type to the third country in question.
5. At the appropriate time, the Commission shall enter into negotiations with a view to remedying the situation resulting from the finding made pursuant to paragraph 4.
6. The Commission may find, in accordance with the procedure referred to in Article 31 (2), that a third country ensures an adequate level of protection within the meaning of paragraph 2 of this Article, by reason of its domestic law or of the international commitments it has entered into, particularly upon conclusion of the negotiations referred to in paragraph 5, for the protection of the private lives and basic freedoms and rights of individuals. Member States shall take the measures necessary to comply with the Commission's decision.

OECD Guidelines

15. Member countries should take into consideration the implications for other Member countries of domestic processing and re-export of personal data.

16. Member countries should take all reasonable and appropriate steps to ensure that transborder flows of personal data, including transit through a Member country, are uninterrupted and secure.

17. A Member country should refrain from restricting transborder flows of personal data between itself and another Member country except where the latter does not yet substantially observe these Guidelines or where the re-export of such data would circumvent its domestic privacy legislation. A Member country may also impose restrictions in respect of certain categories of personal data for which its domestic privacy legislation includes specific regulations in view of the nature of those data and for which the other Member country provides no equivalent protection.

18. Member countries should avoid developing laws, policies and practices in the name of the protection of privacy and individual liberties, which would create obstacles to transborder flows of personal data that would exceed requirements for such protection.

EU Data Protection Directive

Article 26 Derogations
1. By way of derogation from Article 25 and save where otherwise provided by domestic law governing particular cases, Member States shall provide that a transfer or a set of transfers of personal data to a third country which does not ensure an adequate level of protection within the meaning of Article 25 (2) may take place on condition that: (a) the data subject has given his consent unambiguously to the proposed transfer; or (b) the transfer is necessary for the performance of a contract between the data subject and the controller or the implementation of precontractual measures taken in response to the data subject's request; or (c) the transfer is necessary for the conclusion or performance of a contract concluded in the interest of the data subject between the controller and a third party; or (d) the transfer is necessary or legally required on important public interest grounds, or for the establishment, exercise or defence of legal claims; or (e) the transfer is necessary in order to protect the vital interests of the data subject; or (f) the transfer is made from a register which according to laws or regulations is intended to provide information to the public and which is open to consultation either by the public in general or by any person who can demonstrate legitimate interest, to the extent that the conditions laid down in law for consultation are fulfilled in the particular case.
2. Without prejudice to paragraph 1, a Member State may authorize a transfer or a set of transfers of personal data to a third country which does not ensure an adequate level of protection within the meaning of Article 25 (2), where the controller adduces adequate safeguards with respect to the protection of the privacy and fundamental rights and freedoms of individuals and as regards the exercise of the corresponding rights; such safeguards may in particular result from appropriate contractual clauses.
3. The Member State shall inform the Commission and the other Member States of the authorizations it grants pursuant to paragraph 2. If a Member State or the Commission objects on justified grounds involving the protection of the privacy and fundamental rights and freedoms of individuals, the Commission shall take appropriate measures in accordance with the procedure laid down in Article 31 (2). Member States

OECD Guidelines

[There is no comparable counterpart to the derogations from the onward transfer obligations]

EU Data Protection Directive

shall take the necessary measures to comply with the Commission's decision.
4. Where the Commission decides, in accordance with the procedure referred to in Article 31 (2), that certain standard contractual clauses offer sufficient safeguards as required by paragraph 2, Member States shall take the necessary measures to comply with the Commission's decision.

Appendix B: Synopsis of US Federal Privacy Legislation

The Fair Credit Reporting Act (1970) (updated in 1992): Congress enacted the Fair Credit Reporting Act ("FCRA") to protect consumers from the disclosure of inaccurate and arbitrary personal information held by consumer reporting agencies. While the FCRA regulates the disclosure of personal information, it does not restrict the amount or type of information that can be collected. Under the FCRA, consumer reporting agencies may disclose personal information to third parties under specified conditions only. Additionally, information may be released to a third party only with the written consent of the subject of the report, or when the reporting agency has reason to believe the requesting party intends to use the information:

1. For a credit, employment, or insurance evaluation
2. In connection with the grant of a license or other government benefit
3. For another "legitimate business need" involving the consumer

The Privacy Act of 1974: The Privacy Act of 1974 was designed to protect individuals from an increasingly powerful and potentially intrusive federal government. The statute was triggered by the report published by the Department of Health, Education and Welfare (HEW), which recommended a "Code of Fair Information Practices" to be followed by all federal agencies. The code emphasized five principles:

- There should be no records whose very existence is private.
- Individuals must be able to discover what information is contained in their record, and how it is used.
- Individuals must be able to prevent information collected for one purpose from being used for another purpose without their consent.

- Individuals must be able to correct or amend erroneous information.
- Any organization creating, maintaining, using, or disseminating records of identifiable personal data must ensure the reliability of the data for its intended purpose, and must take precautions to prevent misuse.

The Privacy Act incorporates the Code of Fair Information Practices recommended by HEW, and empowers individuals to control the federal government's collection, use, and dissemination of sensitive personal information. The act prohibits agencies from disclosing records to third parties or other agencies without the consent of the individual to whom the record pertains. The prohibition is, however, weakened by several exceptions. As early as 1977, the Privacy Protection Study Commission found that the Privacy Act was vague, and would likely not meet its stated purposes.

The Family Education Rights and Privacy Act (1974): Congress passed the Family Educational Rights and Privacy Act (also known as the Buckley Amendment) to protect the accuracy and confidentiality of student records; it applies to all schools receiving federal funding. The act prevents educational institutions from disclosing student records or personally identifiable information to third parties without consent, but does not restrict the collection or use of information by schools. The statute also requires educational institutions to give students and their parents access to school records, and an opportunity to challenge the content of records that they believe is inaccurate or misleading.

The Right to Financial Privacy Act (1978): The Right to Financial Privacy Act was designed to preserve the confidentiality of personal financial records by creating a statutory Fourth Amendment protection for bank records. The Right to Financial Privacy Act states that "no Government authority may have access to or obtain copies of, the information contained in the financial records of any customer from a financial institution unless the financial records are reasonably described," and:

- The customer authorizes access.
- There is an appropriate administrative subpoena or summons.
- There is a qualified search warrant.
- There is an appropriate judicial subpoena.
- There is an appropriate written request from an authorized government authority.

The statute prevents banks from requiring customers to authorize the release of financial records as a condition of doing business, and states that customers have a right to access a record of all disclosures.

The Privacy Protection Act of 1980: Congress enacted the Privacy Protection Act ("PPA") to reduce the chilling effect of law enforcement searches and seizures on publishers. The PPA prohibits government officials from searching or seizing any work product or documentary materials held by a "person reasonably believed to have a purpose to disseminate to the public a newspaper, book, broadcast, or other similar form of public communication," unless there is probable cause to believe the publisher has committed, or is committing, a criminal offense to which the materials relate. The PPA effectively forces law enforcement to use subpoenas or voluntary co-operation to obtain evidence from those engaged in First Amendment activities.

Many commentators believe the PPA extends protection to computer bulletin boards and online systems under the "other form of public communication" clause of the act. However, the only case to present this question to a court, *Steve Jackson Games, Inc. v. the United States Secret Service,* failed to resolve the issue. In *Steve Jackson Games,* the Secret Service seized a computer game publisher's electronic bulletin board system, e-mail, and electronic files to search for evidence involving an employee of the company. The court decided the PPA protected the seized property, but based its decision on the fact that the company published traditional books, magazines, and board games.

The Cable Communications Policy Act of 1984: The Cable Communications Act establishes a comprehensive framework for cable regulation, and sets forth strong protections for subscriber privacy by restricting the collection, maintenance, and dissemination of subscriber data. Congress passed the Cable Communications Policy Act ("1984 Cable Act" or "Cable Act") to amend the Communications Act of 1934. The act prohibits cable operators from using the cable system to collect "personally identifiable information" concerning any subscriber without prior consent, unless the information is necessary to render service or detect unauthorized reception. The act also prohibits operators from disclosing personally identifiable data to third parties without consent, unless the disclosure is either necessary to render a service provided by the cable operator to the subscriber, or if it is made to a government entity pursuant to a court order.

The Electronic Communications Privacy Act (1986): Congress passed the Electronic Communications Privacy Act ("ECPA") to expand the scope of existing federal wiretap laws, such as the Wiretap Act, to include protection for electronic communications. ECPA expands the privacy protections of the Wiretap Act in five significant ways:

1. ECPA broadens the scope of privileged communications to include all forms of electronic transmissions, including video, text, audio, and data.
2. ECPA eliminates the requirement that communications be transmitted via common carrier to receive legal protection.
3. ECPA maintains restrictions on the interception of messages in transmission and adds a prohibition on access to stored electronic communications.
4. ECPA responds to the Supreme Court's ruling in *Smith v. Maryland* that telephone toll records are not private, and restricts law enforcement access to transactional information pertaining to users of electronic communication services.
5. ECPA broadens the reach of the Wiretap Act by restricting both government and private access to communications.

The Video Privacy Protection Act of 1988: Congress passed the Video Privacy Protection Act in response to the controversy surrounding the release of Judge Robert Bork's video rental records during his failed Supreme Court nomination. The act prohibits video tape service providers from disclosing customer rental records without the informed, written consent of the consumer. Furthermore, the act requires video service providers to destroy personally identifiable customer information within a year of the date it is no longer necessary for the purpose for which it was collected. However, the act contains several exceptions and limitations.

The Telephone Consumer Protection Act of 1991: The Telephone Consumer Protection Act of 1991 ("TCPA") was enacted in response to consumer complaints about the proliferation of intrusive telemarketing practices and concerns about the impact of such practices on consumer privacy. The act amends Title II of the Communications Act of 1934, and requires the Federal Communications Commission ("FCC" or "Commission") to promulgate rules "to protect residential telephone subscribers' privacy rights." In response to the TCPA, the FCC issued a report and order requiring any person or entity engaged in telemarketing to maintain a list of consumers who request not to be called.

The Driver's Privacy Protection Act of 1994: Congress passed the Driver's Privacy Protection Act as an amendment to the Omnibus Crime Act of 1994; it restricts the public disclosure of personal information contained in the State Department of Motor Vehicles ("DMV") records. While Driver's Privacy Protection Act generally prohibits DMV officials from knowingly disclosing personally identifiable information contained in department records, it delineates several broad exceptions. In January, 2000, the Supreme Court unanimously upheld the act in the case of *Reno v. Condon*. The Court held that personal, identifying information from drivers' licenses and motor vehicle registrations is a "thing in interstate commerce" that can be regulated by Congress like any other commodity.

The Communications Assistance for Law Enforcement Act of 1994: Congress passed the Communications Assistance for Law Enforcement Act ("CALEA", also commonly known as the Digital Telephony Act) to preserve the government's ability, pursuant to court order or other lawful authorization, to intercept communications over digital networks. The act requires phone companies to modify their networks to ensure government access to all wire and electronic communications, as well as to call-identifying information. Privacy advocates were able to remove provisions from earlier drafts of the legislation that would have required online service providers to modify their equipment to ensure government access. The law also included several provisions enhancing privacy, including a section that increased the standard for government access to transactional data.

The Telecommunications Act of 1996: In the massive Telecommunications Act of 1996, Congress included a provision addressing widespread concern over telephone companies' misuse of personal records, requiring telephone companies to obtain the approval of customers before using information about users' calling patterns (or CPNI) to market new services. While the statute requires telephone companies to obtain approval before using customer's information, Congress did not specify how companies should obtain such approval. Responding to several requests from the telecommunications industry for guidance, the FCC issued an order interpreting the "approval" requirements in February 1998. Under the FCC's rule, telephone companies must give customers explicit notice of their right to control the use of their CPNI and obtain express written, oral, or electronic approval for its use. In August 1999, the US Court of Appeals for the Tenth Circuit abandoned the FCC privacy regulations regarding the use and disclosure of CPNI.

The Health Insurance Portability and Accountability Act of 1996: Congress created the first guarantee of a federal policy to govern the privacy of health information in electronic form by passing the Kennedy-Kassebaum Health Insurance Portability and Accountability Act. The act contains a section known as "Administrative Simplification," which mandates the development and adoption of standards for electronic exchanges of health information. It also requires that Congress or the Secretary of Health and Human Services develop privacy rules to govern such electronic exchanges; these rules, however, may not be in place before the electronic system is implemented. The provisions of the act mandating the speedy development and adoption of standards for electronic exchanges of health information are troublesome, given the lack of strong, enforceable laws protecting patient privacy; the act required either the Congress or the Executive Branch to enact privacy rules before August 21, 1999. In October 1999, after Congress failed to meet its self-imposed deadline, the Clinton administration issued the first set of federal privacy rules to protect medical information. The proposal, known as the Clinton-Gore initiative, aims to require consumer consent before companies share medical data or detailed information about consumer spending habits. The proposal also requires companies to disclose their privacy policies prior to engaging in data transactions with users.

The Children's Online Privacy Protection Act (COPPA) of 1998: Congress passed COPPA to protect children's personal information from its collection and misuse by commercial websites. On October 20, 1999, the Federal Trade Commission issued a Final Rule implementing the act, which went into effect on April 21, 2000. COPPA requires commercial websites and other online services directed at children twelve years and under, or which collect information regarding users' age, to provide parents with notice of their information practices, and obtain parental consent prior to the collection of personal information from children. The act further requires such sites to provide parents with the ability to review and correct information about their children collected by such services. COPPA was designed to ensure that the children's ability to speak, seek out information, and publish would not be adversely affected.

The Financial Services Modernization Act (Gramm-Leach-Bliley Act) (1999): The Gramm-Leach-Bliley Act regulates the sharing of personal information about individuals who obtain financial products or services from financial institutions. It attempts to inform individuals about the privacy policies and practices of financial institutions, so that consumers can use that information to make choices about the financial institutions with whom they wish to do business. The law gives consumers limited control, via opt-out, over how financial institutions use and share the consumers' personal information.

Source: Consumer Privacy Guide, available at http://www.consumerprivacyguide.org/law/

Bibliography

Aaron, David. 2001. Prepared Testimony Before the Subcommittee on Commerce, Trade, and Consumer Protection of the House Committee on Energy and Commerce. "Hearings on The EU Data Protection Directive: Implications for the U.S. Privacy Debate," March 8, 2001. available at http://energycommerce.house.gov/107/hearings/03082001Hearing49/Aaron102.html

Abbate, Janet. 2000. *Inventing the Internet.* Cambridge, MA: MIT Press.

Abbott, Kenneth, and Duncan Snidal. 2001. "International 'Standards' and International Governance," *Journal of European Public Policy* 8(3).

Agre, Philip E., and Marc Rotenberg, eds. 1998. *Technology and Privacy: The New Landscape.* Cambridge, MA: MIT Press.

Allen, Benjamin. 2002. "Consumption Taxation of Electronic Commerce: A Comparison of United States (US) and European Union (EU) Policies, 1997 to 2000." Ph.D. dissertation, George Mason University.

American Institute for Contemporary German Studies. 1998. *Protecting Privacy: The Transatlantic Debate over Data Protection.* Conference Report. Washington, DC available at http://www.aicgs.org/Publications/PDF/data.pdf

Annenberg Public Policy Center of the University of Pennsylvania. 2003. "Americans and Online Privacy: The System is Broken" available at http://www.appcpenn.org/reports/2003/turow-privacy-no-cover.pdf.

Austin, Marc T., and Helen V. Milner. 2001. Strategies of European Standardization, *Journal of European Public Policy* 8(3): 411–431.

Bainbridge, David. 1996. *EC Data Protection Directive.* London: Butterworths.

Bainbridge, David, et al. 1994. "An Evaluation of the Financial Impact of the Proposed European Data Protection Directive," Report to the European Commission.

Baird, Zoë. 2002. "Governing the Internet: Engaging Government, Business and Nonprofits," *Foreign Affairs* 81(6): 15–20.

Ballmann, Alexander, David Epstein, and Sharyn O'Halloran. 2002. "Delegation, Comitology, and the Separation of Powers in the European Union," *International Organization* 56(3): 551–574.

Bangemann, Martin, et al. 1994. "Europe and the Global Information Society: Recommendations to the European Council" available at http://europa.eu.int/ISPO/infosoc/backg/bangeman.html

Bellman, Steve, Eric J. Johnson, Stephen J. Kobrin, and Gerald L. Lohse. 2004.

"International Differences in Information Privacy Concerns: A Global Survey," *The Information Society* 20: 313–324.

Bennett, Colin J. 1992. *Regulating Privacy: Data Protection and Public Policy in Europe and the United States*. Ithaca, NY: Cornell University Press.

Bennett, Colin J., and Rebecca Grant, eds. 1999. *Visions of Privacy: Policy Choices for the Digital Age*. Toronto: University of Toronto Press, Inc.

Bennett, Colin J., and Charles D. Raab. 1997. "The Adequacy of Privacy: The European Union Data Protection Directive and the North American Response," *The Information Society* 13: 245–263.

Berger, Suzanne, and Ronald Dore, eds. 1996. *National Diversity and Global Capitalism*. Ithaca, NY: Cornell University Press.

Bergkamp, Lucas. 2002. "EU Data Protection Policy: The Privacy Fallacy: Adverse Effects of Europe's Data Protection Policy in an Information-Driven Economy," *Computer Law and Security Report* 18(1): 31–48.

Berners-Lee, Tim, with Mark Fischetti. 2000. *Weaving the Web: The Original Design and Ultimate Destiny of the World Wide Web by Its Inventor*. New York: HarperCollins, Inc.

Bhagwati, Jagdish. 2004. "Don't Cry for Cancun," *Foreign Affairs* 83(1): 52–63.

Bouwen, Pieter. 2002. "Corporate Lobbying in the European Union: the Logic of Access," *Journal of European Public Policy* 9(3): 365–390.

Braman, Sandra. 2004. "The Emergent Global Information Policy Regime," in Braman, ed. *The Emergent Global Information Policy Regime*. New York: Palgrave Macmillan Ltd.

Brühann, Ulf. 1999. "La Directive Européenne Relative à la Protection des Données: Fondement, Histoire, Points Forts," *Revue Française d'Administration Publique* 89: 7–19.

Business Week Harris Poll. 2000. "Privacy on the Net" available at http://businessweek.com/2000/00_12/b3673006.html

Cate, Fred H. 1995. "The EU Data Protection Directive, Information Privacy and the Public Interest," *Iowa Law Review* 80(3): 431–443.

———. 1997. *Privacy in the Information Age*. Washington, DC: Brookings Institution Press.

Clinton, William J., and Albert Gore, Jr. 1997. "Framework for Global Electronic Commerce" available at http://www.technology.gov/digeconomy/framewrk.html

Commission of the European Communities. 1990. Commission Communication on the Protection of Individuals in Relation to the Processing of Personal Data in the Community and Information Security. COM (90) 314 final. Brussels: 13 September, 1990.

———. 1997. "A European Initiative in Electronic Commerce," Communication to the European Parliament, the Council, the Economic and Social Committee and the Committee of the Regions. COM (97) 157. available at http://www.cordis.lu/esprit/src/ecomcom3.html

———. 2003. "First report on the implementation of the data privacy directive." COM (2003) 265 final available at http://europa.eu.int/eur-lex/en/com/rpt/2003/com2003_0265en01.pdf.

———. 2004. Commission Staff Working Document: The implementation of Commission Decision 520/2000/EC on the adequate protection of personal data provided by the Safe Harbour privacy principles and related Frequently

Asked Questions issued by the US Department of Commerce. available at http://europa.eu.int/comm/internal_market/privacy/docs/adequacy/sec-2004-1323_en.pdf.

Consumers International. 2001. "Privacy@Net: An International Comparative Study of Consumer Privacy on the Internet" available at http://www.consumersinternational.org/document_store/Doc30.pdf

Council of Europe. 1981. "Convention for the Protection of Individuals with Regard to Automatic Processing of Personal Data" (ETS No. 108) available at http://www.coe.int/T/E/Legal_affairs/Legal_co-operation/Data_protection/

Cowles, Maria Green. 2001. "Who Writes the Rules of E-Commerce? A Case Study of the Global Business Dialogue on e-Commerce (GBDe)," Washington, DC: American Institute for Contemporary German Studies Policy Paper #4.

Cranor, Lorrie Faith, Joseph Reagle, and Mark Ackerman. 1999. "Beyond Concern: Understanding Net Users' Attitudes About On-Line Privacy" available at http://www.research.att.com/resources/trs/TRs/99/99.4/99.4.3/report.html

Cummings, Maeve L., and Jan L. Guynes. 1994. "Information System Activities in Transnational Corporations: A Comparison of U.S. and Non-U.S. Subsidiaries," *Journal of Global Information Management* 1994, 2(1): 12–27.

Currie, Wendy. 2000. *Global Information Society.* New York: John Wiley and Sons, Ltd.

Cutler, A. Claire, Virginia Haufler, and Tony Porter, eds. 1999. *Private Authority and International Affairs.* Albany, NY: State University of New York Press.

Dhont, Jan, María Verónica Pérez Asinari, and Yves Poullet. 2004. "Safe Harbour Decision Implementation Study" available at http://europa.eu.int/comm/internal_market/privacy/docs/studies/safe-harbour-2004_en.pdf

Donahue, John D., and Joseph S. Nye, eds. 2002. *Market-Based Governance.* Washington, DC: Brookings Institution.

Drake, William J. 1993. "Territoriality and Intangibility: Transborder Data Flows and National Sovereignty," in Kaarle Nordenstreng and Herbert I. Schiller, eds., *Beyond National Sovereignty: International Communications in the 1990s.* pp. 259–313. Norwood: Ablex.

———. 1995. "The National Information Infrastructure Debate: Issues, Interests and the Congressional Process," in Drake, William J., ed., *The New Information Infrastructure: Strategies for U.S. Policy.* Washington, DC: Twentieth Century Fund, Inc.

Egan, Michelle. 2001. *Constructing a European Market.* Oxford: Oxford University Press.

Ellger, Reinhard. 1999. "Konvergenz oder Konflikt bei der Harmonisierung des Datenschutzes in Europa?" *Computer und Recht* 10: 558–69.

Eurostat. 2004. *Yearbook, 2004.* Luxembourg: European Communities available at http://epp.eurostat.cec.eu.int/cache/ITY_OFFPUB/KS-CD-04-001-3/EN/KS-CD-04-001-3-EN.PDF.

Evenett, Simon J., Alexander Lehmann, and Benn Steil, eds. 2000. *Antitrust Goes Global: What Future for Transatlantic Cooperation?* Washington, DC: Brookings Institution Press.

Farrell, Henry. 2002. "Negotiating Privacy across Arenas – The EU-US "Safe Harbor" Discussions," in Adrienne Héritier, ed., Common Goods: Reinventing European and International Governance. Lanham, MD: Rowman and Littlefield Publishers, Inc.

———. 2003. "Constructing the International Foundations of E-Commerce—The EU-U.S. Safe Harbor Arrangement," *International Organization* 57 (2): 277–306.

Federal Trade Commission. 2003. "Identity Theft Survey Report," available at http://www.ftc.gov/os/2003/09/synovatereport.pdf.

Fogg et al. 2002. "How Do People Evaluate a Web Site's Credibility? Results from a Large Study," available at http://www.consumerwebwatch.org/news/report3_credibilityresearch/stanfordPTL.pdf.

Frye, Curtis D. 2001. *Privacy-Enhanced Business: Adapting to the Online Environment*. Westport, CT: Quorum Books.

Gandy, Oscar H. 2003. "Public Opinion Surveys and the Formation of Privacy Policy," *Journal of Social Issues* 59(2): 283–299.

Garfinkel, Simson. 2000. *Database Nation: the Death of Privacy in the 21st Century*. Cambridge, MA: O'Reilley.

Gauthronet, Serge, and Frederic Nathan. 1998. "On-line Services and Data Protection and the Protection of Privacy," Study for the Commission of the European Community (Directorate General XV) available at http://europa.eu.int/comm/internal_market/privacy/docs/studies/online-serv.pdf.

———. 1998. "On-line Services and Data Protection and the Protection of Privacy;" 50–51 available at http://europa.eu.int/comm/internal_market/en/media/dataprot/studies/serven.pdf.

———. 1996. "Can Privacy be Regulated Effectively on a National Level? Thoughts on the Possible Need for International Privacy Rules." *Villanova Law Review* 41(1): 129–172.

Gellman, Robert. 1997. "Conflict and Overlap in Privacy Regulation: National, International and Private," in Kahin, Brian, and Charles Nesson, eds. *Borders in Cyberspace: Information Policy and the Global Information Infrastructure*. Cambridge: MA: MIT Press.

Genschel, Phillipp, and Thomas Plümper. 1997. "Regulatory Competition and International Cooperation," *Journal of European Public Policy* 4: 626–642.

Gillies, James, and Robert Cailliau. 2000. *How the Web Was Born: The Story of the World Wide Web*. Oxford: Oxford University Press.

Glassman, Cynthia. 2000. "Customer Benefits of Information Integration by Financial Services Companies," available at http://www.privacyalliance.org/resources/glassman.pdf.

Godwin, Mike. 1998. *Cyber Rights: Privacy and Free Speech in the Digital Age*. New York: Times Books.

Gordon, Robert J. 2000. "Does the New Economy Measure Up to the Great Inventions of the Past?" *Journal of Economic Perspectives* 4(14).

Gormley, Ken. 1992. "One Hundred Years of Privacy," *Wisconsin Law Review*, pp. 1335–1441.

Greenwood, Justin. 1997. *Representing Interests in the European Union*. New York: St. Martin's Press.

———. 2002. *Inside the EU Business Associations*. New York: Palgrave.

Greenwood, Justin, ed. 2002. *The Effectiveness of EU Business Associations*. New York: Palgrave.

Greenwood, Justin, and Mark Aspinwall, eds. 1998. *Collective Action in the European Union: Interests and the New Politics of Associability*. New York: Routledge.

Guadamuz, Andres. 2001. "Habeas Data vs the European Data Protection

Directive." Journal of Information, Law and Technology (JILT) available at http://elj.warwick.ac.uk/jilt/01-3/guadamuz.html.

Gurak, Laura J. 1997. *Persuasion and Privacy in Cyberspace: The Online Protests over Lotus Marketplace and the Clipper Chip*. New Haven, CT: Yale University Press.

Hafner, Katie, and Matthew Lyon. 1996. *Where Wizards Stay Up Late: The Origins of the Internet*. New York: Simon & Schuster.

Hahn, Robert. 2001. "An Assessment of the Costs of Proposed Online Privacy Legislation" available at http://www.bbbonline.org/UnderstandingPrivacy/library/whitepapers/HahnStudy.pdf.

Hall, Peter A., and David Soskice, eds. 2001. *Varieties of Capitalism*. Oxford: Oxford University Press.

Hall, Peter A., and Rosemary Taylor. 1996. "Political Science and the Three New Institutionalisms." *Political Studies* 44(5): 936–957.

Hamilton, Daniel S., and Joseph P. Quinlan. 2004. *Partners in Prosperity: The Changing Geography of the Transatlantic Economy*. Baltimore, MD: Johns Hopkins University Press.

Haufler, Virginia. 1999. "Self-Regulation and Business Norms: Political Risk, Political Activism," in Cutler, A. Claire, Virginia Haufler, and Tony Porter, eds. *Private Authority and International Affairs*. Albany: State University of New York Press.

———. 2001. *A Public Role for the Private Sector: Industry Self-Regulation in a Global Economy*. Washington, DC: Carnegie Endowment for International Peace.

Heisenberg, Dorothee. 2005. "The Institution of 'Consensus' in the EU: Formal versus Informal Decisionmaking in the Council." *European Journal of Political Research*.

Heisenberg, Dorothee, and Marie-Helene Fandel. 2004. "Projecting EU Regimes Abroad: The EU Data Protection Directive as Global Standard," in Braman, ed. *The Emergent Global Information Policy Regime*. New York: Palgrave Macmillan Ltd.

Hiltzik, Michael A. 1999. *Dealers of Lightning: Xerox Parc and the Dawn of the Computer Age*. New York: HarperCollins Publishers, Inc.

Hine, Christine, and Juliet Eve. 1998. "Privacy in the Marketplace," *The Information Society* 14: 253–262.

Hoffman, Donna L., and Thomas P. Novak. 1997. "A New Marketing Paradigm for Electronic Commerce," *The Information Society* 13: 43–54.

Hondius, Frits W. 1980. "Data Law in Europe," *Stanford Journal of International Law* 16: 87–111.

Hull, Roger. 1993. "Lobbying Brussels: A View From Within," in Mazey Sonia, and Jeremy Richardson, eds., *Lobbying in the European Community*. Oxford: Oxford University Press.

Imparato, Nicholas, ed. 2000. *Public Policy and the Internet: Privacy, Taxes, and Contract*. Stanford, CA: Hoover Institution Press.

Kahin, Brian, and James H. Keller, eds. 1997. *Coordinating the Internet*. Cambridge, MA: MIT Press.

Kalathil, Shanthi, and Taylor C. Boas. 2003. *Open Networks, Closed Regimes: The Impact of the Internet on Authoritarian Rule*. Washington, DC: Carnegie Endowment for International Peace.

Kamarck, Elaine C. 2002. "The End of Government as We Know It," in Donahue,

John D., and Joseph S. Nye, eds. 2002. *Market-Based Governance*. Washington, DC: Brookings Institution.

Katz, James E., and Annette Tassone. 1990. "Public Opinion on Computer and Telecommunications Privacy." *Public Opinion Quarterly* 40 (Spring): 125–143.

Katzenstein, Peter, ed. 1978. *Between Power and Plenty: Foreign Economic Policies of Advanced Industrial States*. Madison: University of Wisconsin Press.

Klosek, Jacqueline. 2000. *Data Privacy in the Information Age*. Westport, CT: Quorum Books.

Korff, Douwe. 1992. *The Effects of the EC Draft Directive on Business,"* in Dumortier, J. ed. *"Recent Developments in Data Privacy Law*. Leuven: Leuven University Press.

Krasner, Stephen D. 1991. "Global Communications and National Power: Life on the Pareto Frontier," *World Politics* 43: 336–356.

Kuper, Richard. 1998. *The Politics of the European Court of Justice*. Maidstone, Kent, UK: Kogan Page, Limited.

Lessig, Lawrence. 1999. *Code and Other Laws of Cyberspace*. New York: Basic Books.

Levy, Jonah D. 1999. *Tocqueville's Revenge: State, Society, and Economy in Contemporary France*. Cambridge, MA: Harvard University Press.

Lindblom, Charles E. 1977. *Politics and Markets*. New York: Basic Books.

———. 2001. "The Market System: What It Is, How it Works and What to Make of It." New Haven, CT: Yale University Press.

Lipset, Seymour Martin. 1996. *American Exceptionalism: A Double-Edged Sword*. New York: W. W. Norton and Company.

Litan, Robert E. 1999. *Balancing Costs and Benefits of New Privacy Mandates*. AEI-Brookings Joint Center For Regulatory Studies Working Paper, 99–103.

Loader, Brian D. 1997. *Governance of Cyberspace: Politics, Technology and Global Restructuring*. New York: Routledge.

Long, William J., and Marc Pang Quek. 2002. "Personal Data Privacy Protection in an Age of Globalization: the US-EU Safe Harbor Compromise," *Journal of European Public Policy* 9(3): 325–344.

Magaziner, Ira. 1998. Transcript of a Speech given at IBM Colloquium, "Privacy in a Networked World: Demands, Technologies, and Opportunities" available at http://www.research.ibm.com/iac/transcripts/internet-privacy-symp/iramagaziner.html.

Magaziner, Ira, and Robert Reich. 1982. *Minding America's Business: The Decline and Rise of the American Economy*. New York: Harcourt.

Majone, G. 1996. *Regulating Europe*. London: Routledge.

Mann, Catherine L., Sue E. Eckert, and Sarah Cleeland Knight. 2000. *Global Electronic Commerce: a Policy Primer*. Washington, DC: Institute for International Economics.

Marlin-Bennett, Renee. 2004. *Knowledge Power: Intellectual Property, Information & Privacy*. Boulder, CO: Lynne Rienner Publishers.

Marsden, Christopher T., ed. 2000. *Regulating the Global Information Society*. New York: Routledge.

Mattli, Walter, and Tim Büthe. 2003. "Setting International Standards: Technological Rationality or the Primacy of Power?" *World Politics* 56(1): 1–42.

Maxeiner, James R. 1995. "Business Information and 'Personal Data': Some

Common-Law Observations About the EU Draft Data Protection Directive," *Iowa Law Review* 80(3): 619–638.

McCown, Margaret. 2003. "The European Parliament before the bench: ECJ precedent and EP litigation strategies," *Journal of European Public Policy* 10(6): 974–995.

McLaughlin, Andrew M., Grant Jordan, and William A. Maloney. 1993. "Corporate Lobbying in the European Community," *Journal of Common Market Studies* 31(2): 191–212.

Milberg, Sandra J., H. Jeff Smith, and Sandra J. Burke. 2000. "Information Privacy: Corporate Management and National Regulation," *Organization Science* 11(1): 35–57.

Milne, George R., and Mary J. Culnan. 2002. "Using the Content of Online Privacy Notices to Inform Public Policy: A Longitudinal Analysis of the 1998–2001 U.S. Web Surveys," *The Information Society* 18: 345–359.

Moravcsik, Andrew. 1997. "Taking Preferences Seriously: A Liberal Theory of International Politics" *International Organization* (Autumn 1997) 51, no. 4 pp. 513–553.

Morgan, Eleanor J., and Steven McGuire. 2004. "Transatlantic divergence: GE–Honeywell and the EU's merger policy," *Journal of European Public Policy* 11(1): 39–56.

Murphy, Dale D. 2004. *The Structure of Regulatory Competition: Corporations and Public Policies in a Global Economy*. New York: Oxford University Press.

Newman, Abraham. 2004. "Creating privacy: the politics of personal information in the US and Europe." Ph.D. Dissertation, University of California, Berkeley.

Newman, Abraham, and David Bach. 2004. "In the Shadow of the State: Self-Regulatory Trajectories in a Digital Age," *Governance* 17(3): 387–413.

Nugter, A. C. M. 1990. *Transborder Flow of Personal Data within the EC*. Boston: Kluwer Law and Taxation Publishers.

Nye, Joseph S., and John D. Donahue, eds. 2000. *Governance in a Globalizing World*. Washington, DC: Brookings Institution.

O'Harrow, Robert. 2005. *No Place to Hide*. New York: Free Press.

Olson, Mancur. 1971. *The Logic of Collective Action*. Cambridge, MA: Harvard University Press.

Organization of Economic Cooperation and Development. 2002. "OECD Guidelines on the Protection of Privacy and Transborder Flows of Personal Data" available at http://www1.oecd.org/publications/e-book/9302011E.pdf.

Palafoutas, John. 2002. Prepared Witness testimony before the House Subcommittee on Commerce, Trade, and Consumer Protection. "H.R. 4678, the Consumer Privacy Protection Act of 2002" available at http://energycommerce.house.gov/107/Hearings/09242002hearing724/Palafoutas1180.html.

Papapavlou, G. 1992. "Latest Developments concerning the E.C. Draft Data Protection Directives," in Dumortier, J., ed. *Recent Developments in Data Privacy Law*. Leuven: Leuven University Press.

Pearce, Graham. 2001. "Regulating Electronic Commerce in the European Union." Aston Business School Research Paper, RP0102.

———. 1998. "Achieving Personal Data Protection in the European Union," *Journal of Common Market Studies* 36(4): 529–547.

Pearce, Graham, and Nicholas Platten. 2000. "Managing Personal Data Flows Between the EU and US." Aston Business School Research Paper, RP0013.

Peterson, John, and Elizabeth Bomberg. 1999. *Decisionmaking in the European Union*. London: Palgrave.

Pew Internet & American Life Project. 2000. "Trust and Privacy Online: Why Americans Want to Rewrite the Rules," available at http://www.pewinternet.org/reports/pdfs/PIP_Trust_Privacy_Report.pdf.

Pierson, Paul. 2000. "Increasing Returns, Path Dependence, and the Study of Politics," *American Political Science Review* 94(2): 251–267.

———. 2004. *Politics in Time: History, Institutions and Social Analysis*. Princeton, NJ: Princeton University Press.

Pipe, G. Russell, Carol Charles, and Symon Visser, eds. 1997. *Assessing Data Privacy in the 1990's and Beyond*. Center for Strategic & International Studies.

Pitofsky, Robert. 1998. Prepared Statement of the Federal Trade Commission on "Consumer Privacy on the World Wide Web," Before the Subcommittee on Telecommunications, Trade and Consumer Protection of the House Committee on Commerce available at http://www.techlawjournal.com/privacy/80721ftc.html.

———. 2000. Prepared Statement of The Federal Trade Commission on "Privacy Online: Fair Information Practices In the Electronic Marketplace," Before the Committee on Commerce, Science, and Transportation, United States Senate available at http://www.ftc.gov/os/2000/05/testimonyprivacy.html.

Platten, Nick. 1996. "Background to and History of the Directive," in Bainbridge, David. *EC Data Protection Directive*. London: Butterworths.

Price, Monroe E., and Stefaan G. Verhulst. 2000. "In Search of the Self: Charting the Course of Self-Regulation on the Internet in a Global Environment," in Marsden, ed. *Regulating the Global Information Society*. New York: Routledge.

Princeton Survey Research Associates. 2002. "A Matter of Trust: What Users Want from a Web Site" available at http://www.consumerwebwatch.org/news/report1.pdf.

Privacy International. 2003. "Privacy and Human Rights 2003: Country Reports" available at http://www.privacyinternational.org/survey/phr2003/index.html.

Prosser, William. 1960. "Privacy," *California Law Review* 48: 383–423.

Putnam, Robert D. 1988. "Diplomacy and Domestic Politics: The Logic of Two-Level Games," *International Organization* 42 (Summer): 427–460.

Raab, Charles D. 1997. "Privacy, Democracy, Information," in Loader, Brian D. *Governance of Cyberspace: Politics, Technology and Global Restructuring*. New York: Routledge.

Raab, Charles D., and Colin J. Bennett. 1998. "The Distribution of Privacy Risks: Who Needs Protection?" *The Information Society* 14: 263–274.

Raskopf, Robert, and David Bender. 2003. "Cross-Border Data," *New York Law Journal* (230) July 29, 2003: 5–16.

Regan, Priscilla M. 1995. *Legislating Privacy: Technology, Social Values, and Public Policy*. Chapel Hill: University of North Carolina Press.

———. 2003. "Safe Harbors or Free Frontiers? Privacy and Transborder Data Flows," *Journal of Social Issues* 59(2): 263–282.

Reid, Robert H. 1997. *Architects of the Web: 1000 Days That Built the Future of Business*. New York: John Wiley & Sons.

Reidenberg, Joel. 1995. "Information Flows on the Global Infobahn: Toward New U.S. Policies," in Drake, William J. ed. *The New Information Infrastructure: Strategies for U.S. Policy*. Washington, DC: Twentieth Century Fund, Inc.

———. 2001. "E-commerce and Transatlantic Privacy," *Houston Law Review* 38: 717–738.

Reidenberg, Joel, and Paul Schwartz. 1998. "Data protection law and on-line services: regulatory responses." Study for the Commission of the European Community (Directorate General XV) available at http://europa.eu.int/comm/internal_market/privacy/docs/studies/regul_en.pdf.

Rosen, Jeffrey. 2000. *Unwanted Gaze: The Destruction of Privacy in America*. New York: Random House Publishers.

Rubin, Paul H., and Thomas M. Lenard. 2002. *Privacy and the Commercial Use of Personal Information*. Boston: Kluwer Academic Publishers.

Schoeman, Ferdinand D., ed. 1984. *Philosophical Dimensions of Privacy: An Anthology*. Cambridge: Cambridge University Press.

Schwartz, Paul. 1995a. "Privacy and Participation: Personal Information and the Public Sector Regulation in the United States," *Iowa Law Review* 80(3): 553–618.

———. 1995b. "European Data Protection Law and Restrictions on International Data Flows," *Iowa Law Review* 80(3): 471–496.

Schwartz, Paul, and Joel R. Reidenberg. 1996. *Data Privacy Law: A Study of United States Data Protection*. Michie Publishing.

Shaffer, Gregory. 2000. "Globalization and Social Protection: the Impact of EU and International Rules in the Ratcheting Up of U.S. Privacy Standards," *Yale Journal of International Law* 25(1): 1–88.

Sheehan, Kim Bartel. 2002. "Toward a Typology of Internet Users and Online Privacy Concerns," *The Information Society* 18: 21–32.

Simitis, Spiros. 1992. "New Trends in National and International Data Protection Law," in Dumortier, J. ed. *Recent Developments in Data Privacy Law*. Leuven: Leuven University Press.

———. 1995. "From the Market To the Polis: the EU Directive on the Protection of Personal Data," *Iowa Law Review* 80(3): 445–469.

Siu, Perri. 1998. *The Future of Privacy; Volume 1: Private Life and Public Policy*. London: Redwood Books.

Six, Perri, with Kristen Lasky and Adrian Fletcher. 1998. *The Future of Privacy; Volume 2: Public Trust and the Use of Private Information*. London: Redwood Books.

Smith, H. Jeff. 1994. *Managing Privacy: Information Technology and Corporate America*. Chapel Hill: University of North Carolina Press.

Spar, Debora L. 1999. "Lost in (Cyber)space: The Private Rules of Online Commerce," in Cutler, A. Claire, Virginia Haufler, and Tony Porter, eds. 1999. *Private Authority and International Affairs*. Albany: State University of New York Press.

———. 2001. *Ruling the Waves: From the Compass to the Internet, a History of Business and Politics along the Technological Frontier*. New York: Harcourt, Inc.

Swire, Peter P. 2001. "New Study Substantially Overstates Costs of Internet Privacy Protections" available at http://www.peterswire.net/hahn.html.

Swire, Peter P., and Robert E. Litan. 1998. *None of Your Business: World Data Flows, Electronic Commerce and the European Privacy Directive*. Washington, DC: Brookings Institution Press.

Tetlock, Philip E., and Aaron Belkin, eds. 1996. *Counterfactual Thought Experiments in World Politics: Logical, Methodological, and Psychological Perspectives*. Princeton, NJ: Princeton University Press.

Turner, Michael A. 2001. "The Impact of Data Restrictions on Consumer Distance Shopping" available at http://www.privacyalliance.org/resources/turner.pdf.

Vogel, David. 1989. *Fluctuating Fortunes: the Political Power of Business in America*. New York: Basic Books.

———. 1995. *Trading Up: Consumer and Environmental Regulation in a Global Economy*. Cambridge, MA: Harvard University Press.

———. 1996. *Kindred Strangers: The Uneasy Relationship Between Politics and Business in America*." Princeton, NJ: Princeton University Press.

Walczuch, Rita M., and Lizette Steeghs. 2001. "Implications of the New EU Directive on Data Protection for Multinational Corporations," *Information Technology & People* 14(2): 142–162.

Warren, Samuel, and Louis Brandeis. 1890 . "The Right to Privacy," *Harvard Law Review* (4): 193–220.

Wellbery, Barbara. 2002. "Privacy and the EU: Is Change Coming?" *Privacy & American Business Newsletter*, October.

Westin, Alan. 1967. *Privacy and Freedom*. New York: Atheneum.

———. 1996. Testimony before the Subcommittee on Domestic and International Monetary Policy of the Committee on Banking and Financial Services, U.S. House of Representatives. Washington, D.C., June 11, 1996, available at http://www.privacyexchange.org/iss/testimony/westin96.html.

———. 1999. Report on the Japan National Consumer Privacy Survey available at http://www.privacyexchange.org/japan/japanindex.html.

———. 2001. Testimony Before the Subcommittee on Commerce, Trade, and Consumer Protection of the House Committee on Energy and Commerce; "Opinion Surveys: What Consumers Have To Say About Information Privacy." Washington, DC, May 8, 2001 available at http://energycommerce.house.gov/107/hearings/05082001Hearing209/Westin309.html.

Whitener, Rebecca. 2003. Prepared Witness testimony before the House Subcommittee on Commerce, Trade, and Consumer Protection. "H.R. 4678, the Consumer Privacy Protection Act of 2002" available at http://energycommerce.house.gov/107/Hearings/09242002hearing724/Palafoutas1180.html.

Wilson, James S. 2000. "The Use of Survey Data in Privacy Research." Master's Thesis, University of North Carolina at Chapel Hill, November, 2000.

Working Party on the Protection of Individuals With Regard to the Processing of Personal Data. 1997. "First Orientation on Transfers of Personal Data to Third Countries—Possible Ways Forward in Assessing Adequacy," XV D/5020/97-EN available at http://europa.eu.int/comm/internal_market/privacy/docs/wpdocs/1997/wp4_en.pdf.

———. 1998. "Transfers of Personal Data to Third Countries: Applying Articles 25 and 26 of the EU Data Protection Directive," Directorate General XV D/5025/98 available at http://europa.eu.int/comm/internal_market/privacy/docs/wpdocs/1998/wp12_en.pdf.

———. 1999a. Third Annual report on the Situation Regarding the Protection of Individuals with Regard to the Processing of Personal Data and Privacy in the Community and in Third Countries Covering the Year 1998 available at http://europa.eu.int/comm/internal_market/privacy/docs/wpdocs/2000/wp35en.pdf.

———. 1999b. Opinion 1/99 concerning the level of data protection in the United States and the ongoing discussions between the European Commission and the United States Government available at http://europa.eu.int/comm/internal_market/privacy/docs/wpdocs/1999/wp15en.pdf.

———. 2002. "Opinion 6/2002 on transmission of Passenger Manifest Information and other data from Airlines to the United States," available at http://europa.eu.int/comm/internal_market/privacy/docs/wpdocs/2002/wp66_en.pdf.

———. 2005. "Working document on Data protection issues Related to RFID Technology," 10107/05/EN WP 105 January 19. Available at http://europa.eu.int/comm/internal_market/privacy/docs/wpdocs/2005/wp105_en.pdf.

Index

About the Book

How did the European Union come to be the global leader in setting data privacy standards? And what is the significance of this development? Dorothee Heisenberg traces the origins of the stringent EU privacy laws, the responses of the United States and other governments, and the reactions and concerns of a range of interest groups.

Analyzing the negotiation of the original 1995 EU Data Protection Directive, the 2000 Safe Harbor Agreement, and the 2004 Passenger Name Record Agreement, Heisenberg shows that the degree to which business vs. consumer interests were factored into governments' positions was the source not only of US-EU conflicts, but also of their resolution. She finds, too, that public opinion in Europe and the US has been remarkably similarCand thus cannot account for official US reaction to the issues raised by the EU privacy directive. More broadly, *Negotiating Privacy* sheds important light on both the relationship between the US and the EU and the relationship between domestic issues and the development of international rules.

Dorothee Heisenberg is associate professor of European studies at the Johns Hopkins University School of Advanced International Studies. She is author of *The Mark of the Bundesbank: Germany's Role in European Monetary Cooperation.*